Who Were the Early Israelites
and Where Did They Come From?

Who Were the Early Israelites and Where Did They Come From?

William G. Dever

WILLIAM B. EERDMANS PUBLISHING COMPANY
GRAND RAPIDS, MICHIGAN / CAMBRIDGE, U.K.

© 2003 Wm. B. Eerdmans Publishing Co.
All rights reserved

Published 2003 by
Wm. B. Eerdmans Publishing Co.
2140 Oak Industrial Drive N.E., Grand Rapids, Michigan 49505 /
P.O. Box 163, Cambridge CB3 9PU U.K.

Paperback edition 2006

Printed in the United States of America

11 10 09 08 07   8 7 6 5 4 3

ISBN 978-0-8028-4416-3

www.eerdmans.com

In loving memory of my son
Sean William Dever
1969-2001

Contents

CONTENTS

Introduction

For nearly two thousand years the so-called "Western cultural tradition" has traced its origins back to ancient Israel. In Israel's claims to have experienced in its own history revealed truth of a higher, universal, and eternal order, we in Europe and much of the New World have seen a metaphor for our own situation. We considered ourselves the "New Israel," particularly we in America. And for that reason we knew who we were, what we believed in and valued, and what our "manifest destiny" was.

But what if ancient Israel was "invented" by Jews living much later, and the biblical literature is therefore nothing but pious propaganda? If that is the case, as some revisionist historians now loudly proclaim, then there was no ancient Israel. There was no actual historical experience of any real people in a real time and place from whom we could hope to learn anything historically true, much less anything morally or ethically enduring. The story of Israel in the Hebrew Bible would have to be considered a monstrous literary hoax, one that has cruelly deceived countless millions of people until its recent exposure by a few courageous scholars. And now, at last, thanks to these social revolutionaries, we sophisticated modern secularists can be "liberated" from the biblical myths, free to venture into a Brave New World unencumbered by the biblical baggage with which we grew up. Our gurus will be those renegade biblical scholars — along with the "new historians," anti-humanists, and cultural relativists whom the historian Keith Windschuttle has described so well in his devastating critique *The Killing of History: How Literary Critics and Social Theorists Are Murdering Our Past* (1996).

Anyone who is uninspired by this vision of a postmodern utopia, who wishes to salvage something of the biblical story of ancient Israel and its value for our cultural traditions, will have to begin at the beginning with the biblical accounts of Israel's origins in Egypt and Canaan, the so-called Exodus and Conquest. But are these dramatic, memorable stories "historical" at all in the modern sense? Where might we turn for external, corroborative (or corrective) evidence? And finally, why should the biblical narratives about ancient Israel, factual or fanciful, matter to anyone any longer?

It is to these questions that this book is addressed.

A word about methodology may be helpful, with particular reference to my task here — that of using archaeological evidence as a "control" (not "proof") in rereading the biblical texts. I would argue that there are at least five basic approaches to doing so, in a continuum from the right to the left. One can

1. Assume that the biblical text is *literally* true, and ignore all external evidence as irrelevant.
2. Hold that the biblical text is *probably* true, but seek external corroboration.
3. Approach the text, as well as the external data, with *no preconceptions*. Single out the "convergences" of the two lines of evidence, and remain skeptical about the rest.
4. Contend that nothing in the biblical text is true, *unless* proven by external data.
5. Reject the text and any other data, since the Bible *cannot* be true.

In the following, I shall resolutely hold to the middle ground — that is, to Approach 3 — because I think that truth is most likely to be found there.

I should acknowledge that in my attempt to tell the "story" of early Israel and to make it accessible to the average educated reader, I have indulged in some oversimplifications. This has been necessary, but nevertheless I have tried to give a balanced account of the data and an honest account of the views of other scholars. The reader will find more details in the works cited at the end of the book. As for my own biases, they will be clear enough.

Since I approach this topic as an archaeologist and historian, not a literary critic of the Hebrew Bible, I have not discussed the numerous works that deal simply with the relevant texts as "literature." Most of these works, oddly enough, including those both to the left and to the right, eschew the problem of actual historical reconstruction. Such works tend to be a "history of the literature *about* the history of ancient Israel," whereas I focus more on what Albright termed the *realia*.

Finally, by way of introduction, when referring to time periods I shall use some shorthand, thus:

"Late Bronze Age" = *ca.* 1500-1200 B.C.
"Iron I" = *ca.* 1200-1000 B.C.

Also, for the sake of convenience, I shall often refer to the former as the "Canaanite" era, the latter as the "Israelite" (or "proto-Israelite") era. Throughout I capitalize "Exodus" and "Conquest" when I am referring specifically to the biblical stories and their traditions, without necessarily prejudging their historicity.

I have not encumbered the text with footnotes, although I do cite year of publication and page numbers for authors whom I quote directly. These and a few other basic works are listed by subject matter at the end of the book, so that readers who wish may delve further into the sources.

I owe a debt to nearly all of the scholars whose works I quote throughout, because I have been privileged to know nearly all of them personally, even those of the pioneer generation, and I have built on their foundations. In particular, I am grateful to my many Israeli colleagues, with whom I have worked for years "viewing the land" (Josh. 2:11), trying to learn the facts on the ground.

I also wish to thank my colleague Professor J. Edward Wright, who read the first draft and made many helpful suggestions on the biblical side — although of course he is not to be held accountable for any idiosyncrasies that remain.

I wrote this book in the few weeks following the death of my son Sean in the spring of 2001, since work is the only therapy I know. His memory inspired me then and now. I dedicate this work, although still in progress, to Sean, for he taught me that it is the journey, not the destination, that matters.

Tucson, Arizona
May 2001

CHAPTER 1

The Current Crisis in Understanding
the Origins of Early Israel

Until modern literary-critical biblical scholarship began to emerge in the mid-to-late 19th century, the Hebrew Bible or Christian Old Testament was regarded as Scripture, as Holy Writ. Its stories were taken at face value and were read more or less literally by Jews, by Christians, and by the public at large. Indeed, in some circles this is still the case: as my favorite bumper-sticker (usually to be found on a pickup with a rifle rack) puts it: "God said it; I believe it; that settles it!" If only it were that simple.

The Birth of Skepticism

Biblical scholars have long known that all the books of the Hebrew Bible were written long after the events that they purport to describe, and that the Bible as a whole was produced by composite writers and editors in a long and exceedingly complex literary process that stretched over a thousand years. Furthermore, the biases of those orthodox nationalist parties who wrote the Bible are often painfully obvious, even to pious believers. Finally, many of the biblical stories are legend-like and abound with miraculous and fantastic elements that strain the credulity of almost any modern reader of any religious persuasion. All these factors have contributed to the rise of doubts about the Bible's trustworthiness.

The Public Catches On

Gradually the skepticism — in some cases nihilism — of scholars has trickled down to the general public. And in the past few years, readers who value the biblical traditions have become puzzled and even alarmed by what they perceive as a concerted, hostile attack on the Bible — much of it coming from reputable biblical scholars themselves. Now even a few Syro-Palestinian (or "biblical") archaeologists are entering the fray.

A sampling of recent book titles, many intended for the general reader, will indicate the direction some current biblical scholarship is taking:

Philip R. Davies, *In Search of "Ancient Israel"* (1992).
Keith W. Whitelam, *The Invention of Ancient Israel: The Silencing of Palestinian History* (1996).
Lester Grabbe (ed.), *Can a "History of Israel" Be Written?* (1997).
Thomas L. Thompson, *The Mythic Past: Biblical Archaeology and the Myth of Israel* (1999).
Israel Finkelstein and Neil A. Silberman, *The Bible Unearthed: Archaeology's New Vision of Ancient Israel and the Origin of Its Sacred Texts* (2001).

I have even published a recent book myself, although it attempts to counterbalance the skepticism of most of these, *What Did the Biblical Writers Know and When Did They Know It? What Archaeology Can Tell Us about the Reality of Ancient Israel* (2001; to sum up my argument, the biblical writers knew a lot, and they knew it early on).

Journalists have already seized on the controversies over "the Bible as history," especially now that archaeology has become involved. Thus the recent popular exposé by Amy Dockser Marcus, a former Middle East correspondent for the *Wall Street Journal,* entitled *The View from Nebo: How Archaeology Is Rewriting the Bible and Reshaping the Middle East* (2000). Even though this book's treatment of archaeology is superficial and tends toward the sensational, it has been influential in some circles (more on this in Chapter 12).

Largely as a result of these and a few similar books, the public is becoming aware that long-cherished notions about the "Bible as history" are being questioned, undermined, and often rejected, not only by a generation of younger, disaffected, postmodern scholars, but even by members of the religious and institutional Establishment. In seminaries the Bible and biblical history are being rewritten by deconstructionist literary critics, political activists, New Left ideologues, radical feminists, Third World Liberation theologians, social constructivists, multiculturalists, New Age pop-pyschologists, and the like. Nor is this a "quiet revolution."

Sensational stories about these developments in our understanding of the Bible have appeared not only in popular specialty magazines like the *Biblical Archaeology Review,* but also in such mainstream media as *Time, Newsweek, U.S. News and World Report, Science,* the *Atlantic Monthly,* the *Chronicle of Higher Education,* and even the *Wall Street Journal.* In July of 2000 the *New York Times* ran a lead story entitled "The Bible, as History, Flunks New Archaeological Tests." Finkelstein and Silberman's recent book, despite its controversial themes and (as we shall see) many flaws, has become an instant bestseller. Its authors, along with myself and others, have recently appeared in many newspaper stories, in interviews with National Public Radio, on television programs for the History Channel and the Learning Channel, and in documentaries filmed for a BBC educational television subsidiary.

"Exodus" and "Conquest": Hot Topics

Whenever I give popular lectures, I find that one of the principal concerns of laypeople is the question of the "Exodus and Conquest." Anyone even remotely acquainted with Jewish and Christian traditions instinctively grasps that these are fundamental issues, as they have to do with the *origins,* as well as the distinctive nature, of the people of the Bible. People rightly ask, "If the story of the Exodus from Egypt is all a myth, what *can* we believe?"

In Israel, the suddenly-fashionable denial of the biblical stories of the Exodus and Conquest takes on a special urgency for many because it calls into question early Zionism's fundamental rationale for Jewish claims to the land. A seemingly harmless report of recent archaeological interpretation by Ze'ev Herzog, a Tel Aviv University archaeologist, in the *Ha'aretz Magazine* in October, 1999, caused a firestorm (more on this in Chapter 12). Nor have Palestinian activists been slow to see the implications of the new notion that ancient Israel was "invented" (more on this presently).

Toward a Consensus — and Its Dissolution

Both biblical scholars and archaeologists have pursued the question of what I shall call here "Israelite origins" from the very beginnings of modern scholarship in the late 19th century. Scholars did not raise questions of authorship, date, context, authenticity, and theological significance in order to discredit the texts, as laypeople suspicious of "critical" biblical scholarship often thought in the early 20th century debate between fundamentalists and modernists. They rather meant to provide a more reliable "history-of-events" in biblical times. And none of the events described in the biblical narratives was more formative than those enshrined in the stories of the "Exodus and Conquest." God's deliverance of his people from Egyptian bondage to the Promised Land in Canaan — this was the very foundation on which the entire biblical edifice was erected. It was as fundamental to later Israelite history, to the biblical vision of the people's selfhood, as the American Revolution is to the uniquely American experience and sense of destiny.

As for early archaeologists, they, too, sought to probe ancient Israel's origins, equally believing them to be unique. Nearly all of the sites excavated in the infancy of archaeology in the Holy Land were sites known from the Bible, dug precisely for the light it was thought they might shed on early biblical history. The principal items on the agenda of the American founder of the "biblical archaeology school" — the inimitable William Foxwell Albright — were "the historicity of the Patriarchs"; "Moses and Monotheisms"; and "the Exodus and Conquest." Bible in hand, archaeologists excavated sites like Jericho and confidently announced to the waiting world that they had brought to light the very walls that Joshua brought tumbling down. As the English translation of the title of a German journalist's best-selling book put it, "The Bible Was Right After All" (*Und die Bibel hat doch Recht*). Earlier in the 20th century, even more enthusiasm and optimism about "biblical archaeology's" potential for proving the truth of the Bible were common. As one biblical Old Testament scholar put it in the 1930s:

> Not a ruined city has been opened up that has given any comfort to unbelieving critics or evolutionists. Every find of archaeologists in Bible lands has gone to confirm Scripture and confound its enemies. . . . Not since Christ ascended back to heaven have there been so many scientific proofs that God's word is truth.

4

As archaeological evidence mounted, however, in the heyday of "biblical archaeology" between the 1930s and the 1950s, the question of Israelite origins grew more intractable. To everyone's frustration, new data brought more questions than answers. In fact, no one had ever found any archaeological evidence for the Exodus from Egypt. But in order to try to reconstruct the conquest and settlement of Canaan, three competing theories or "models" eventually emerged, to which we shall turn presently.

CHAPTER 2

The "Exodus" — History or Myth?

The story of the Israelites establishing themselves in the Land of Canaan commences with the Exodus from Egypt. It is the beginning of the history of Israel as a nation, and it is recounted in lavish and dramatic detail in the books of Exodus, Leviticus, and Numbers. This epic makes up about one-seventh of the entire material in the history of "all Israel" that extends from Genesis through 2 Kings.

The Biblical Sources and the Background

This sweeping national epic is comprised of two major works that once stood alone: (1) the Pentateuch, or "Five Books of Moses," Genesis through Deuteronomy (probably originally the "Tetrateuch," without Deuteronomy); and (2) the "Deuteronomistic history," the book of Deuteronomy plus Joshua, Judges, Samuel, and Kings. Scholars have long since known that each of these "strands" of the literary tradition in the Hebrew Bible, now so skillfully woven into a whole, is in turn a composite work, written and edited by a group of anonymous authors. The sources of the Pentateuch are thus divided into a "J school" (because of its preference for the divine name Yahweh, or Jahweh in German); and an "E school" (for the other Hebrew divine name, Elohim). Traditionally it was thought that J, dated as early as the 10th century B.C., and E, perhaps composed in the 9th century B.C., were edited together in the 8th century or so. Then a final "Priestly school" (known as P) edited both together into the work that we now have, adding much priestly legislation, sometime during the exilic or post-exilic period (6th century B.C.).

Nowadays, however, there is a tendency to see the Pentateuch (or Tetrateuch) as a more unified work, although dated somewhat later, toward the very end of the Monarchy in the 8th or 7th century B.C. Part of the reason for lowering the date is that archaeologists have recently shown that literacy was not widespread in ancient Israel until the 8th century B.C. at the earliest. The Deuteronomistic history, on the other hand, is almost certainly the work of a school of Mosaic reformers (thus "Deuteronomy," or "Second Law") under Josiah (650-609 B.C.), with final additions concerning the end of Judah added during the exile in the 6th century B.C.

The point here is that both the Pentateuch/Tetrateuch and the Deuteronomistic history were set down in writing in their present form *at least* 500 years after the Exodus and Conquest they purport to describe. That alone should raise the question of their historical trustworthiness. Most scholars, however, will also argue as I do that the biblical tradition rests not only on contemporary and earlier documentary sources now lost to us, but also on even older oral traditions. Some of these may have their roots in pre-Israelite times in the Bronze Age, when the Exodus would have had to occur.

The specific time frame for the Exodus is now confirmed as the middle to late 13th century B.C., not the 15th century B.C. as formerly thought. The old "high" date, based on imprecise and contradictory biblical schemes of chronology, was determined using the following calculations: Work began on the Jerusalem Temple in the fourth year of Solomon's reign, and that was 480 years after the Exodus (1 Kings 6:1). Since we know that Solomon died in 930 B.C. (14:25-28; "Shishak" = Sheshonq I, now *ca.* 945-924 B.C.), and he reigned 40 years (11:42), he would have ascended the throne in 970. Thus we add 480 to 966 to get 1446 B.C. — the exact date of the Exodus. But such a high date does not accord at all with the archaeological record in Palestine; today only a handful of diehard fundamentalists would argue in its favor.

All authorities today agree that the major break in the archaeological sequence in Palestine that would have to be correlated with a shift from "Canaanite" to "Israelite" culture occurred at the end of the Bronze Age, *ca.* 1250-1150 B.C. This, then, is the actual historical context for the biblical story we know, even though the writers do not tell us that (and, writing centuries later, without the benefit of modern scientific knowledge, could not actually have known it). For instance, the biblical writers speak again

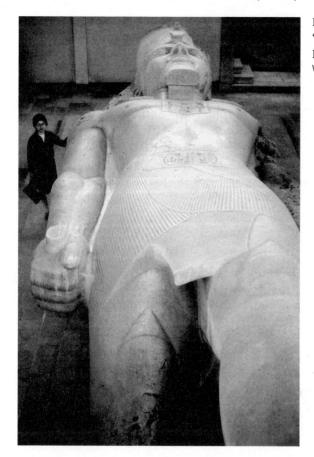

Ramses II, the putative "Pharaoh of the Exodus"
William G. Dever

and again of the villain of the piece, referring to him simply as "Pharaoh." This personage, if historical, can only be the infamous Ramses II of the 19th Dynasty (*ca.* 1290-1224 B.C.). Of the other supposedly "historical details" in the biblical story we shall speak directly.

Virtually everyone is familiar with the basic outline of the biblical story, if not from Sunday school days then from Cecil B. DeMille's movie *The Ten Commandments* (which starred Yul Brynner as a suitably malevolent Ramses and Charlton Heston as a cardboard Moses). But let us take a look at various details of the ancient biblical narrative, the historical veracity of which might be "tested" against the textual or archaeological evidence that we have today.

9

The "Joseph Story"

According to the book of Exodus, trouble for the "children of Israel" in Egypt began with the accession of a "new king . . . who did not know Joseph" (1:8). That is all the Bible tells us. However, as long ago as the Roman period, scholars were looking for a context in which to place Joseph's story. The Jewish historian Josephus connected it with the rule of the once-mysterious Hyksos, or "foreign rulers." The Hyksos were kings of Asiatic descent, interlopers from Canaan who prevailed in the Delta during the 15th dynasty, *ca.* 1640-1500 B.C., and rivaled the contemporary 16th and 17th Dynasty in central and southern Egypt. Archaeologists have even located and extensively excavated the long-lost Hyksos capital of Avaris, at Tell ed-Dab'a on the Pelusiac branch of the Nile. And its pottery, burial customs, architectural style, and other material culture remains all suggest that the Hyksos were Canaanite in origin. Furthermore, three of the names of the six Hyksos kings that are known from the ancient Egyptian "King Lists" are demonstrably Semitic: one of them is the Amorite/Canaanite name "Yaqub" — the exact equivalent of the Hebrew name of the biblical Patriarch Jacob. The same name occurs on a scarab of the Hyksos period found recently at a site near the coast of Israel.

In Josephus's scenario, the "new king" who did not know the Hyksos Joseph would have been one of the early rulers of the renascent 18th Dynasty. These vigorous leaders founded the New Kingdom and expelled the Asiatics from the Delta, destroying Avaris and pursuing the survivors all

Wall painting from a tomb at Beni Hassan in Egypt, depicting a trading party of Asiatics from Canaan; note the "coat of many colors" resembling that of Joseph (Gen. 37:23). Early 12th Dynasty (ca. 1900 B.C.).

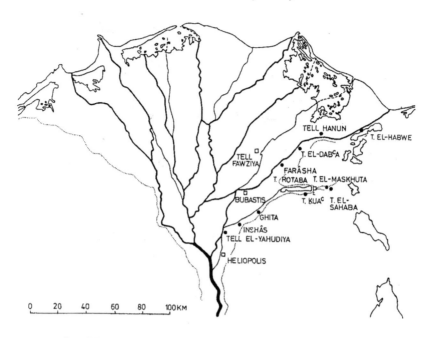

Map of Middle Bronze Age sites in the eastern Nile Delta, ca. 1900-1500 B.C.
Manfred Bietak, *Avaris: The Capital of the Hyksos*

the way back to Canaan. There, in a series of annual campaigns from *ca.* 1524 to 1450 B.C., the 18th Dynasty Egyptian kings ruthlessly destroyed almost every fortified Middle Bronze site. All this is corroborated by both the Egyptian texts and recent archaeological excavations at Tell ed-Dabʿa in Egypt and at numerous sites in Israel and the West Bank. Josephus goes so far as to identify the "new king" specifically with Thutmosis III, whose annual campaigns in Canaan following his accession in 1457 B.C. are well-attested. And of course that date, along with biblical synchronisms, was once thought to point to *ca.* 1446 B.C. as the date of the Exodus. We can see from all this that Josephus's recasting of the traditional biblical stories that he knew is far from being fantastic; it may even seem to have some genuine historical basis. But the archaeological evidence we have today tells us that the "new king" who persecuted Joseph's descendants could not have been Thutmosis. It would have to have been Ramses II, some two centuries later. I shall come back to the Joseph story later, at the end of this book, because it turns out to be significant whatever the supposed historical background

11

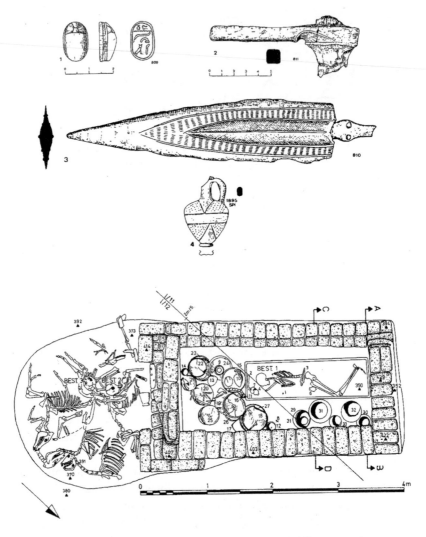

Tomb and grave goods of typical Asiatic (Canaanite) Middle Bronze Age types
from Tell ed-Dab'a; ca. 1900-1750 B.C.
Manfred Bietak, *Avaris: The Capital of the Hyksos*

and date of composition. But now the stage is set for the events of the Exodus that are to unfold; and so far the story is credible, at least to the extent that we can realistically expect accuracy from ancient historians and their sources. As we continue, however, it must be borne in mind that no

Egyptian text ever found contains a single reference to "Hebrews" or "Israelites" in Egypt, much less to an "Exodus." Of course, true believers will explain the silence by supposing that the proud Egyptians would never have admitted such a defeat. But archaeology may tell us a different story.

Bondage in Egypt

According to the biblical story, what precipitated the crisis was the fact that the Egyptian king enslaved the Hebrews, who had been long-time resident aliens in Egypt, in order to construct royal "store cities, Pithom and Ramses" (Exod. 1:11). Scholars have long searched for Egyptian sites by

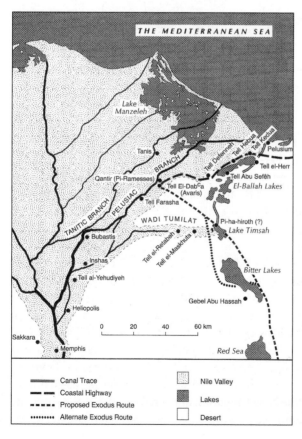

Map of the eastern
Nile Delta, showing
possible location of
"Pithom" and
"Ramses"
James K. Hoffmeier,
Israel in Egypt

Ramses II smiting a foreigner

these names. "Pithom" (Per-Atum) has been plausibly identified with the mound of Tell el-Maskhuta, or possibly nearby Tell el-Retabeh. Both sites have been partially excavated by archaeologists, and they turn out to have been occupied in the "Hyksos" or Middle Kingdom period. The latter, however, was abandoned throughout the New Kingdom and the early Ramesside period, resettled only in the 12th century B.C. And the former has no occupation after the Middle Kingdom until the Saite period (late 7th century B.C.). Thus our best candidates for "Pithom" do not fit the required historical circumstances in the mid-13th century B.C.

Biblical "Ramses," however, has now been conclusively identified with Avaris, the old Hyksos capital located at Tell ed-Dabʿa, mentioned above. And Dabʿa provides extensive evidence for a possible historical setting for some of the biblical memories and stories. There is an Egyptian destruction that took place around 1530 B.C.; a long period of abandonment during most of the New Kingdom; and a refounding as the royal city of "Ramses" (or "Pi-Ramesse") in the time of Ramses II. Of course, no actual building remains have been found, much less the slave camps (of which little could be expected to be preserved, and nothing definitive). But Asiatic slaves — among them possibly the ancestors of the Israelites — may indeed have been employed in making mudbricks (Exod. 5:5-21) for Ramses II's construction projects there and elsewhere in the Delta.

The Ten Plagues

At this point the biblical writers bring the character of Moses to the fore. As a result of Pharaoh's increasing oppression, Moses, born a Hebrew but reared an adopted son of the royal household, becomes a protagonist for the Hebrew slaves. He challenges Pharaoh, but Pharaoh's "heart is hardened" (Exod. 7:14). So Yahweh, Moses' newly revealed patron deity, sends terrible plagues upon the Egyptians until Pharaoh finally relents and frees the slaves (chs. 8-12).

The story of the ten plagues has intrigued and troubled both lay readers and scholars for centuries. The events are all presented as miracles: dramatic and conclusive proof of Yahweh's intervention in nature and history on behalf of his people, and also of course an exhibition of the impotence of Pharaoh and the gods of Egypt. Yet since these "fantastic" events are scarcely credible to sophisticated modern readers, it is tempting to seek naturalistic explanations. And most of the plagues are susceptible to such common-sense explanations — indeed are all too familiar to those who live in the Middle East and have experienced them as typical "natural disasters." Periodic infestations by frogs, gnats, flies, and locusts (plague nos. 2, 3, 4, and 8) are common in the region. Contagious diseases whose causes are unknown but which afflict cattle (no. 5) are nearly as common today as they were in antiquity. Adverse weather conditions like unseasonal flooding, hail, and dark storms (nos. 7, 9) are characteristic of the eastern Mediterranean climate. And anyone who has traveled widely in the Middle East has seen the ubiquitous skin diseases (no. 6, "boils") of the area, among them the "Baghdad boil" or the "Jericho rose," now identified and treated as subcutaneous Leischmaniasis, a pernicious infection caused by a parasite carried by sand flies (as I know from contracting it in Jordan in 1962).

The last and most terrible plague, however — the death of all firstborn males among the Egyptians (Exod. 12:29-32) — is not easily explained. Even some deadly contagious disease that is documentable could not have been that selective. There is simply no naturalistic way of accounting for this particular plague (and whether there is a moral way of accounting for the actions of such a vengeful deity is another question altogether).

Impressive though various attempts at rational explanations of the ten plagues of Exodus may be, they all miss the point of the biblical narrative, which is that such events *cannot be explained.* They are miracles, supernatural events. To say otherwise would be to negate Yahweh's power over Nature; and that is among the most damnable of all heresies. Attempting to "explain away" the biblical miracles is profoundly against the spirit and intent of the biblical writers. You either accept them, incredible as they may seem, or you do not. It is a matter of faith, not of reason — nor archaeology. Archaeological data can illuminate the historical context of the biblical narratives; to think it can (or should) prove or disprove miracles is, again, to miss the point.

The Crossing of the Red (Reed) Sea

Following Pharaoh's capitulation, the biblical story has the freed slaves setting out on their perilous journey through the Sinai Desert in the direction of faraway Canaan, the "Land of Promise." First another, stupendous miracle: thousands upon thousands of the helpless refugees from Pharaoh's wrath flee across the Red Sea, crossing on dry land as Moses parts the waters. Pharaoh's horses and chariots pursue, only to be drowned when the waters close over them (Exod. 14:21-31; who can forget this scene in *The Ten Commandments?*). As with the plagues, naturalistic explanations have long been sought for this miracle. For instance, it has been pointed out that the Hebrew text in Exodus does not actually mean "Red Sea"; the correct rendering of the term *yam sûf* here and elsewhere (Isaiah 11:15) is "Reed Sea." Some suggest that the Reed Sea was a shallow, marshy area somewhere where the northern section of the Suez Canal is today, where it was possible for people on foot to ford the water, but which would have bogged horses and heavy iron chariots down in the mud. In any case it is unlikely to refer to any part of the Red Sea, which is salt water and thus devoid of reeds. Furthermore, an exhaustive analysis of the topography of the northern Nile Valley in ancient times does not reveal any place where the water could easily have been forded, although various "routes" have been proposed. But again, all this rationalization misses the point of the biblical story.

16

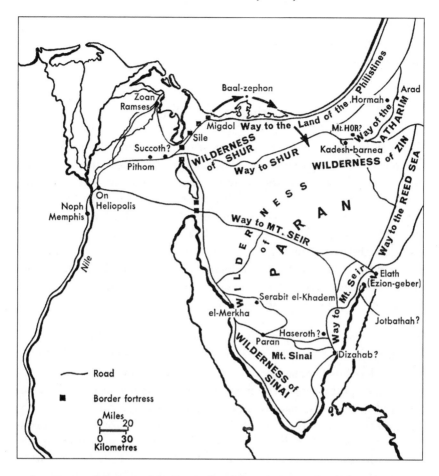

Proposed "routes of the Exodus" and "wandering in the wilderness"
Yohanan Aharoni, *The Land of the Bible*

(Some time ago, I was visited by a frustrated entrepreneur, obviously a pious believer, who claimed that he knew exactly where the Israelites had crossed the Red Sea. He even predicted where the remains of the Egyptian chariots would be found, well preserved in the deep salt water. But he explained that the Egyptian authorities had refused to grant him a license to do underwater archaeology. If I would only come in with him, as a professional archaeologist, we would get the permit, carry out a fabulous project, and would both become, as he put it, "rich and famous." I told him that I

17

was already sufficiently rich and famous, and suggested another destination where the good man might go. I never heard from him again, but I imagine that he is still a believer.)

Wandering in the Wilderness

Much of the biblical story of the escape from Egypt and its aftermath is devoted to the crossing of the Sinai Desert, largely because of the literary and theological themes that the writers intend to develop in this setting. Among the events are the census of the people; the revelation of Yahweh at Sinai; the giving of the Ten Commandments; the establishment of a covenant relationship with Israel's new god Yahweh (who soon supplants the old Canaanite-style deity El); Yahweh's miraculous guidance and sustenance in the "great and terrible wilderness" (Deut. 8:15); the establishment of the tabernacle, priesthood, and cult; the people's faithlessness and disobedience; the punishment of an entire generation, forced to camp for thirty-eight years at the oasis of Kadesh-barnea; the renewal of the promise of the Land of Canaan and the demarcation of the Israelite boundaries; and, finally, instructions for the conquest of the land after making a forced entry at Jericho (Exodus 15–40; Leviticus 1–24; Numbers 1–36).

Much of this long account is very detailed, listing dozens if not hundreds of individuals, place-names, commandments, regulations, and the like. But the account is often disjointed, and scholars have long regarded it as a composite work of the so-called J and E schools of authors in the 8th-7th centuries B.C., extensively reworked by the P (or "Priestly") editors in the 6th-5th centuries B.C. (for instance, the addition of almost the whole of Leviticus; see further above). What evidence from either textual or archaeological data can be brought to bear on the question of the historicity of the Sinai epic? The biblical texts themselves are suspect, for many reasons.

1. The cumbersome detail throughout often seems superfluous, and since it can scarcely have been handed down accurately for centuries in oral tradition, it must have been partly invented to give the story credence.
2. Some of the information is clearly fanciful, as for instance the tribal census lists (Num. 1), which total 603,550; similarly the contradictory claim that the tribes could field a fighting force of 600,000 men

(Exod. 12:37), which would work out to a total population of some 2.5-3 million. There is simply no way that the Sinai Desert, then or now, could have supported more than a very few thousand nomads.

3. Much of the incredibly complex priestly legislation (especially throughout Leviticus) can only reflect the later institutional cult of urban life in the Monarchy, not the experience of desert wanderers. And even then, the tradition clearly represents a priestly ideal, not the realities of either State or folk religion. Most of Leviticus, for instance, simply does not have the "ring of truth" about it; and, not surprisingly, historians and lay readers alike tend to ignore it, or find it lacking in moral edification. (Try to read the book sometime!)

4. Then there is the problem of the itinerary, or the "stages" of the journey as Numbers 33 puts it in summary. Dozens of sites are listed matter-of-factly here and there in the overall account, as though the reader of a later day knew of their existence. But the fact is that only a few sites in the entire biblical text have ever been persuasively identified (if indeed so many ever existed in the barren and hostile Sinai). One is "Migdol," which is probably to be located at the site of a fortress on the Sinai coast near Lake Bardawil. But Israeli excavations have shown that Migdol was an Egyptian fortress on the border of the eastern Nile Delta, and it was occupied only in the Saite period (7th-6th centuries B.C.). That is when many scholars think that the Priestly version was written and the J and E accounts re-edited. That would explain why the biblical editors knew where the site of "Migdol" actually was, although they did not know that it lacked any earlier history.

The only other known site is "Kadesh-barnea," where the Israelites are said to have sojourned for some 38 years (Num. 13, 14, 20). It has long been identified with Tell el-Qudeirat near the oasis at 'Ain Qudeis in the northeastern Sinai, on the border with Canaan, which still preserves in Arabic the ancient Hebrew name. The mound near the springs was extensively excavated by Israeli archaeologists in 1956 and again in 1976-1982, when Israel temporarily occupied the Sinai. Yet despite high hopes of shedding light on what would have amounted to a national shrine, Israeli archaeologists found that there was only a small fort there, with several phases dating to the 10th-7th centuries B.C.

There was not so much as a potsherd from the 13th-12th centu-

The small mound of Tell el-Qudeirat, probably biblical Kadesh-barnea
William G. Dever

ries B.C., the time frame required, as we have seen, for the Exodus. It would appear that Kadesh-barnea was not occupied earlier, but became a pilgrim-site during the Monarchy, no doubt because it had come to be associated with the biblical tradition which by then would have begun to take shape. Thus after a hundred years of exploration and excavation in the Sinai Desert, archaeologists can say little about "the route of the Exodus," even where the dry desert sands would likely have preserved the evidence. Both a "northern" and a "southern" route have been proposed, but these are almost entirely speculative (see the illustration on p. 17 above).

5. Finally there is the recurrent problem of miracles — the whole of the biblical story of the crossing of the Sinai is miraculous, and deliberately so. Yahweh himself goes at the head of the column, guiding the wandering hordes with "a pillar of cloud by day and in a pillar of fire by night" (Num. 14:14). He provides water from rocks; multitudinous birds for prey; and a breadlike substance, "manna," that can be gathered fresh each morning. The desert miraculously feeds several million people.

Once again, attempts have been made to explain these miracles as natural phenomena. It has been suggested that the heavenly fire and smoke may have been caused by the well-known volcanic eruption on Santorini, ancient Thera, debris from which might have drifted and been visible in the atmosphere this far away. As long as that eruption was dated *ca.* 1450 B.C., the chronology seemed to work, at least for the traditional 15th century B.C. date (above). But now the date of the "Exodus" must be lowered to the 13th century B.C.; and meanwhile a growing consensus based on scientific chronometric methods dates the eruption at Thera to *ca.* 1675 B.C.

The reference to abundant quails that are said to have "covered the camp" (Exod. 16:13) may be explained by the fact that low-flying migrating birds do come in over the northern Sinai coast in great numbers, and even today Bedouin catch them easily in nets rigged on the sand dunes (but not inland). The description of the mysterious "manna" (the Hebrew name means "What is it?"; Exod. 16:14-21) has been connected to the secretion of a sweet sticky substance by tamarisk shrubs in the desert, caused by two species of scale insects. Considerable quantities of the edible stuff could have been gathered; but it is seasonal, and in any case would hardly have been enough to feed several million people for even a short time. Once again, such "naturalistic" explanations beg the question of miracles and their religious significance in the Hebrew Bible. The events are the *magnalia dei*, the "mighty acts of God," or they are nothing.

CHAPTER 3

The Conquest of Transjordan

The Biblical Accounts

Near the very beginning of their wanderings, the Israelites contemplate entering Canaan "by way of the land of the Philistines," that is, the coastal route or the later *Via Maris* (Exod. 13:17-18). This route would seem to make sense; it is the most direct one from Egypt to their destination. But the reference to Philistines is an anachronism. That people did not settle in Canaan until the time of Ramses III, *ca.* 1180 B.C. The biblical writers would not have known this, but they were aware that the Philistines' establishment at sites along the coast would have been a barrier. Thus the reference is inserted into the Exodus account, and thus the alternate route described in Numbers. After the Israelites do their 40-year penance at Kadesh-barnea, they attempt unsuccessfully to invade Canaan directly from the south, through the Negev Desert, despite Moses' warning that their attack will be a failure (14:39-45).

But now the Israelites are repulsed by "Canaanites who lived in that hill country" and are turned back to "Hormah," which some have identified with Tel Masos, southeast of Beersheba (more on this below). Since Moses explains their defeat by the fact that they still have not repented sufficiently, counseling that "the Lord will not be with you," the account continues with a long passage, apparently inserted later. It contains detailed laws regarding sacrifices and ritual purity and recounts the rebellion of factions that were still opposed to the leadership of Moses and Aaron (Num. 15-19).

Finally "the people of Israel and the whole congregation" are assembled in the "Wilderness of Zin," poised at last to enter the Land of Canaan. The Wilderness of Zin lies mostly in Egypt today, in the northeastern Sinai on the border with Israel, in the greater region of the oasis at Kadesh-barnea. This desert area was brought to prominence again by the explorations and romantic account of Sir Leonard Woolley and T. E. Lawrence ("of Arabia") in 1914-1915. By chance I camped at Beerotayim, Lawrence and Wooley's deserted campsite, in the 1970s, while directing the excavation of nearby pastoral nomadic encampments from a period a thousand years earlier than the supposed stay of the Israelites. Like them, I was anxious to move on to "the land flowing with milk and honey." All we had was brackish water and sand-flies (Numbers 20:2 acknowledges that "there was no water for the congregation").

From the Wilderness of Zin the Israelites commence their conquest of the Negev Desert and Transjordan; this is summarized in Numbers 20-36. It may be helpful to outline the major campaigns and sites as follows:

1. From Kadesh-barnea eastward across the Negev to Edom, in southern Transjordan. There the king of Edom refuses the Israelites passage (20:14-21).
2. On to Mt. Hor in Edom, where Aaron dies (20:22-29).
3. Back to Arad, in the Negev Desert, where the Israelites destroy all the cities of the region and change the name to "Hormah" (Hebrew "destruction"; 21:1-3).
4. From Arad southward (and apparently eastward), so as to bypass Edom; Moses deals with a plague of snakes (21:4-9).
5. Encamped at Oboth and Iyeabarim, in eastern Moab; then on to the Zered and Arnon gorges, on the border between Moab and the "Amorites"; finally to Mattaneh, Nahaliel, Bamoth and on to Pisgah overlooking Jericho and the Jordan Valley (21:10-20).
6. A great battle against "Sihon, king of the Amorites," at Heshbon, with follow-up victories at Jahaz and Dibon, which gave the Israelites control of the whole territory "from the Arnon to the Jabbok" (21:21-32).
7. Campaign northward to Bashan, and a victory against Og the king at Edrei (21:33-35).

With this, the conquest of Transjordan would appear to be complete, extending north to Gilead and Bashan near the Syrian border. In

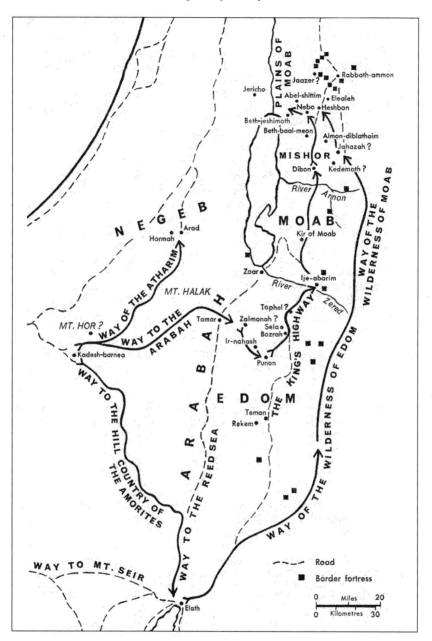

Proposed routes to Transjordan
Yohanan Aharoni, *The Land of the Bible*

the story of the tribal allotments, the northern region is assigned to Manasseh, the southern region to the tribes of Gad and Reuben. This is attributed to the fact that none of these tribes apparently could retain a foothold west of the Jordan (cf. Josh. 13:8).

There then follows a very long passage (Num. 22–30) that covers matters such as the strange story of a local prophet named Balaam, who has a talking donkey and who gives oracles favoring the Israelites even though he is hired to curse them; further apostasy with the Moabites; more plagues; a census of the tribes; explanations of why none of the present generation except Caleb and Joshua would be allowed to cross the Jordan; and regulations for sacrifices, feasts, and festivals. Again, these passages appear to have been inserted later into the original itinerary.

Next the writers and editors turn their attention southeast to the Land of Midian, where Moses had much earlier met his wife Zipporah and where according to tradition he had first learned of the deity Yahweh from her father Jethro (sometimes called Reuel). A great victory is claimed over five kings and all their cities, with many slaughtered, others taken captive, and the place entirely looted (Num. 31:1-12).

Finally, Numbers 33, as we have already seen, provides a summary of the "stages" of the journey all the way from the border of Egypt to the desert east of Jericho — setting the stage, of course, for the dramatic story of the latter's conquest in the book of Joshua (below). Numbers 33 notes the "encampment" of the Israelites at place after place, more than fifty of these places being named. Oddly enough, Mt. Sinai, where Moses received the Ten Commandments, is not mentioned in this summary.

An Archaeological Critique of the Story

Applying our principle of letting both the texts and the archaeological data speak for themselves and in dialogue with each other, let us now look at the "Israelite conquest" of Transjordan from an archaeological perspective. First, let us try to identify some of the sites on the itinerary after Kadesh-barnea.

"Hormah," the hoped-for gateway from the northern Negev Desert into the fertile hill country south of Hebron, is as we have seen often identified with Tel Masos, seven miles southeast of Beersheba. The site was extensively excavated between 1972 and 1975 by a joint German-Israeli team.

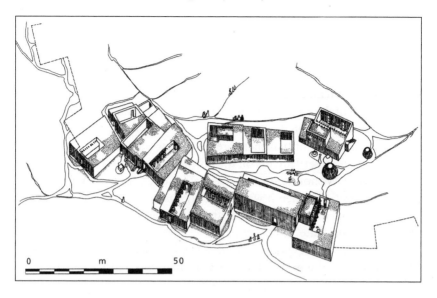

A reconstruction of the Str. II settlement at Tel Masos, ca. 1100-1050 B.C.
V. Fritz

They brought to light what may indeed have been a small Israelite village of four acres, which probably dates from *ca.* 1225-1100 B.C. It is an unwalled agricultural village with "four-room" houses and pottery types that characterize other early Israelite villages in the hill country (more on these distinctive houses and pots below). But the relatively high percentage of cattle bones (26%) found, as well as the appearance of some decorated coastal pottery, suggest that this site is not necessarily a typical 12th century rural Israelite village. In fact, it may not even be biblical Hormah; some scholars identify Tel Masos rather with Baʿalat Beer (Josh. 19:8); Amalek (a non-Israelite city); Bethel-of-the-Negev (1 Sam. 30:27); or Ziklag (1 Sam. 27:6). Regardless of its identity, the significant point here is that there is no Late Bronze Age Canaanite occupation of the 13th century B.C. at Tel Masos, so the Israelites can hardly have battled the native inhabitants of the land there. Nor is there any such occupation *anywhere* in the northern Negev — not so much as a single Late Bronze Age site. Even if biblical Hormah is located somewhere else nearby, the archaeological record remains silent regarding the context of this first attempt at the Israelite invasion of Canaan.

The account that picks up again in Numbers 20 and extends through chapter 36 seems to ignore Hormah (possibly because of the defeat there).

It skips back to Kadesh-barnea, where as we have seen there is again no archaeological evidence of occupation before the 10th century B.C. The story then passes over the Negev sites entirely in order to place the Israelites in Edom, in southern Transjordan. The area is well enough defined geographically, stretching south from the Wadi Hasa toward Petra, but the biblical account does not mention any specific sites. But that is just as well, because there are none. Recent surveys and excavations have shown beyond reasonable doubt that there are only a few possible Late Bronze Age (13th century B.C.) settlements on the northern plateau of Edom, and none south of those. We now know that occupation of Edom did not begin until much later, and even then it was extremely sparse. And the area remained largely nomadic until perhaps the 7th century B.C., when a sort of semi-sedentary "tribal state" finally emerged.

It is true that Egyptian topographical lists dating from the times of Thutmosis III in the mid-15th century through those of Ramses II in the 13th century B.C. list names such as Iyyin (cf. Num. 33:44); Dibon (below); and Abel (there are several sites known later by that name). Typically, however, the Egyptian texts refer to the entire region of Edom (as well as Moab) as "Mt. Seir," the homeland of the "Shasu," clearly Bedouin-like semi-nomadic pastoralists.

Some conservative scholars like John Currid, Kenneth Kitchen, and Charles Krahmalkov have attempted to interpret the Egyptian textual references as evidence that Edom was extensively occupied and even had urban sites during the Late Bronze Age. As Krahmalkov stated some years ago:

> The Israelite invasion route described in Numbers 33:45b-50 was in fact an official, heavily trafficked Egyptian road through the Transjordan in the Late Bronze Age (1994).

But newer archaeological evidence states otherwise. It offers nothing to suggest that the places in Edom named by the Egyptian scribes were anything more than larger regions of Transjordan, occupied sparsely by nomadic tribes.

What this means is that there cannot have been a king of Edom to have denied the Israelites access, since Edom did not achieve any kind of statehood until the 7th century B.C. The obvious solution to this dilemma is to suppose that the writers and editors of Numbers (the "J" and "E" schools), which as we have seen was probably composed in the 7th century

B.C., naturally "read back" into their story the Edom that they knew from their own day. It was by then indeed a rival state of sorts, for which we have very good archaeological evidence.

After passage through Edom is refused in chapter 20, the narrative in Numbers 21 jumps for some reason back to Arad, in the northern Negev, near Hormah. Were the biblical writers compensating, as it were, for the Israelites being stymied in Edom? Or were they aware of the lack of evidence for Israel's presence there? In any case, Arad poses another archaeological dilemma. The site is indisputably to be identified with Arabic Tell 'Urad, 18 miles east of Beersheba. Yohanan Aharoni, a leading Israeli archaeologist of his generation and author of the standard handbook on biblical topography (*The Land of the Bible*, 1962), excavated the Iron Age upper part of the mound in 1963-1964. Like other northern Negev sites, Arad has no Late Bronze Age occupation. Indeed, it was not founded until one small, isolated village was established in the late 10th century B.C. on a promontory above the ruins of another Early Bronze city. That city had been abandoned *ca.* 2600 B.C., and Arad had lain deserted for some 1700 years. The claim in Numbers 21:1-3 that the Israelites had laid Arad waste

The upper Iron Age mound at Arad, as seen from the Early Bronze Age lower city
William G. Dever

and then destroyed all the cities in the vicinity simply cannot be based on actual historical events. Therefore some scholars have either regarded the reference to "Arad" as denoting the larger district, or have sought Arad rather at nearby Tell el-Milh. But this seems like a counsel of despair. There are no Late Bronze Canaanite cities to be found anywhere in the northern Negev.

The next leg of the Israelite journey is back to Transjordan, via a roundabout southern route bypassing recalcitrant Edom. Then there are listed several sites, such as Oboth and Iyeabarim, that are said to have been somewhat to the north, "bordering Moab toward the sunrise," which would have been to the east, between the Zered and Arnon gorges. We have no clues about Oboth; but Iyeabarim has been tentatively identified with Arabic Kh. el-Medeiyineh some ten miles northeast of Dhiban in northern Moab, on the Wadi Thamad. The site is currently being excavated; it appears to be a major fortified Moabite town, with a double city wall and an impressive towered gate with three sets of flanking chambers, all erected probably in the 8th or 7th century B.C. But if biblical Iyeabarim is indeed Medeiyineh, then there is no city there before the 8th century B.C., at the earliest. Once again, it is plausible that the biblical writers of the 8th-7th century B.C. assumed that the city of their day had existed much earlier, and they thus incorporated it into their story of the conquest of Moab. The destination of this leg of the journey is Pisgah. Pisgah is associated in other biblical texts with Mt. Nebo, where Moses looked out over the Jordan Valley toward the Promised Land before his death.

Some Troublesome Sites

The account of the destruction of Heshbon in Numbers 21:21-32, the seat of "Sihon, king of the Amorites," is extremely difficult to synthesize with archaeological evidence. Biblical Heshbon must certainly be located at Tell Hesbân, thirteen miles south/southwest of Amman, the Arabic name of which is identical. The site was excavated in 1968-1976 in a large interdisciplinary project sponsored by a group of Seventh Day Adventist scholars who perhaps intended to "prove" the biblical traditions of the Israelite conquest of the site. Much to their consternation, however, the town turned out to be founded only in the Iron II period — long after any supposed conquest. There were only a few scattered remains of the 12th-11th

Tell Hesbân, seen from the north
William G. Dever

century B.C. (pottery, but no architecture), and no trace whatsoever of occupation in the 13th century B.C. The excavators resolutely published their results, however, and reluctantly conceded that something was drastically wrong with the biblical story about Heshbon.

A related victory was claimed at Jahaz, possibly Arabic Kh. Libb, on the road from Hesbân to Madeba. The site of Jahaz is mentioned on the 9th century B.C. royal inscription of Mesha, king of Dibon in Moab, which was recovered in the late 19th century and is now held in the Louvre, but it has never been definitively located or excavated. Strangely enough, the text of Numbers 21:21-32 does not mention any other sites in Moab, yet it claims that the whole region clear up to Amman (ancient Rabbath-Ammon) fell into Israelite hands. Such inconsistencies make several authorities doubt whether an actual Moabite campaign ever occurred. Certainly the biblical writers and editors show little familiarity with the topography and settlement patterns of the early Iron Age. What they do know seems to fit much better into the context of the 7th century B.C. as we finally understand the area through modern archaeological investigation.

Dibon, some 22 miles south of Hesbân, on the north bank of the

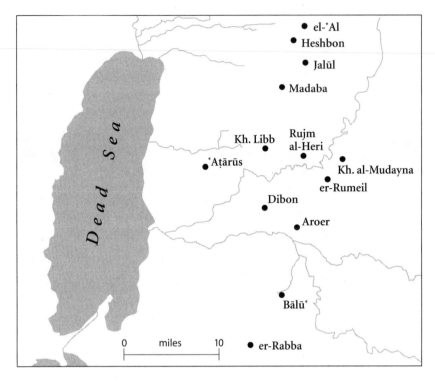

Iron I sites east of the Dead Sea, on the plains of Moab

Arnon Gorge in southern Moab, is an equally great embarrassment. Again, the identification is certain. Dibon is Arabic *Dhibân,* the names being identical (and the Moabite stone, above, was discovered there — obviously it was Mesha's capital). It was excavated by devout believers, in this case Southern Baptist biblical scholars who were searching for corroboration of Scripture when they worked there in the 1950s. And again the results were disappointing (to say the least). There are remains of city walls and some buildings of the 9th century B.C. — Mesha's city — but very little earlier in the Iron Age. And there are no Late Bronze Age remains whatsoever. Once again, the silence of the archaeological record is deafening.

According to Numbers, the northernmost penetration of the Israelites into Transjordan was opposite the Sea of Galilee, where a victory over "Og, king of Bashan" is claimed to have been won at Edrei. Edrei is no

Tell Dhibân and adjacent sites, with presumed biblical
identifications in parentheses

doubt modern Der'a, the border town between Jordan and Syria. But there is a sprawling modern town there now; any ancient remains will remain hidden under it forever.

The excursion into Midian remains a mystery. The biblical Land of Midian lies in the northwest Arabian Peninsula, on the east shore of the Gulf of Aqaba on the Red Sea (the "Hejaz"). Archaeologists have cursorily surveyed this area since the 1960s, and there have been small soundings of a few sites like Qurayyah and Teima. Midian, however, like southern Transjordan, was never extensively settled until the 8th-7th century B.C.

Deep cut on west side of Tell el-'Umeiri showing fortifications below and Iron Age structures at top
William G. Dever

Neo-Assyrian texts of the mid-8th century B.C. mention the subjugation of the region, still a center for camel caravans crossing the desert. The "five kings and all their cities" claimed to have been subjugated to the Israelites remain entirely undocumented. Once again, the book of Numbers seems to reflect conditions of the 8th-7th century B.C., not those of an earlier time period. Midian plays a role in other biblical narratives; but there is no evidence that ancient Israel had any presence there during the conquest, much less exercised any control.

There is one curious exception to the lack of Israelite destructions in Transjordan: the site of Tell el-'Umeiri on the southern outskirts of modern Amman. There stood a strongly fortified town, exceptional for the region, with built-up residential quarters and a well-developed socio-economic system, as well as evidence of cultic activities. What is remarkable at 'Umeiri is not only the heavy fortifications — a dry moat, an outer revetment wall, a tamped earthen embankment, and an upper double (casemate) city wall — but the fact that the town suffered a massive destruction sometime in the late 13th or more probably the early-mid 12th century B.C. The excavator Larry Herr tentatively attributes this town to early Israelite tribes, perhaps Reuben, a once-prominent tribe that in the biblical tradition is first located west of the Jordan but seems to have ended up in Transjordan (cf. Num. 32; Josh. 13:8-13). But could it be the Reubenites, struggling to gain a foothold somewhat later in the settlement process, who attacked the Canaanite town of 'Umeiri and destroyed it? If so, they did not settle there, because the town revived only slowly. In any case, this would be the first clear archaeological evidence obtained of any actual Israelite occupation or destruction in Transjordan; ironically it is at a site that is not mentioned in the biblical accounts.

CHAPTER 4

The Conquest of the Land West of the Jordan: Theories and Facts

The Biblical Accounts

It is universally agreed that the book of Deuteronomy is a later addition to the Pentateuch (probably it was inserted not earlier than the late 7th century B.C.). For that reason we shall skip from Numbers to Joshua in order to give a connected account of the Israelite conquest, focusing now on Cisjordan, or the land west of the Jordan.

The book of Joshua in many ways does take up where Numbers leaves off — with Moses at the end of his life, and the Israelites camped opposite Jericho. After Moses' death his former right-hand man Joshua commences the military campaigns that, according to the biblical account, culminate in the conquest of the heartland of Canaan west of the Jordan — the story of this book.

An outline of the contents may be helpful at this point:

Chapter 1	Introduction of Joshua
Chapters 2–6	The conquest of Jericho
Chapters 7–8	Conquest of 'Ai; altar at Mt. Ebal
Chapter 9	Campaigns at Gibeon and in the Central Hills
Chapter 10	Campaigns at Jerusalem and in the south: Beth-horon, Gezer, Azekah, Makkedah, Libnah, Eglon, Hebron, Debir
Chapter 11	The fall of Hazor
Chapter 12	Summary of sites destroyed

37

Chapters 13–24   Allotments of territories to the 12 tribes;
instructions and commandments; establishment
of a tribal center at Shechem and an altar on
Mt. Ebal; the death of Joshua

We have already discussed the general character of the "Deuteronomistic history" (that is, Deuteronomy through II Kings) of which Joshua is a
critical component. We noted that mainstream scholars date the composition and first editing of this great national epic toward the end of the Israelite
Monarchy, probably during the reign of Josiah (640-609 B.C.). But the compilers must have had many separate "sources," so we need to look now more
closely at the special character of the sources that went into the making of
the book of Joshua. (Obviously Joshua himself did not write it!) Specifically,
what did its editors actually know? How did they weave their information
into the apparently connected story that we now have? And what were their
motives in this composition, which is unique in the Hebrew Bible?

The book of Joshua has long been controversial. Even a superficial
reading reveals it to be an extraordinarily chauvinistic work, glorifying the
military exploits of a ruthless, brilliant general who makes Patton look like
a teddy bear. Joshua carries out a systematic campaign against the civilians
of Canaan — men, women, and children — that amounts to genocide.
Consider the case of Jericho: all its inhabitants were slaughtered except one
— Rahab the prostitute, who had been an informer. And the first unsuccessful attempt to take 'Ai, up in the hills, is explained by the failure of the
Israelites to "devote" the entire city to Yahweh — its inhabitants and all the
spoils of war — in a holocaust or "burnt offering" (the custom of *herem*;
see Josh. 7). Achan, one of the offenders, is stoned to death along with his
children and even his animals. Then, when a second attack is successful,
the entire population of 12,000 is butchered, even the fleeing survivors.

And so it goes in Joshua's campaigns throughout the entire land.
"Amorites, Canaanites, Perizzites, Hivites, and Jebusites" (Josh. 9:1) are annihilated. Only the Shechemites are spared, possibly because of old tribal
alliances dating back to Patriarchal times (Gen. 12:4-9); and the Gibeonites, who however are enslaved as "hewers of wood and carriers of water"
(Josh. 9:22-27). By the end of the story, Joshua had

> defeated the whole land, the hill country and the Negev and the low-
> lands and the slopes, and all their kings; he left no one remaining, but

destroyed all that breathed, as the Lord God of Israel commanded. (Josh. 10:40; cf. 11:23)

Is this literary hyperbole? Or did these horrifying events really happen, just as recounted? And what sensitive modern reader can condone genocide — "ethnic cleansing" — on a grand scale? Because that appears to be what is going on here. These are stories that we might well *hope* have no basis in fact. Why not just excise them from the Bible, as unworthy of its grand themes? How did they ever get into the Canon, or collection of Holy Writ, in the first place?

The Book of Joshua: "Historicized Fiction"?

Many scholars would indeed reject the book of Joshua not (I regret to say) on moral grounds, but on the ground that the work is of little historical value. One of today's leading Israeli biblical historians and a relatively moderate critical scholar, Nadav Na'aman of Tel Aviv University, puts it this way.

> The comprehensive conquest saga in the Book of Joshua is a fictive literary composition aimed at presenting the occupation of the entire Land of Israel, initiated and guided by the Lord and carried out by the twelve tribes under Joshua. Military events that took place in the course of the later history of Israel were used by the author as models for his narratives. These military episodes were entirely adapted to the new environment, so that in no case can we trace a direct literary relationship between the story/tradition and its literary reflection. (1994: 280-81)

Na'aman concludes that the "conquest stories" of the book of Joshua make only a "minor contribution" to the early history of Israel. Among the few possibly early, authentic narratives are the brief anecdotes concerning the subjugation of sites in the south: Hebron, Debir, Hormah, Bethel, and Dan. Conversely, the authors and editors betray their "ignorance of the history of the northern tribes." Na'aman concludes: "The biblical conquest description . . . save for its underlying very thin foundation, has only a tenuous contact with historical reality" (1994: 281).

More conservative biblical scholars, along with evangelical and fundamentalist Christians, as well as Orthodox Jews, pick up the book of Joshua and read it uncritically, quite literally (sometimes even a bit gleefully; the underdog triumphs for once). Thus one of the few remaining defenders of the old "high date" of the Exodus, the British scholar John Bimson, attempted in 1978 an idiosyncratic re-working of the archaeological evidence for the Conquest. Bimson concluded:

> Such widespread destruction of fortified cities could only have been achieved through the concerted efforts of a large body of people. It is therefore likely that the situation sketched in the biblical traditions — a large and fairly unified group of people migrating from Egypt to Canaan — should be given credence. (1981: 223)

Another evangelical scholar, John Currid, in his book *Ancient Egypt and the Old Testament* (1997), declared that

> The writer (of Numbers) knew the geography and topography of Egypt, Sinai, and Transjordan; he understood the ecology of those areas; and he was well acquainted with the road system that was in use in the second millennium B.C. (1997: 141)

Easily the best survey of the evidence from a conservative viewpoint is the recent work of James K. Hoffmeier, *Israel in Egypt: The Evidence for the Authenticity of the Exodus Tradition* (1996). The last words of the book argue for a historical exodus:

> There is ample supporting evidence from Egypt, some of which has been presented here, to come to this conclusion, not to mention hundreds of references and allusions to the Israel in Egypt and exodus events in the remainder of the Hebrew Bible. Because of the weight of these two lines of evidence, it seems premature to dismiss the biblical traditions of Israel's birth as a nation in Egypt, an event still commemorated annually by Jews when Passover is observed. (1996: 226)

Reviewers have pointed out, however, that Hoffmeier only makes a case that the Exodus (or "an exodus") *could* have happened, according to the Egyptian evidence, not that it *did*.

Models for Reconstructing the
Conquest of Western Palestine

But what archaeological evidence is there for each of these viewpoints? We need to examine the material culture data and the historical-cultural context that it provides to see to what degree Joshua looks "real," without drawing any firm conclusions in advance about its historicity, or (insofar as possible) holding any theological preconceptions about what the book "should" mean. But before surveying the evidence, let us assess several hypotheses, or models, that have governed the discussion up to the present. Each reflects a different methodology, and methodology is very important in determining the outcome of an inquiry. This foray into theory, then, is by way of acknowledging up front — and to some degree compensating for — the presuppositions that all scholars hold, whether consciously or unconsciously.

Paraphrasing Joshua: The Conquest Model

The oldest model for attempting to reconstruct "what really happened" in the Israelite conquest of Canaan overall is drawn, not surprisingly, directly from the book of Joshua. This view has been espoused not only by recent conservative scholars such as those quoted above, but also by some of the giants of mainstream scholarship of the past.

For instance, the legendary Orientalist William Foxwell Albright, the "Father of Biblical Archaeology," defended the "conquest model" from the 1920s until his death in 1971. Some quotations from his magnum opus, *From the Stone Age to Christianity* (1940), will suffice.

> Archaeological excavation and exploration are throwing increasing light on the character of the earliest Israelite occupation (of Canaan), about 1200 B.C. (1940: 279)

> The Israelites . . . proceeded without loss of time to destroy and occupy Canaanite towns all over the country. (1940: 278)

And it seems that Albright was not bothered all that much about genocide, for he concludes:

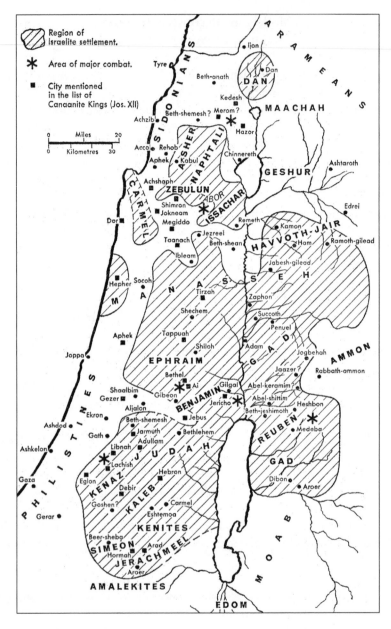

An older reconstruction of the "Conquest of Canaan" and the allotment
of conquered territories to the twelve tribes
Yohanan Aharoni, *The Land of the Bible*

It was fortunate for the future of monotheism that the Israelites of the Conquest were a wild folk, endowed with primitive energy and ruthless will to exist, since the resulting decimation of the Canaanites prevented the complete fusion of the two kindred folk which would almost inevitably have depressed Yahwistic standards to a point where recovery was impossible. Thus the Canaanites, with their orgiastic nature-worship, their cult of fertility in the form of serpent symbols and sensuous nudity, and their gross mythology, were replaced by Israel, with its pastoral simplicity and purity of life, its lofty monotheism, and its severe code of ethics. (1940: 281)

Albright was far from being the only advocate of the "conquest model." His protégé (and my own teacher) G. Ernest Wright followed him. In his influential 1957 handbook *Biblical Archaeology,* he acknowledged that the biblical sources are problematic in some ways. But nonetheless he rejected the German view that the conquest was "nothing more than a gradual process of osmosis." After reviewing the archaeological evidence then available, Wright stated matters this way:

Late-13th-century-B.C. destruction of the "palace" at Dan
William G. Dever

We may safely conclude that during the 13th century a portion at least of the later nation of Israel gained entrance to Palestine by a carefully planned invasion, the purpose of which was primarily loot, not land. (1957: 83)

The leading Israeli archaeologist of his generation, Yigael Yadin, argued that his excavations at the great Upper Galilee site of Hazor in 1955-58 actually proved the historicity of the account in Joshua 11:10-13 of the fall of Hazor, "formerly the head of all those kingdoms." Despite conflicting biblical accounts (cf. Josh. 11:10-11 and Judges 4 and 5), Yadin argued overall that

Archaeology broadly confirms that at the end of the Late Bronze Age (13th century B.C.E.), semi-nomadic Israelites destroyed a number of Canaanite cities; then gradually and slowly, they built their own sedentary settlements on the ruins, and occupied the remainder of the country. (1982: 23)

The standard reference when I was a graduate student at Harvard forty years ago was the work of Albright's pupil John Bright, *A History of Israel* (1959). Bright, although assuming that "we have no means of testing the details of the Bible's narratives," nevertheless marshaled the archaeological evidence of the time in such a way as to conclude:

The external evidence at our disposal is considerable and important. In the light of it, the historicity of such a conquest ought no longer to be denied. (1959: 117)

For many, the conquest model had in its favor the fact that it took the biblical account (in Joshua, though not in Judges) seriously, if naively. And the archaeological evidence known up until the 1960s from such sites as Bethel, Debir, Lachish, and Hazor seemed to corroborate at least some sort of pan-military campaigns by foreign invaders in Canaan in the late 13th-early 12th centuries. Why not the Israelites? Give the Bible the benefit of the doubt.

By the late 1960s, however, the assault or conquest model was assaulted itself. And the threat came from the same quarter that once staunchly upheld the theory — archaeology. We have already noted the ab-

The mound of Jericho as seen from the foothills to the west
William G. Dever

sence not only of destruction levels at Dibon and Heshbon in Transjordan, but also any possible occupational context for such. This evidence was known already in the late 1960s, but it was often ignored or rationalized away by scholars still anxious to salvage something of the traditional theory.

Another crushing blow to the conquest model came from the excavations of the great British archaeologist Dame Kathleen Kenyon at Jericho between 1955 and 1958. Another British archaeologist, John Garstang, had already dug there in the 1920s, sponsored by an evangelical foundation, the Wellcome-Marston Trust. He brought to light a massive destruction of mud brick city walls that he confidently dated to the 15th century B.C. As a result, he announced triumphantly that he had found the very walls that Joshua and his men had brought tumbling down (dating the Exodus, of course, *ca.* 1446 B.C., as was fashionable at the time).

Kenyon, however, equipped with far superior modern methods, and proclaiming herself unencumbered by any "biblical baggage" (so she once told me in Jerusalem), proved that while this destruction indeed dated to *ca.* 1500 B.C., it was part of the now well-attested Egyptian campaigns in the course of expelling the Asiatic "Hyksos" from Egypt at the beginning

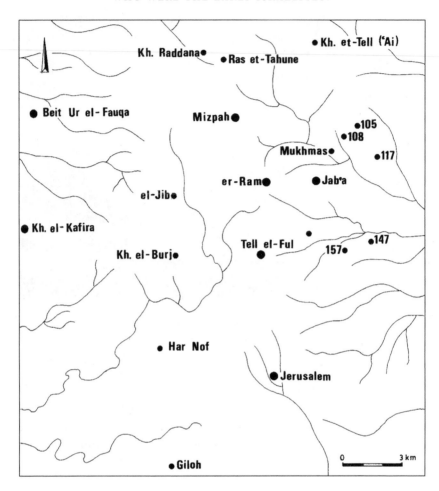

Map of Iron I sites north of Jerusalem, showing 'Ai, as well
as other possible early Israelite villages
Israel Finkelstein and Nadav Na'aman, *From Nomadism to Monarchy*

of the 18th Dynasty. Moreover, Kenyon showed beyond doubt that in the
mid-late 13th century B.C. — the time period now required for any Israelite
"conquest" — Jericho lay completely abandoned. There is not so much as a
Late Bronze II potsherd of that period on the entire site. This seems a blow
to the biblical account indeed. (Nevertheless, I always reassure those who
need it that here we have a stupendous "miracle": Joshua destroyed a site

46

that was not even there!) Even Kenyon searched for an answer; she suggested perhaps later erosion had removed all traces of the Israelite "destruction layer." But regardless of possible explanations, no trace remains of Late Bronze Age II occupation. Nor is there any other possible candidate for biblical Jericho anywhere nearby in the sparsely settled lower Jordan Valley. Simply put, archaeology tells us that the biblical story of the fall of Jericho, miraculous elements aside, cannot have been founded on genuine historical sources. It seems invented out of whole cloth.

The next site on the Israelite itinerary across the Jordan and up into the central hill country is ʿAi, about ten miles north/northeast of Jerusalem. It was extensively excavated in 1933-35 by a French Jewish archaeologist, Mlle. Judith Marquet-Krause. She brought to light a massively fortified Early Bronze Age city-state, with monumental temples and palaces, all destroyed sometime around 2200 B.C. After scant reoccupation in the early 2nd millennium B.C., ʿAi appears to have been entirely deserted from *ca.* 1500 B.C. until sometime in the early 12th century B.C. Thus it would have been nothing more than ruins in the late 13th century B.C. — that is, at the time of the alleged Israelite conquest.

Albright suggested a response to Marquet-Krause's discovery that attempted to salvage much of the biblical account. He proposed that the events set at ʿAi in Joshua 7–8 actually took place at Bethel. Bethel was a mile away from ʿAi, and the archaeological record there does indeed reveal a 13th-century-B.C. destruction. But because the name ʿAi in Hebrew means "ruin-heap," and because the ruins there would have been a highly visible landmark, it could have eventually become part of oral tradition that ʿAi, not Bethel, was annihilated by the Israelites. Thus over the centuries it became to them an "etiology" — a story of origins. The biblical writers would have been familiar with this tradition, but they would have had no way of knowing that it was false. Albright's solution was novel, but it was ultimately not satisfying.

Between 1965 and 1972 Joseph Callaway, an American archaeologist and Southern Baptist Theological Seminary professor who had studied method with Kenyon, reopened the investigation. And he confirmed Marquet-Krause's results beyond doubt. To his credit, he acknowledged the excavations of ʿAi as a major blow to the "conquest theory." He put it this way in 1985:

For many years, the primary source for the understanding of the settlement of the first Israelites was the Hebrew Bible, but every reconstruc-

The 12th-11th century-B.C. Israelite village at 'Ai,
showing typical four-room courtyard houses
William G. Dever

tion based upon the biblical traditions has floundered on the evidence
from archaeological remains. . . . (Now) the primary source has to be archaeological remains. (1985: 72)

Moreover, Callaway — a southern gentleman of great moral character —
took early retirement from his very conservative seminary rather than risk
being the cause of theological embarrassment.

The next site in the Joshua account, Gibeon, fares little better archaeologically. To be sure, the Gibeonites in the rather convoluted biblical story
devise a ruse to save their town; and despite being discovered they are
somehow spared (although forced into servitude). Thus no actual destruction is claimed in the biblical text. The problem, however, is that Gibeon
was apparently not occupied in either the late 13th or the early 12th century
B.C. The American excavator who dug there in the 1960s — James Pritchard, a well-known archaeologist and Professor of Religious Thought at the
University of Pennsylvania — found Iron Age remains, but nothing earlier
than the 8th century B.C.

The mound of Tell el-Jîb, as seen from the north, with the Arab village on top
William G. Dever

Nor is the problem misidentification, for here the identity of the site is certain. The Arabic name, *el-Jib,* is the exact equivalent of Hebrew "Gibeon," as the great American Semitist and topographer Edward Robinson pointed out as long ago as 1838. And Pritchard found 56 broken jar handles inscribed "Gibeon" in Hebrew in a deep water system of the 8th-7th century B.C. The fact that this water system is probably the same one that is mentioned in 2 Samuel 2:13 suggests that the book of Joshua belongs to the 8th-7th century B.C., when the Gibeon known to the biblical writers really did exist.

Several other sites formerly thought to corroborate the biblical account have also in the last few years been reinterpreted in light of fresh evidence. For instance, Albright's own site of Tell Beit Mirsim, excavated in 1926-32, and identified by him with biblical Debir, is probably not Debir at all, even though it does reflect a late 13th century B.C. destruction. Most scholars now locate Debir, at Kh. Rabûd, seven miles southeast of Tell Beit Mirsim. This site has been excavated by Israeli archaeologists, but it exhibits no destruction on the 13th-12th century B.C. horizon.

Albright and others were once fond of citing the massive Late Bronze

Age destruction at Lachish, after which it was abandoned for as long as two centuries. Albright dated the relevant destruction to *ca.* 1225 B.C. But large-scale excavations carried out by Israeli archaeologists in 1973-87 have proven that the destruction in question took place perhaps as late as 1170 B.C., as shown by an inscribed bronze bearing the cartouche of Ramses III (*ca.* 1198-1166 B.C.). That is some fifty years too late for our commander-in-chief Joshua — unless he was leading troops into battle well into his eighties. The evidence, published in 1983, has not, however, attracted much attention.

The major site where excavations seemed to favor the conquest model was Yadin's site of Hazor. But since Hazor is being reexcavated as I write this book, and Yadin's postivist conclusions are being reexamined, let us postpone our discussion until we survey the rest of the current data. Meanwhile, let us look at an alternative to the conquest model.

An Alternative Model: Peaceful Infiltration

In the 1920s and 1930s leading German biblical scholars such as Albrecht Alt and Martin Noth put forward what soon came to be known as the "peaceful infiltration" model as an alternative to the largely American "conquest" model, which they thought essentially fundamentalist. It comprised two elements. The first was the biblical tradition of Israel's ancestors as mobile, tent-dwelling shepherds, as recalled vividly in the Genesis narratives. The second was modern ethnographic studies of the sedentarization of Middle Eastern pastoral nomads, which documented that for millennia tribal peoples in this part of the world had migrated over long distances, but that many had eventually settled down to become peasant farmers or townspeople. The ubiquitous Bedouin of the Middle East were taken as the modern counterparts of the ancestors of the ancient Israelites.

According to the peaceful infiltration model, those who settled the highlands of Canaan, or western Palestine, in the 13th-12th centuries B.C. had originally been nomadic tribespeople of the semi-arid regions of Transjordan. Crossing the Jordan River on their annual trek in search of pasture and water, some of them had stayed on longer and longer each season in the cooler, well-watered, fertile hill country. Eventually they settled there and emerged in the light of written history as the biblical "Israelites."

The peaceful infiltration model had many attractions, and it held

Flock of Bedouin sheep in the Syrian desert near Palmyra
William G. Dever

sway for several years. For one, it accorded well with the Bible's memories of Israel's nomadic and tribal origins, its sojourn in Transjordan before entering Canaan, and its gradual transformation into a small-scale rural agricultural society with "egalitarian" ideals. Then, too, the ethnographic parallels adduced for this model seemed to offer a convincing modern secular explanation for who the earliest Israelites had been and where they had come from, a witness independent of the Bible. It all seemed too good to be true. And it was.

For one thing, the biblical stories of tribal origins are suspiciously like the "foundation myths" of many other peoples. In other words, many scholars believe they are largely fictitious — a "nomadic ideal" perpetuated by later biblical writers who were disillusioned by the ills of urban life during the Monarchy and were nostalgic for the presumably simpler lifestyle of Israel's formative years during the "period of the Judges." Furthermore, the basic notion here of small-scale, gradual "peaceful sedentarization" of nomads conflicts sharply with other strands of the biblical tradition. We cannot simply ignore the emphasis on the massive, well-organized, lightning-quick military invasion of Canaan celebrated in the book of Joshua.

On the ethnographic side, the "peaceful infiltration" model is badly flawed by its dependence on typical 19th-century European misconceptions about Bedouin life. At that time, most investigators of Middle Eastern pastoral nomadic societies and lifestyles knew little Arabic. They had observed local tribespeople only superficially — rarely, for example, accompanying them year-round throughout their entire annual cycle of migrations so as to experience firsthand all aspects of the lives of tribal peoples on the move. Above all, these amateur ethnographers had "romanticized" Bedouin life and had consequently failed to comprehend the real dynamics of sedentarization.

We now know that Bedouin typically are not "land-hungry hordes," that they do not usually "infiltrate" or settle of their own initiative. Sometimes drought, famine, or adverse political conditions compel them to settle. But even then they attempt to return as soon as possible to Bedouin life — always the ideal of the "true Arabs of the desert." More often than not, nomads are *forcibly* settled by urban authorities because they are considered nuisances, in particular a hindrance to state control. Nor is this only a modern situation. Dozens of 18th century B.C. cuneiform texts found at the great city-state of Mari, on the Euphrates, deal with the complex interaction of the urban authorities and the nomads of the nearby steppe, the ancient "Amorites" remembered by the writers of the Bible. Officials at Mari had long been attempting to take a census of the nomads in order to control their migrations and to tax or draft them. But this was no easy task. Eventually the Amorites did become largely sedentarized, but the Mari and other texts tell us that the process took as long as 500 years.

Revolting Peasants?

The two models of the Israelite Conquest that I have introduced thus far date mostly from pre–World War II days, and already by the early 1950s they had begun to seem a bit obsolete. Then in 1962, one of Albright's students who had always been a maverick of sorts, Professor George Mendenhall of the University of Michigan, published a brief article entitled "The Hebrew Conquest of Palestine." It is a classic — one of the most highly original contributions to American biblical scholarship in the 20th century. Mendenhall, although of conservative theological leanings, concluded that despite their appeal both the "conquest" and "peaceful infiltration" models of the Conquest were fatally flawed. They could not actually account for the phenomenon of the rise of early Israel, which he thought unique. He proposed instead an internal revolution that was religiously motivated. As he put it in a later book, *The Tenth Generation: The Origins of the Biblical Tradition:*

> There was chaos, conflict, war, but of one thing we can be absolutely certain. Ancient Israel did not win because of superior military weapons or superior military organization. It did not drive out or murder en masse whole populations. The gift of the land meant merely that the old political regimes and their claim to ownership of all land was transferred to God Himself. (1973: 225)

In Mendenhall's opinion, then,

> [T]here was no real conquest of Palestine in the sense that has usually been understood; what happened instead may be termed, from the point of view of the secular historian interested only in socio-political processes, a peasant's revolt against the network of interlocking Canaanite city states. (1962: 73)

Mendenhall's innovative model of indigenous or local origins for the early Israelites was widely read. But it seemed too radical to most scholars; and there was little, if any, archaeological evidence to support it at the time. Brilliant? Undoubtedly; but perhaps too precocious.

Then in 1979 another American biblical scholar, Berkeley's Norman Gottwald, published what is probably one of the most influential works of American biblical scholarship in the 20th century, *The Tribes of Yahweh: A Sociology of the Religion of Liberated Israel, 1250-1050 B.C.E.* The title itself gives away several unique aspects of this monumental work: "Yahweh"; "Sociology"; "Liberated Israel." Gottwald, a committed Marxist with a long history of both liberal Christian theological involvement and social activism, was the first to crystallize the then-experimental *sociological* approach to ancient Israel's history and religion. And he also made what use he could of the newer archaeological data — at least what was available when he was writing in the mid-1970s (when I was one of his informants).

Gottwald's distinctive contribution to our subject revolved around two of his fundamental propositions. First, "Early Israel" was the result not of an overnight military conquest of foreigners, but rather of long, drawn-out socio-cultural and religious "revolution." It was mounted by local Canaanite peasants of the Late Bronze/Early Iron I horizon, who revolted against their corrupt overlords and gradually formed a new ethnic entity and society. Second, the driving force behind this revolution was largely religious, the "liberating" power of faith in Israel's unique national deity Yahweh.

Gottwald's book, highly controversial at the time and still provocative, was much admired in the 1980s for its refreshing boldness. But it did not find much sympathy, even among liberal biblical scholars in America and Europe. For one thing, some biblical scholars, unfamiliar with this discipline, dismissed its heavily anthropological discourse as jargon. A more widespread and serious objection was Gottwald's obviously Marxist orientation. His model of class struggle and "peasant revolts" was clearly borrowed from modern 20th century wars of liberation, and it was couched in Marxist-style rhetoric that was still anathema at the time. Few appreciated his stress on indigenous origins or his emphasis on ideological and societal factors in long-term cultural change. But these insights, as we shall see, have proven brilliantly correct, even if largely intuitive at the time. Gottwald was *right:* the early Israelites were mostly "displaced Canaanites" — displaced both geographically and ideologically.

Ironically, Gottwald's peasant revolt model was violently opposed by Mendenhall, despite the obvious affinity between their two theories. The two differed primarily over what "Yahwism" was. And archaeologists, parochial as usual, ignored the discussion. This in particular was unfortunate, for as Gottwald succinctly put it, "Only as the full *materiality* of ancient Israel is more securely grasped will we be able to make proper sense of its *spirituality*" (1979: xxv).

Major Excavated Sites in Western Palestine

Scholars are fond of models because they provide a convenient and often instructive intellectual framework within which to manipulate data — in this case for coming up with plausible reconstructions of the past. But the data, not the theory, are fundamental. So as archaeologists we try to stay "close to the ground." And as we shall see, because of extensive archaeological surveys and excavations over the past twenty-five years or so, we now must confront many "ugly facts that kill the elegant theories" regarding the

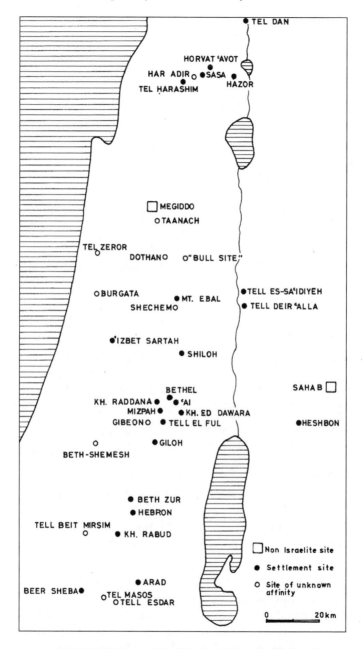

Principal excavated Iron I or "early Israelite" sites
Israel Finkelstein, *The Archaeology of the Israelite Settlement*

Table 4.1. Cities in Joshua 12:9-24

Ancient Place Name	Biblical References	Archaeological Evidence
1. Jericho	Joshua 12:9; 6; 24:11	Meager LB II occupation
2. Ai	Joshua 12:9; 7:2–8:29	No occupation from 2250 to 1200
3. Jerusalem	Joshua 12:10; Judges 1:21	No destruction at the end of LB II
4. Hebron	Joshua 12:10; 10:36-37; 14:13-15; 15:13-14; Judges 1:10	No evidence
5. Jarmuth	Joshua 12:11; 10:5	LB II to Iron I occupation
6. Lachish	Joshua 12:11; 10:31-32	City VII destroyed in late thirteenth century; City VI destroyed ca. 1150
7. Eglon	Joshua 12:12; 10:34-35	Tell ʿAitun; LB occupation unclear
8. Gezer	Joshua 12:12; contra Judges 1:29	LB destruction, probably Merneptah or Philistines
9. Debir	Joshua 12:13; 10:38-39; 15:15-17; Judges 1:11-13	Tell er-Rabud, no destruction at end of LB
10. Geder	Joshua 12:13	Khirbet Jedur; LB II and Iron I pottery; not excavated
11. Hormah	Joshua 12:14	Identification unknown
12. Arad	Joshua 12:14	No LB occupation
13. Libnah	Joshua 12:15; 10:29-31	Identification unknown
14. Adullam	Joshua 12:15	Khirbet ʿAdullam; not excavated
15. Makkedah	Joshua 12:16; 10:28	Identification unknown
16. Bethel	Joshua 12:16; 8:17; Judges 1:22-26	Destruction in the late thirteenth century
17. Tappuah	Joshua 12:17	Tell Sheikh Abu Zarad; not excavated

Israelite settlement in Canaan west of the Jordan River. Let us look at excavated sites first, moving from north to south.

I summarized the data in 1990 in a popular book entitled *Recent Archaeological Discoveries and Biblical Research*. At that time I was able to list sixteen sites mentioned in the Hebrew Bible as having been taken by the Israelites, which we could now identify and for which we had at least some

18. Hepher	Joshua 12:17	Tell el-Muhaffer; not excavated
19. Aphek	Joshua 12:18	LB destruction followed by Iron I "Sea Peoples" occupation
20. Lasharon	Joshua 12:18	Identification unknown
21. Madon	Joshua 12:19	Identification unknown
22. Hazor	Joshua 12:19; 11:10-13; Judges 4:2	LB city, Stratum XIII, destroyed in thirteenth century
23. Shimron-meron	Joshua 12:20	Identification unknown
24. Achsaph	Joshua 12:20	Khirbet el-Harbaj: LB II and Iron I pottery
25. Taanach	Joshua 12:21; contra Judges 1:27	Meager LB II remains; Iron I village destroyed in latter half of twelfth century
26. Megiddo	Joshua 12:21; contra Judges 1:27	LB II/Iron I city, Stratum VIIA, destroyed in latter half of twelfth century
27. Kedesh	Joshua 12:22	Tell Abu Qudeis; Iron I settlement, Stratum VIII, destroyed in latter half of twelfth century
28. Jokneam	Joshua 12:22	LB II settlement, Stratum XIX, destroyed in late thirteenth or twelfth century; gap follows
29. Dor	Joshua 12:23; contra Judges 1:27	"Sea Peoples" known as Sikils occupy city in twelfth century; transition from LB to Iron I not yet determined
30. Goiim	Joshua 12:23	Identification unknown
31. Tirzah	Joshua 12:24	Tell el-Farah (N); LB II and Iron I occupation; no evidence of destruction

archaeological evidence. By 1998, however, my colleague Lawrence Stager at Harvard could list thirty-one such sites. His chapter in *The Oxford History of the Biblical World,* entitled "Forging an Identity: The Emergence of Ancient Israel," is now the most up-to-date popular treatment of the overall subject. But I shall go into more detail on a number of individual sites, specifically in order to "test" the theoretical models summarized above.

Ta'anach

Biblical Ta'anach is certainly to be located at the imposing mound named in Arabic Tell Ti'innik. It is situated five miles southeast of Megiddo in a pass guarding the southern reaches of the Jezreel Valley. In the summary account in Joshua 12:21, Ta'anach is listed as one of the Canaanite cities whose king was defeated. Judges 1:27, however — the well-known list of "cities not taken" — includes "Ta'anach and its villages."

The site was excavated by German biblical scholars in 1902-4, and then investigated again extensively by the noted American archaeologist Paul Lapp (a student of Albright and Wright) in 1964-68. The site has some meager Late Bronze II Canaanite remains, followed by an early Iron Age village that was destroyed *ca.* 1150 B.C. This 12th-century village has been regarded as Israelite on the basis of the Song of Deborah in Judges 5:19, which places the battle between Sisera and Barak at "Ta'anach, by the waters of Megiddo." Yet the destruction, although well attested, *follows* rather than precedes this village.

The most reasonable explanation of the archaeological evidence is that the Late Bronze Canaanite village continued into the early 12th century before being destroyed by Israelites (or others) because of its strategic location. Ta'anach was largely deserted thereafter until the 10th century B.C., when there is indication that it became one of Solomon's district administrative centers, governed by one Baana (1 Kings 4:12). It was destroyed again *ca.* 925 B.C., as we know from its being listed on the "Victory Stele" of Pharaoh Shishak (Biblical "Sheshonq") found at Karnak in Egypt. In sum, the only evidence for Ta'anach having been an "Israelite" city at all before the 10th century B.C. comes from a few biblical references, all penned much later.

Megiddo

Ta'anach's larger sister city, Megiddo, was one of the most important sites in ancient Palestine. It guarded the major pass that led from the Coastal Road (Hebrew *derek ha-yām*) through the northern Samaria hills, across the Jezreel Valley, and ultimately to Damascus and beyond. Its Hebrew name, *har-megiddo,* "Mount Megiddo," was later rendered into Greek as "Armageddon," and because of all the famous battles fought in the vicinity,

Looking north across the Jezreel Valley from the mound at Megiddo
William G. Dever

it became synonymous with apocalyptic visions of the end of the world. Joshua 12:21 lists it as taken, but Judges 1:21 contradicts that.

The site was excavated by German archaeologists in 1903-5, and then again from 1925-39 in a major American project sponsored by John D. Rockefeller and directed by the Oriental Institute of the University of Chicago. Since 1994 it has been under excavation by a large Israeli team. Thus Megiddo's history is exceptionally well known.

As in the case of nearby Ta'anach, the Canaanite city continued into the mid- to late 12th century B.C., at which point it was violently destroyed. After a brief gap in occupation, a major rebuilding in a new style took place in the 11th century B.C. Substantial findings from this level suggest that the population at this point was still Canaanite. These Canaanites met their end in a violent conflagration that left heaps of debris still visible today near the surface of the mound. This destruction (Str. VI) has been attributed traditionally to David (*ca.* 1000-960 B.C.), but the current excavations would date it somewhat later (even as late as Shishak's raid, *ca.* 925 B.C., above). If we are to believe this evidence, no Israelite destruction took place in the late 13th or even in the 12th century

B.C. Megiddo seems to have come into their hands in the 10th century B.C. at the earliest.

Jokneam

Jokneam, seven miles northwest of Megiddo, is said in Joshua 12:22 to have been another site whose king the Israelites killed. But unlike Megiddo and Ta'anach, it is not listed in Judges 1 among the sites still occupied by the Canaanites. The site was excavated in 1977-88 by a large Israeli team. They unearthed a settlement belonging to the end of the Late Bronze Age, which was destroyed *ca.* 1200 B.C. (Str. XIX). A gap in occupation followed, eventually replaced by a small, unfortified settlement in the late 12th-early 11th century B.C. There is no evidence whether the inhabitants were Canaanites or Israelites.

The mound of Jokneam, looking north across the Jezreel Valley
William G. Dever

Kedesh

Kedesh, mentioned in Joshua 12:21, is identified with Arabic Tell Abu Qudeis, midway between Megiddo and Taʿanach. It was excavated by Israeli archaeologists in 1968. There is an early Iron Age village there; it was destroyed in the mid-12th century B.C. There is no evidence regarding the ethnic identity of either the inhabitants or the destroyers.

Tell el-Farʿah

Tell el-Farʿah, strategically located ten miles south of Megiddo in the northern Samaria hills at the head of major springs and a deep valley leading down to the Jordan, is almost certainly biblical Tirzah. Joshua 12:24 claims that its king was killed. Later, in the 9th century B.C., Tirzah functioned briefly as one of the early capitals of the northern kingdom, before Omri and Ahab relocated to Samaria.

Tell el-Farʿah was excavated by the inimitable French Dominican biblicist and archaeologist Roland de Vaux from 1946-60. Although Père de Vaux did not live to produce a final publication, preliminary reports make it clear that the Late Bronze Age Canaanite occupation (Period VI), extended from the 13th century B.C. well into the Iron Age (the 12th or even 11th century B.C.), with no evidence of a destruction at the end.

Shechem

Biblical Shechem has always been identified with the imposing mound of Tell Balâtah in the pass between Mount Ebal and Mount Gerizim, a few miles east of modern Nablus, and 35 miles north of Jerusalem. Because of its central location in the hill country of Samaria, Shechem was remembered in later tradition as "the navel of the Land." It played a major role in biblical history, from the first visit of the Patriarch Abraham (Genesis 12) to the days when it served as one of the earliest centers of tribal assembly and covenant-making under Joshua (Joshua 24). Indeed, according to biblical tradition, the Israelite twelve-tribe confederation was founded at Shechem. Later, Abimelech established an abortive rule there before being killed in a rebellion (Judges 9).

The mound of Shechem, as seen from Mount Gerizim
William G. Dever

Shechem was excavated by German biblical scholars in 1913-14 and again in 1934-36. And major American excavations were directed there from 1958-73 by G. Ernest Wright and his students (this writer among them). When Wright commented on Shechem in 1957 in his *Biblical Archaeology* (see above), he had not yet begun the excavations and could only note on the basis of the inconclusive German work that "numerous problems still defy convenient solution" (1957: 83). Yet the picture is now quite clear. There is no interruption whatsoever in the occupation layers at Shechem from the Late Bronze Age well into the 12th century B.C.

And here at last we meet an archaeological discovery that is fully in accord with biblical tradition, since Shechem is nowhere mentioned in Joshua or Judges among the cities either conquered or reconquered. That Shechem was the site of a great covenant renewal ceremony between Yahweh and the Israelites (Joshua 24) has suggested to many biblical scholars (such as Wright) that the Israelites and the Shechemites coexisted peacefully. Perhaps Israel found a "pre-Israelite" population there dating back to common ancestral (Patriarchal) traditions. The town could thus have been "co-opted" into the new tribal confederation by treaty, leaving no need for destruction.

Gezer

Gezer has a similar story. The 33-acre site, undoubtedly to be identified with the mound of Tell el-Jezer, is prominently situated on the edge of the foothills of the northern border of the valley known as the Shephelah. One of the largest and most important Bronze and Iron Age mounds of ancient Palestine, Gezer was among the first excavations of the modern era, with work directed there in 1902-9 by the Irish archaeologist R. A. S. Macalister. A large American project was carried out in 1964-73 for the Hebrew Union College and the Harvard Semitic Museum; several associates and I directed it.

According to Joshua 10:33ff., Horam, the king of Gezer, joined a coalition of Canaanite kings from Lachish and other Judean sites to oppose the Israelite campaign in the area. And while the text implies that he was captured and executed (and it says so in Josh. 12:12) along with the others, nowhere does the Bible claim that Gezer itself was actually conquered. On the contrary, texts such as Joshua 16:10 and Judges 1:29 state explicitly that the Israelites "did not drive out the Canaanites in Gezer," who continued to

Tell Gezer as seen from the south
William G. Dever

dwell there "to this day" — that is, until the time when the oral tradition began or until it was set down in writing (probably in the 8th-7th century B.C.). Elsewhere, 1 Kings 9:15-17 observes that Gezer did not come into Israelite hands until the days of Solomon, who fortified it as a regional capital, along with Hazor and Megiddo.

Our excavations have documented this sequence of events in rather astonishing detail (and we did not go there, so to speak, with a Bible in one hand and a trowel in the other). True, there is a partial destruction of some areas in the late 13th century B.C., but this is almost certainly the work of the Egyptian Pharaoh Merneptah, who on his "Victory Stela" of *ca.* 1210 B.C. claims to have captured Gezer (more on this below). Here, then, there is a destruction; but it is demonstrably not Israelite in origin.

Jarmuth

Jarmuth is listed in the summary of sites in Joshua 12 whose kings are said to have been killed. Ongoing French excavations at this site have revealed a 3rd millennium Canaanite town with massive defenses, which flourished again briefly in the Late Bronze and early Iron Age. But there is no sign of a 13th/12th century destruction there, despite the prominent *tell* and its strategic location guarding the corridor up into the central hills (like nearby Beth-shemesh). Thus its role in the famous battle against the "five kings of the Amorites" (Josh. 10:5ff.) is archaeologically unattested.

The other four kings in the account just mentioned are those of Jerusalem, Hebron, Lachish, and Eglon. Jerusalem has not been excavated systematically within the present walls of the Old City. But large-scale clearance of the City of David to the south by Dame Kenyon and the late Yigal Shiloh have revealed little that dates from before the 10th century B.C. The Late Bronze Age "Jebusite city" of Joshua 18:28, Judges 19:10, and other passages is attested to only by a few possible terrace walls and some potsherds. But Jerusalem is also known from the 14th century B.C. cuneiform letters from local kings there written to Pharaoh Amenophis IV ("Akhenaten") in Egypt and found just a century ago at his capital at Tell Amarna. Thus we can say with certainty that there was a Late Bronze Age city there; yet there is no destruction on the 13th/12th century B.C. horizon. The alternate biblical tradition that the Israelites took Jerusalem by force only in the time of David (2 Sam. 5:6-9) seems far more accurate.

Hebron, too, was part of the coalition against Israel. But it has been investigated only superficially, so archaeology has no evidence to offer regarding its involvement. Biblical Eglon is probably to be located at Tell 'Eitun, in the Hebron hills. On the present border between Israel and the West Bank, it has never been systematically excavated. But a salvage operation after the Six Day War in 1967 brought to light some material that suggests a largely Philistine occupation in the 12th century B.C. The final coalition site is Lachish, the ruin of which Albright mistakenly dated *ca.* 1225 B.C., as we saw above. But the destruction, now securely dated *ca.* 1160 B.C., does not appear to be either Israelite or Philistine in origin.

Debir

This site is rather prominently mentioned in the biblical accounts of the Conquest (Josh. 12:13; cf. 10:38, 39; 15:15-17; Judg. 1:11-13), the editors consistently noting that its former name was Kirath-sepher. We have already noted that Albright's excavations at Tell Beit Mirsim in the 1920s-1930s, though originally identified as Debir, are probably not relevant. The identification of Albright's site remains unknown; but biblical Debir is now better sought at nearby Kh. Rabûd (see above). There is no destruction there at the end of the Late Bronze Age, although there is a small village dating from the 12th century B.C.

Makkedah

The Makkedah of Joshua 12:16 and 10:28 is usually identified with Kh. el-Qôm, a dozen miles west of Hebron in the Judean foothills, at the inner reaches of the pass leading up from Lachish. I excavated the site in 1967-71 and discovered a walled settlement and dozens of Iron Age tombs, some with revelatory Hebrew inscriptions (one, for example, mentioning "Yahweh and his Asherah," that is, the old Canaanite mother goddess). But occupation began no earlier than the late 10th or 9th century B.C., and the town did not really flourish until the 8th-7th century B.C., the date of the cemetery and inscriptions. I found no trace of Late Bronze Age Canaanite remains.

Kh. el-Qôm and the robbed cemetery
William G. Dever

Hazor

I have saved Hazor for last even though it is a distant northern site and out of geographical sequence here. We have already brought both the biblical texts as well as Yadin's excavations in the 1950s into the picture. Renewed excavations in the 1990s directed by Yadin's protégé Amnon Ben-Tor, now a senior Israeli archaeologist in his own right, have greatly expanded Yadin's already dramatic evidence of a mid-late 13th century destruction layer.

It has been known for some time that the whole of the 200-acre Canaanite lower city, which would have had a population of some 20,000 in the 13th century b.c., was so thoroughly destroyed that its Bronze Age history of 1500 years came to an abrupt and permanent end. Now we also know that the smaller Late Bronze Age upper city, or acropolis, was also violently destroyed. Ben-Tor has discovered a monumental Canaanite royal palace complex of the 14th-13th century b.c., very similar to those well known from Syria, which was deliberately looted and then burned in a fire

 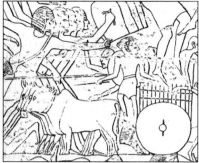

Reliefs of Ramses III, showing invasion of the Delta by "Sea Peoples,"
coming via the Mediterranean and overland, ca. 1180 B.C.
Courtesy of The Oriental Institute of The University of Chicago

so intense that it left great blocks of dense basalt (of volcanic origin) masonry blackened, cracked, and shattered. One can still see today heaps of burned mudbrick from the upper courses of the walls, standing six feet high, the bricks calcimined and turned bright red by the heat of the fire. Among the few items left behind by the destroyers, who piled up enormous quantities of brush and timber to set the buildings afire, were six or seven Egyptian statues that must have been deliberately mutilated. Heads and arms were chopped off, the chisel marks still visible on the torsos. Everywhere in the debris there are signs of what Ben-Tor describes as rage. Who were these bloodthirsty, vengeful assailants? Ben-Tor has been cautious so far about identifying them — partly because the destruction is still not closely dated; it may have been anytime within the latter half of the 13th century B.C. (this cautious assertion stands in marked contrast to Yadin's confident date of *ca.* 1225 B.C.). But he does suggest that the Israelites (or "proto-Israelites," together with other ethnic elements living in the region) may well be guilty of Hazor's destruction — at least, there are currently no better candidates (1999: 39).

One intriguing bit of evidence comes from a fragment of a mid-2nd millennium B.C. cuneiform clay written in Akkadian, the East Semitic language of Mesopotamia that had become by this time the medium of international correspondence. The tablet contains a reference to a king named Ibni, who was apparently part of a dynasty by that name in the 18th-16th centuries B.C. The same name appears in cuneiform documents found at the great city-state of Mari on the Euphrates, referring to trade between Mari and Hazor in the 18th century B.C. Now it happens that Akkadian "Ibni" is the *exact* linguistic equivalent of Hebrew "Yabin," the name of the king of Hazor in Joshua 11:1. It would appear that the authors of this passage in the Hebrew Bible, however late, had *some* knowledge of an Ibni (that is, a Yabin) dynasty at Hazor, stretching all the way back to the Middle Bronze Age centuries earlier. To me, this suggests strongly that the writers of the book of Joshua did not entirely "invent" the story of the fall of Hazor. They had reliable historical sources, oral and/or written. They also knew correctly that Hazor had indeed formerly been "the head of all those kingdoms" or city-states in the north, as the current excavations have made abundantly clear. Hazor easily rivals the most important Late Bronze sites known in Syria all the way up to the present Turkish border. And it may turn out that the current archaeological data does indeed support the idea of an "Israelite conquest" at Hazor.

Other Late Bronze/Iron I Destructions and Their Possible Causes

Of the more than thirty sites claimed in Joshua 12 to have been destroyed in western Palestine by incoming Israelites, I have discussed all those for which we have significant archaeological evidence. There remain, however, the following:

Site	Status
Geder	Kh. Jebur; unexcavated
Libnah	Unidentified
Adullam	Kh. Adullam; unexcavated
Tappuah	Tell Sheikh Abu Zarad; unexcavated
Hepher	Tell el-Muhaffer; unexcavated
Aphek	Philistine destruction
Lasharon	Unidentified
Madon	Unidentified
Shimron-meron	Unidentified
Achshaf	Kh. Harbaj; unexcavated
Dor	Philistine destruction?
Goiim	Unidentified

At a few of these unexcavated sites there is some Late Bronze and Iron I pottery from the surface, but nothing else. As noted, there are destructions at coastal sites that are listed in Joshua 12, such as those at Aphek and Dor. But today it is beyond doubt that these destructions were caused by groups of "Sea Peoples," among them the biblical Philistines, who invaded Palestine en masse after they were turned back from the Egyptian delta by Ramses III *ca.* 1180 B.C. in a battle that is well described and illustrated by the Egyptian sources. The Philistines, having destroyed many sites along the coast and in the foothills, then colonized large areas in the 12th century B.C., expanding throughout the 11th century B.C. until they were checked by David *ca.* 1000 B.C.

We know that for certain the coastal destructions and settlements were indeed Philistine, not Israelite, because of the former's distinctive material culture. This included urban planning, building styles, tomb types, pottery, metallurgy, cultic items, and even dietary preferences that stem ultimately from the Mycenaean world. The Israelites were West Semitic peoples; the Philistines were European in origin.

There are, of course, many other Philistine or "Sea Peoples" destructions beyond the two mistakenly attributed to the Israelites in Joshua 12. Among those that have been excavated are:

Two Philistine anthropoid coffin lids from Beth-shan, 12th century B.C.
Amnon Ben-Tor, *The Archaeology of Ancient Israel*

Tell Abu-Hawam VC
Tel Keisan 13
*Miqne/Ekron VIIIA
*Ashdod XIV
Tel Zeror XII
*Ashkelon V
Tel Batash VI
Beth-shemesh IVA
Tel Sippor III
Tel Haror D

*sites attributed by the Bible to the "Philistine Pentapolis"; Gath and Gaza are either unknown or unexcavated but may be Tell es-Sâfi and modern Gaza

There are at least a dozen other sites that have revealed destructions between *ca.* 1225 and 1175 B.C.; these are not mentioned in the Bible or in any other written sources. For these the agents of destruction (or even the ancient names) are unknown. In a few cases, natural disasters such as earthquakes may have been the cause. There are, however, other possibilities, since there were other ethnic groups in movement at the same time as the Israelites — the early Phoenicians along the northern coast, for example, or the early Aramaeans in upper Galilee and southern Syria. These peoples were long enigmatic except for scattered references in the Hebrew Bible to their later, hostile relations with the established Israelites from the 10th century B.C. on. Now, however, recent archaeological exploration in Lebanon and Syria has shown that the early history of these other West Semitic peoples in the Iron Age — "first cousins" to the Israelites — closely paralleled that of Israel. They, too, began to emerge in the light of history sometime in the 12th-11th centuries B.C. But we have no Bible to illuminate them (or, perhaps, to further obscure them?).

Closer to home, in Transjordan, Israel's indigenous neighbors — the Ammonites, Moabites, and Edomites — are also beginning to be better known, thanks to extensive archaeological surveys and excavations of just the past twenty years. As noted, however, there is very little Late Bronze Age Canaanite or early Iron Age *sedentary* occupation anywhere in southern Transjordan. Only in the 7th century did the ethnic groups in Ammon, Moab, and Edom begin to coalesce into "tribal states." Thus it is unlikely, despite the biblical stories, that any of these peoples either suffered or caused destructions in the late 13th or early 12th century B.C. (the one possible exception being Tell el-'Umeiri, discussed above).

Testing the Conventional Models for the Israelite Settlement in Canaan

We have now surveyed in some detail both the evidence preserved in the literary traditions of the Hebrew Bible and the current archaeological evidence from both sides of the Jordan. We have also set forth the principal hypotheses or theoretical models that scholars have conventionally employed to reconstruct the overall process of the Israelite settlement in Canaan. Now we need to test those models against the archaeological data, especially the recently accumulated data, to see how they fare — whether or not they really explain anything satisfactorily. Or are *new,* more sophisticated models required?

My working assumption in the following is obviously that the information from archaeological or "material culture" sources is now our *primary* source for history writing — not the biblical texts. Nevertheless, I shall give the Bible the benefit of the doubt, unlike the revisionists who hold it guilty until proven innocent. It is a matter again of genuine, open-ended *dialogue* between our two complementary sources, each with its own integrity, each supplementing and sometimes correcting the other (as I discussed in the Introduction).

The Conquest Model

The foregoing survey of the archaeological data leaves one, I think, with little choice. We must confront the fact that the external material evidence supports almost *nothing* of the biblical account of a large-scale, concerted Israelite military invasion of Canaan, either that of Numbers east of the Jordan, or of Joshua west of the Jordan. Of the more than forty sites that the biblical texts claim were conquered, no more than two or three of those that have been archaeologically investigated are even potential candidates for such an Israelite destruction in the entire period from *ca.* 1250-1150 B.C.

This fact, by now well established, may nevertheless be disturbing at first to many. To be fair, however, as well as to err on the side of caution, I need to reassure readers that the newer archaeological evidence does not mean that there were *no* military conflicts that accompanied Israel's emergence in Canaan. And the fact that we now know that the biblical conquest stories are partly later literary inventions certainly does not mean that the *entire story* of ancient Israel was "invented" by the biblical writers, as many of the revisionists maintain.

Yet even among people who are open-minded and willing to try to accommodate the archaeological data, legitimate questions remain. If the biblical stories as they stand do not give us an adequate account of what *really* happened, how shall we reconstruct the early Israelite settlement? And if the stories are not "true" in a factual sense, how did they come to be told, written, and preserved for so long in the first place? What did the writers and editors of the Hebrew Bible think they were *doing?* And how have Jews and Christians been fooled for so long? To these questions, all appropriate, I shall return presently. The theological issues simply cannot be sidestepped, as most archaeologists tend to think.

The Peaceful Infiltration Model

Not surprisingly, the peaceful infiltration or, as some call it, the "immigration" model, has fared somewhat better than the conquest model. All along, it was less theologically driven; more realistic in terms of depicting long-term cultural change; less rigid and more capable of encompassing new evidence. Moreover, it resonated with the "nomadic ideal" of the Bible. It also had a modern romantic appeal. In the barren Great Desert, far from the corruptions of urban society, wandering pastoralists encountered an austere but just deity, purified their faith by fire, then later introduced their simple, egalitarian ideals among settled folk not by force of arms but by the purity of their lifestyle. A similar ideal of the "Noble Arab of the Desert" still persists in the Middle East. This is especially true among the Bedouin, who consider themselves — not the despised *fellahin,* or peasants, farmers, and villagers — the only true Arabs.

Romantic nonsense aside, however, the fact is that the infiltration/immigration model never had much factual support. The ethnographic theory underlying it was badly flawed, as noted above. And there never was any archaeological evidence to support it, largely because peaceful migrations and movements of people leave far less physical evidence than catastrophic destructions — usually none at all. In the late 1970s, for example, I excavated an ancient camp of late 3rd millennium B.C. pastoral nomads in the western Negev Desert. We hoped also to study the modern Bedouin who frequented the area, so as to compare lifestyles. The Israeli army, however, for security reasons had ordered them all to clear out. So the Bedouin near our tent camp had literally pulled up stakes a few days before we arrived that summer. The only traces left behind were the ashes of their cooking fires, a few non-biodegradable items like tin cans and a plastic sandal, and one live but emaciated puppy. (We adopted him; he thrived and barked all summer.)

Archaeologists and anthropologists have developed a few simple, testable "rules" for recognizing when we are dealing with the immigration of new peoples into an area. (1) The new society and culture must have characteristics that are different and distinguishable, usually marked by observable discontinuities in material culture. (2) The "homeland" of the immigrant group must be known, and its culture well understood there. (3) The route by which the postulated immigration took place must be traceable, so that the actual process may be reconstructed. The infiltration/immigration model for early Israel satisfies none of these requirements. There probably were some former pastoral nomads in the mix of early Israelite peoples, as the Bible remembers, but they have left few if any traces in the archaeological record (see further below, Chapter 9).

The Peasant Revolt Model

However revolting the ancient peasants may have been, they are not likely to have constituted a major component in the mix of early Israelite peoples. Mendenhall and Gottwald had built their hypothesis, which Gottwald often preferred to call a "withdrawal" model, partly on the well-known societal role of certain predecessors of the Israelites in Canaan. Known from the 14th century B.C. Canaanite texts as "'Apiru," or formerly "Habiru," these malcontents were "dropouts," or "social bandits" as anthropologists might dub them. They lived on the fringes of urban society as refugees from the Canaanite city-states, rebels, highwaymen, sometimes mercenaries, but always underminers of the Establishment. Although not numerous, they were around in such sufficient numbers in the Late Bronze Age that they constituted a nuisance, sometimes even a real threat, to the authorities. One 14th century B.C. text, a letter from the king of the Canaanite city-state of Shechem written to his Egyptian overlord Amenophis IV ("Akhenaten"), protests that the king did not know of the report that his son had gone over to the ʿApiru, but says that now he has had the boy arrested and turned over to the resident Egyptian high commissioner.

One can understand why adherents of a social revolution or withdrawal model for early Israel would see parallels between the earlier ʿApiru and the biblical Hebrews. It was even argued by some that "Habiru" and "Hebrew" were etymologically related. Today we know, however, that "Habiru" is not the preferable transliteration; the Akkadian (Mesopotamian) root of "ʿApiru" means something like "freebooter," while the root of "Hebrew" means "to cross over." That is, it refers to those ancestors of Israel who like Abraham came over from Mesopotamia to Canaan. The social roles of these groups in Canaan a century or two apart may, however, have been somewhat similar. And some later "ʿApiru-like" people of the Iron Age may well have been attracted to the Israelite ethnic movement because of its dissident character, and thus joined the confederation as it expanded. (More of this presently.)

But the above is all speculation — and it is all one can say. The crucial archaeological evidence is missing, just as it was for the infiltration/immigration model. That is because we are dealing here with a presumed social revolution, one that would have been based largely on ideological motivations that are extremely difficult to detect in tangible material culture remains. As leading American archaeologist Lewis Binford once remarked, "archaeologists are poorly equipped to be paleo-psychologists." We can dig up things people made; and we can usually ascertain how these things were made and how they were used, discarded, and reused. But rarely can we know what people *thought*, what really "made them tick."

So in summary, the real insight and the continuing value of the peasant revolt model is that it draws attention for the first time to the largely *indigenous* origins of the early Israelite peoples, which previous academics tended to resist but which virtually all scholars now accept. And fortunately, today we can finally deal somewhat better with the societal realities that the model sought to highlight. Largely obsolete today, this model paved the way for newer and better understandings of early Israel (despite the skepticism of many biblicists and the contempt of a few archaeologists). Stripped of its Marxist baggage, the peasant revolt model can still be useful, as we shall see when we come to chart the changes in the 13th-12th century B.C. cultural context that archaeology can now document.

CHAPTER 5

Facts on the Ground: The Excavated Evidence for the Archaeological Rediscovery of the Real Israel

The state of our knowledge up until the 1970s, as well as of much scholarly speculation, has now been summarized in some detail. But what's new regarding the "old" Israel?

Excavated Sites

First, the excavation of several small sites of the 13th-12th century B.C. horizon, beginning in the 1970s, began to change the picture of the settlement process in Canaan. This was particularly true in the central hill country, the "heartland" of ancient Israel.

Raddana

Joe Callaway, the excavator of 'Ai, whose refreshing candor we have already noted, moved from 'Ai to the small hilltop site of Kh. Raddana, on the western outskirts of the present-day Jerusalem suburb of Ramallah, in 1969-74. This was a "salvage campaign," occasioned when the site was discovered by accident as the Jordanians were planning to build a hotel there. It was about to be bulldozed. But Callaway and his associates were able to uncover what had been an isolated farming village, dated by its pottery to the late 13th-early 12th century B.C.

Raddana, which Callaway tentatively identified with biblical Beeroth,

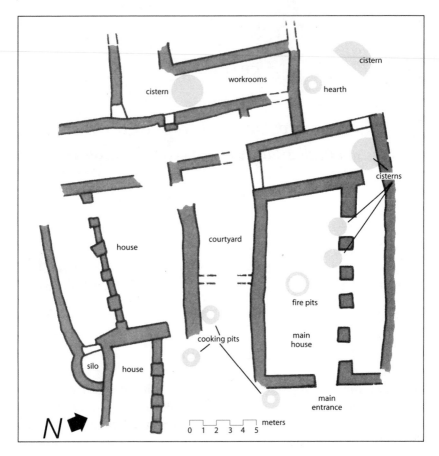

Pillar-courtyard houses at Kh. Raddana
Biblical Archaeology Review 9:5

was established on bedrock, on a site and in a region conspicuously devoid of earlier Late Bronze Age Canaanite occupation. Although on a prominent ridge and naturally defensible, the site was probably chosen not for its strategic location, but rather for its proximity to a spring and its fertile valley below, as well as the surrounding hillsides that were particularly well suited to terrace agriculture. (The terraces are now abandoned, but they are still visible even from a distance).

A relatively large proportion of the site at Raddana was cleared; thus both individual house-plans and the overall village plan have been dis-

12th-century-B.C. pillar-courtyard or "Israelite" type house at Kh. Raddana
William G. Dever

cerned. The houses were of a distinctive type that we may call "pillar-courtyard" in style. It is often called, however, the "four-room" or even "Israelite" house. In a typical example, three banks of rooms are grouped around a central courtyard, usually set off by a row of pillars. At Raddana (and elsewhere), two or three of these individual houses are usually grouped together to form a sort of "family compound." This turns out to be significant because it reflects the biblical ideal of the *mishpaha,* or "extended multiple-generation family," as for instance in the narratives in Judges and Samuel. I shall return to this presently.

Before we leave Raddana, let me note a few individual finds. These include simple utilitarian pottery vessels that are clearly in a degenerate, late 13th century Canaanite style, with no decorated, imported, or painted Philistine-style wares present; simple bronze knives, adzes, and other domestic utensils; and a jar handle inscribed with the Hebrew name "Ahilu(d)," written in the local Canaanite script (compare Ahilud in 1 Kings 4:12; the father of Solomon's district governor Baana, at Megiddo). All of these offer clues as to who the village's ancient inhabitants were.

Tel Masos

I have already mentioned the 1972-75 excavations at Tel Masos in discussing the problem of identifying biblical Hormah, which some scholars would locate there. It is a small site in the semi-arid northern Negev about ten miles southeast of Beersheba. Here archaeologists have revealed a sizeable portion of the seven- to eight-acre village, with about a dozen well-developed pillar-courtyard houses tightly grouped in two or three clusters. Using the accepted factor of about ten square meters of living space per person (a common figure in both New and Old World ethnography) each house might have been home to as many as ten or fifteen people (one house has more than 150 square meters of living space). That estimate would yield a total population of 120-180 for the dozen or so houses at Tel Masos. (Another way of estimating ancient population sizes is to figure about a hundred persons per acre for built-up domestic areas, like that of densely occupied contemporary Middle Eastern cities, such as Old Jerusalem or Damascus. That would give a figure of some seven hundred for the entire site, which is probably much too large, since it is doubtful that the entire area inside the settlement was filled with houses.)

The houses at Tel Masos are built contiguously, forming an oval settlement with a sort of perimeter, although there is nothing like a city wall surrounding the site. Thus defense does not seem to have been a priority, apart from the common-sense protection from animals or marauders that the perimeter would have provided in addition to facilitating the penning up of animals. The economy was based on dry farming, as attested by silos for storage of cereals and grains. But it also included stockbreeding, particularly cattle and sheep/goat herding, as the percentages of animal bones show (26% and 60% respectively). Finally, Tel Masos was located on good trade routes leading through the desert and participated in overland trade, as demonstrated by some decorated pottery of coastal types, perhaps Cypro-Phoenician, a rare phenomenon in the relatively isolated Iron I villages under consideration here. (Thus the contention of some scholars that Masos, Hormah or not, was not Israelite.) The life-span of this small agricultural village extends from its founding just before 1200 B.C. (dated by a scarab of Ramesside type), through its expansion in the 12th century B.C., to its abandonment about 950 B.C.

Whether Tel Masos is biblical Hormah, Bethel-of-the-Negev (cf. 1 Sam. 30:27-31), Ziklag, or even Amalek (a non-Israelite site), most schol-

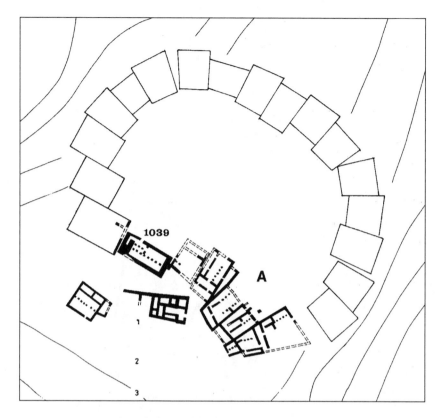

Plan of the northern settlement at Tel Masos,
showing the projected Str. III village layout
Aharon Kempinski and Ronny Reich, eds., *The Architecture of Ancient Israel*

ars take it as typical in many ways of the other Iron I villages that we may
now identify as Israelite (or my "proto-Israelite," below), perhaps only a bit
more sophisticated. (I shall note some disagreement with this contention a
bit later.)

Giloh

In 1978-79 Amihai Mazar did a salvage campaign at a one-period hilltop
hamlet, found when the Jerusalem suburb of Giloh was expanding. The
site is sometimes thought to be identified with the Giloh mentioned in

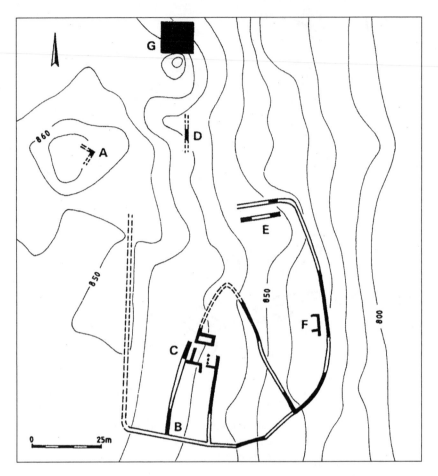

General plan of Giloh
Israel Finkelstein and Nadav Na'aman, *From Nomadism to Monarchy*

Joshua 15:51, but that is unlikely. Mazar's prompt report and discussion of Giloh in 1981 is still one of the best-balanced and most helpful treatments of the issues to be found anywhere.

The settlement produced only the fragmentary remains of a house or two. But significantly these are of the pillar-courtyard or four-room style often associated, as we saw above, with early Israelite villages. If the entire site had been built up (and preserved), Giloh might have had up to ten of those houses by Mazar's estimate, which would yield a total population of

100-150. There is some evidence of a perimeter wall; but this may be later, since there is an Iron II defensive tower at the north end of the site.

Pottery from one of the buildings at Giloh has turned out to be particularly significant: it is a small but representative *corpus* that is analyzed expertly by Mazar. He draws numerous parallels from discoveries at other sites to prove beyond doubt (1) that the Giloh pottery, typical of other early Israelite sites in the hill country, is late 13th-early 12th century B.C. in date; and (2) that it is in the Late Bronze Age Canaanite tradition. One may note especially the transitional cooking pot rims; and the large storejars with a reinforcing band around the neck — the so-called "collar-rim" jars that are thought by many archaeologists to be characteristic of early Israelite sites (more on this below).

'Izbet Sartah

The site of 'Izbet Sartah was excavated in 1976-78 by one of the principal contenders in this debate on Israelite origins, Tel Aviv University's Israel

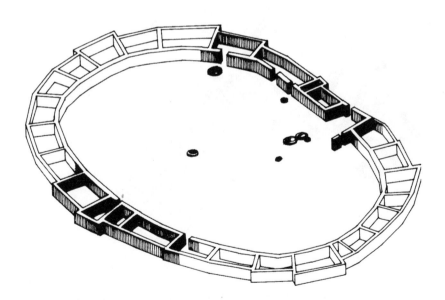

Plan of Str. III at 'Izbet Sartah; only dark portions were excavated
Israel Finkelstein and Neil Silberman, *The Bible Unearthed*

Finkelstein. 'Izbet Sartah, which I think may possibly be identified with biblical Ebenezer, is a small five-acre hilltop site at the extreme western edge of the foothills. It is just three miles inland from the great site of Aphek on the coastal plain, at the headwaters of the Yarkon River.

The third stratum (archaeologists divide their digs into strata, or layers, each representing a different period in a site's history) of remains, on

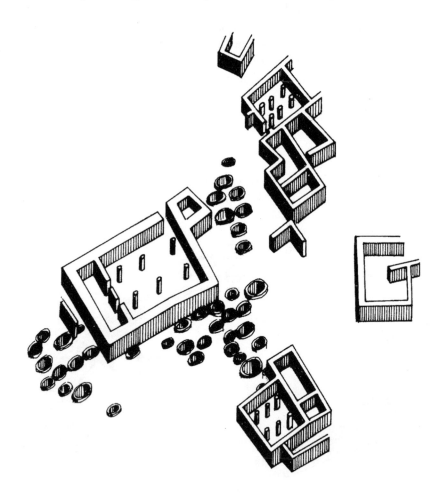

Plan of a sector of Str. II at 'Izbet Sartah, surrounded
by grain silos; 11th century B.C.
Israel Finkelstein and Neil Silberman, *The Bible Unearthed*

bedrock, yielded only tattered architectural remains, a few silos, and what may have been an oval perimeter wall or a row of house walls. Finkelstein dates this level to the late 13th century B.C. on the basis of pottery still in the Late Bronze Age tradition. Due to its oval plan — like "wagons drawn up in a circle" — he regards Stratum III as a sort of "encampment" that reflects the activities of pastoral nomads beginning to settle down.

Stratum II, much more substantial and now expanded to about ten acres, dates to the 11th century B.C., following Stratum III after a gap in occupation sometime during the late 12th century B.C. This level reveals a village of perhaps a hundred people, with several classic pillar-courtyard houses, surrounded by numerous stone-lined silos. The central house was large (*ca.* 1700 sq. ft on the ground floor) and very well built. Forty-three silos surrounded it. In one of them was found an ostracon (that is, a piece of inscribed pottery) on which some eighty characters were written in ink, arranged in five lines. The only legible line, at the bottom, is an abecedary, or a list of the letters of the alphabet — written, unusually, from left to right. Although the script is Canaanite, the writer may have been an Israelite schoolboy practicing his letters. (If this were a take-home exercise, I'd give him a C-.) If this is indeed the case, the 'Izbet Sartah ostracon is our earliest real Hebrew inscription — and also important evidence for the early spread of literacy. Stratum I, extending into the 10th century B.C.,

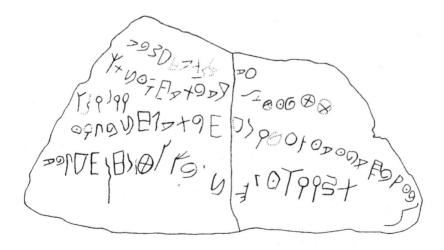

The 12th-century-B.C. abecedary from Str. II at 'Izbet Sartah
Biblical Archaeology Review IV:3

ends the brief occupation of the site, and thereafter it disappears, not to be rediscovered for nearly three thousand years.

'Izbet Sartah is one of the very few early Israelite sites to be extensively excavated and published, not merely described on the basis of surface surveys (see below). Finkelstein sees it as conclusive evidence of the sedentarization of local pastoral nomads, but the support for that is underwhelming. Animals that were almost exclusively domesticated (97%), the substantial presence of cattle bones (34.3%), and the ability to produce a significant surplus all indicated to the specialists on the staff that the economic system of 'Izbet Sartah "was typical of a settlement based on agricultural and animal breeding." These facts led the Field Director to publish a rebuttal of Finkelstein's theories, entitled "Nomads They Never Were." (I shall take up this issue again in Chapter 9.) In any case, 'Izbet Sartah's location only about three miles from the large and extensively excavated Canaanite-Philistine urban site of Aphek gives it special significance. That would be especially true if it really is "Ebenezer," where the Philistines are said to have defeated the Israelites and seized the Ark of the Covenant (1 Sam. 4).

Shiloh

From 1981 to 1984 Finkelstein re-excavated Shiloh, some twenty miles north of Jerusalem, which had been dug in the 1920s by Danish archaeologists. According to biblical tradition, Shiloh (Arabic Kh. Seilûn) served as Israel's religious center during the time of the judges. The Ark rested there, and Samuel dwelled there as the last of the judges and the first of the prophets — Israel's "king-maker" in the days of Saul in the late 11th century B.C.

Finkelstein's new excavations confirmed the fact that after a long abandonment in the Late Bronze Age, Shiloh was resettled in the 12th century B.C. Along the inside perimeter of the old abandoned Middle Bronze Age city wall (17th-16th centuries B.C.), which now served as a sort of terrace wall, there was built an adjoining row of pillar-courtyard houses of early type, surrounded by many stone-lined silos. The abundant pottery consisted of early 12th century B.C. types, including several of the large collar-rim storejars discussed above. Of the biblical cultic center Finkelstein found no trace, although he speculated that an earlier Canaanite

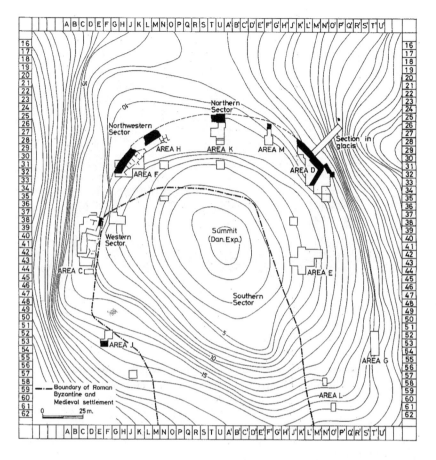

General plan of Shiloh, showing areas of the Danish and Israeli excavations
Israel Finkelstein, *Shiloh*

shrine might have been reused for such an installation. Shiloh was then destroyed in a huge fire around 1050 B.C., which left up to six feet of debris overlying the ruins. It was never again an important town, probably since urbanization during the early Monarchy caused the center of population to shift elsewhere.

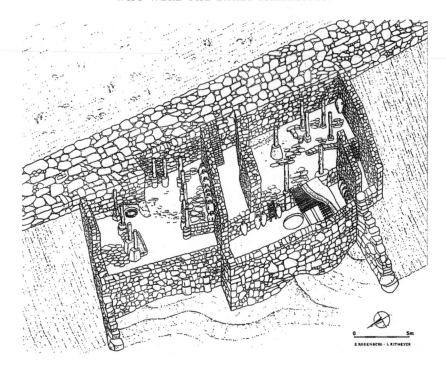

Isometric reconstruction of Shiloh Iron Age pillar-courtyard
buildings of Area C in Str. V, ca. 12th century B.C.
Israel Finkelstein, *Shiloh*

Kh. ed Dawara

In the 1980s Finkelstein also excavated the small hilltop village of Kh. ed-Dawara, dating to the mid-late 11th century B.C. It was built on an oval-shaped plan, with several well-developed pillar-courtyard houses constructed against and bonded into a peripheral wall some six feet thick. Thus far, it is perhaps the only town wall we have from the 12th-11th centuries B.C.

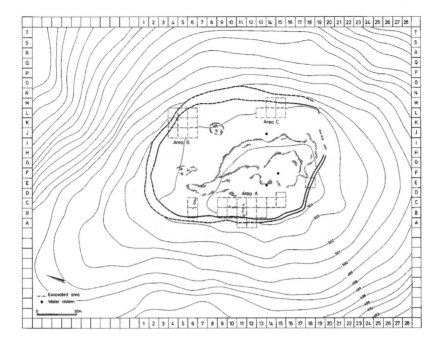

General plan of Kh. ed-Dawara, showing the line of a
"boundary" wall; 11th century B.C.
Tel Aviv 17:2

Beersheba

One of the few of these early Iron I Israelite villages that continued into
Iron II and the period of the Monarchy is Beersheba. The excavations of
the Israeli scholar Yohanan Aharoni there in 1969-76 brought to light the
plan of another apparently oval-shaped village, only about an acre in size.
It had pillar-courtyard houses grouped closely together, as well as stone-
lined silos. Stratum IX, belonging probably to the late 12th century B.C.,
was followed by two rebuilds (Strata VIII-VII) in the 11th century and early
10th century B.C. There was no Late Bronze Canaanite occupation.

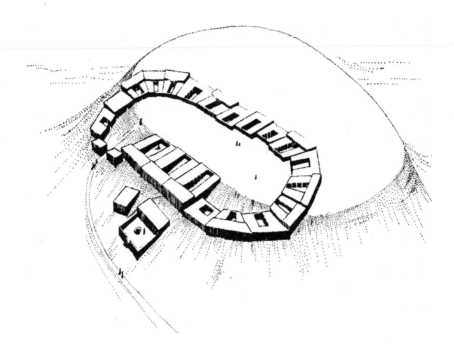

Isometric reconstruction of the Str. VII settlement at Beersheba;
ca. early 10th century B.C.
Israel Finkelstein and Nadav Na'aman, *From Nomadism to Monarchy*

Other Excavated Israelite Sites

There are only a few other early Iron I excavated sites that might be considered "Israelite" (although we have yet to define that term fully). I have
noted above the excavations carried out at Bethel, in the hill country some
ten miles north of Jerusalem, in the 1930s and again in the 1950s. There is a
massive destruction there, followed by an unfortified 12th-11th century B.C.
village. This destruction was attributed to incoming Israelites by Albright
(see above, on 'Ai), but we lack material proof of this, and the argument is
more biblical than properly archaeological. According to biblical tradition,
Bethel was recaptured sometime during the period of the Judges (Judg.
1:22-26); but it is not mentioned in the earlier conquests of Joshua. The
two destructions within the Iron I settlement of the 12th-11th centuries B.C.
may possibly reflect the biblical tradition.

88

A Cultic Site

There is also a 12th century B.C. site of unique character that calls for comment because it has been interpreted as an early Israelite cultic center. It is a small installation on the crest of Mt. Ebal, forty miles north of Jerusalem, overlooking Shechem in the pass below. It was excavated in the 1980s by Adam Zertal, who claimed that he had discovered the very altar that Joshua had built on Mt. Ebal (Deut. 11:29; Josh. 8:30-35). The site has three phases. The first, consisting mostly of an enclosure wall, was dated to the late 13th century B.C. by two Egyptian scarabs of the time of Ramses II or III. The next phase featured the addition of another enclosure wall and a small rectangular building with no apparent entrance, oriented to the points of the compass. Numerous animal bones were found within this structure, even though it had no real living surface. In two courtyards outside the building there were buried several storejars containing some broken pottery, ashes, and the burnt bones of several kinds of animals: sheep, goats, cattle, and roe deer.

Zertal interpreted the central structure as a large altar, approached by a stepped ramp. The burnt bones he took to reflect biblical traditions of animal sacrifice (although deer are not kosher in the Bible). He then made an elaborate reconstruction of the whole hilltop, based on the description

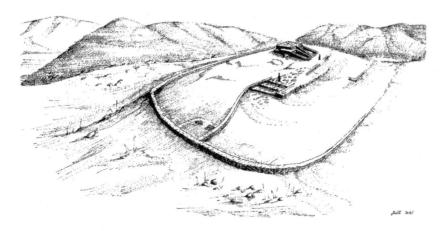

Zertal's reconstruction of the supposed "altar" on Mount Ebal
Tel Aviv 13-14:2

of the altar in Ezekiel, as well as on even later rabbinical sources. Few agreed with Zertal's interpretation, however, and many thought it a particularly egregious example of the excesses of "biblical archaeology." Most Israeli and American archaeologists interpreted the enigmatic structure atop Mt. Ebal as an isolated Iron I farmhouse, or even just a watchtower. (I have suggested somewhat facetiously that the cool and breezy hilltop location, the splendid views, and the burnt bones all indicate that this was a favorite picnic site, especially for summer barbecues.) The other, better attested early Israelite cultic installation is Mazar's "Bull Site" farther north (see below and the illustration on p. 127).

CHAPTER 6

More Facts on the Ground:
Recent Archaeological Surveys

So far our archaeological evidence for the rise of early Israel on the soil of Canaan has consisted of a handful of excavated sites that can plausibly be identified as "Israelite" sites on the basis of texts in the Hebrew Bible. But there is much more evidence from recent archaeological survey work — especially in the West Bank, the "heartland" of ancient Israel.

The West Bank and Other Surveys

In an ironic twist of history, the establishment of the State of Israel in the UN-sponsored partition of Palestine in 1948 left the new nation without its ancient heartland, the West Bank, which was designated part of the Hashemite Kingdom of Jordan, with an Arab population. Thus, in effect, the Israelis became the modern counterparts of the ancient Canaanites, the Palestinians equivalent to the ancient Israelites.

Immediately after the Six Day War in 1967, Israeli archaeologists and others flocked to the newly-conquered territories, keen on rediscovering their supposed historical "roots." At the time of the war I was the Director of the American Hebrew Union College Biblical and Archaeological School in West Jerusalem in Israel. Before that, however, in the earlier 1960s, I had been associated with the other, older American school in Arab East Jerusalem, now the William Foxwell Albright Institute of Archaeological Research. Since the foreign archaeologists in East Jerusalem who were familiar with the West Bank sites had all fled before the war, I was the only archaeologist in Jerusalem who knew the area well, having excavated there in Jordanian times. Of course, a few of the older Israeli archaeologists like Avraham Biran and Benjamin Mazar remembered the area vaguely from their youth. But the younger Israeli archaeologists, although they knew the sites well "on paper," had never dreamed of actually seeing them. I still re-call my excitement when Biran and Mazar asked me about a week after the war if I would conduct a guided tour. Thus a caravan of Israeli cars and a couple dozen of us set out one day to explore sites like 'Ai, Bethel, Gibeon, Shechem (where I had worked), Samaria, and others. It was like coming home — for me in one way, and for the Israelis in another.

Since no one knew how long the Israelis might hold "Judea and Sa-maria" (as they came to be called), Israeli archaeologists soon carried out a sort of "quick and dirty" surface exploration, whose results were published in Hebrew in 1968. Years passed, however, and the Israeli occupation did not end. So in 1978 a much larger and more deliberate archaeological sur-vey was launched, led mostly by young archaeologists of the Tel Aviv Uni-versity. There their mentor, Yohanan Aharoni, had pioneered the then-new "regional approach," based on large-scale surface surveys plus selective ex-cavation in depth of a few key sites.

These surveys in the West Bank continued for nearly a decade and produced such an astonishing wealth of data that they totally revolution-ized our understanding of the origins of ancient Israel. The first systematic presentations were given at the annual Archaeological Conference in Jeru-salem in the spring of 1982, while I was in Israel on sabbatical. I struggled through three days of papers presented in Modern Hebrew, not able to un-derstand everything but aware that I was in at the beginning of a huge ar-chaeological event. By the mid-1980s I was following further reports and began to write on the subject, largely to acquaint non-Israeli biblical schol-ars with what I thought really was a revolution. Then some of the basic data were published by Finkelstein in his preliminary report in 1988, enti-tled *The Archaeology of the Israelite Settlement*. Hebrew final reports began to appear; and by 1997 part of the vast database appeared in English.

The Methodology of Surface Surveys

Before summarizing the results of the Israeli surveys, which were the first systematic explorations of most areas in the West Bank, let us look briefly at the methodology of surface surveys, as well as some of their advantages and limitations. In doing what we call intensive "pedestrian" surveys (as opposed to "windshield," or drive-by surveys), teams of archaeologists grid off a selected region, then spread out in a line and walk the entire area looking for all traces of ancient remains. They carefully record any features that may reveal the nature of the ancient occupation, such as topographic irregularities, wall-lines, and in particular the broken potsherds that provide the best clue to the various periods of occupation below the surface. An attempt is also made to locate any related off-site installations, such as terraces, rock-cut olive presses, springs, irrigated fields, and the like. All the information about the site and its surroundings that can be gleaned from the material remains observed on the surface is thus recorded, and nowadays is computerized. Then, when all the sites in the region have been similarly surveyed, "settlement maps" for each archaeological period are drawn up, showing the location and distribution of all the known sites by estimated size and by type for each period (that is, isolated farmhouse, hamlet, village, town, walled city, industrial site, fort, cemetery, and so on).

The advantage of such methodical surveys are many: (1) They focus on all the sites in a region, giving a more complete picture. (2) They "salvage" many sites that may soon be lost forever to modern development. (3) They produce a lot of information without resorting to excavation in depth, which ultimately becomes a form of systematic destruction. (4) Finally, in these days of limited resources, surface surveys, much cheaper than excavations, yield the "biggest bang for the buck."

There are, however, several drawbacks to surface surveys. (1) They can give a somewhat misleading impression of settlement history for a given region, since many sites — especially smaller and single-period sites — have already been lost to erosion or modern construction, or may simply be buried and invisible under deep alluvial deposits. (2) The remains preserved and picked up on the surface may come principally from the final occupation, while deeper layers (or strata) from earlier periods remain completely invisible. (3) Finally, the material exposed on the surface, which archaeologists can actually see and thus pick up, may be very scant, due to overgrowth, the accidents of preservation, or many other factors. For instance, a small site may yield only a handful of badly worn, obscure shards. For all these reasons, surface surveys are often impressionistic and lacking in absolute statistical validity. Yet for all these variables, surface surveys, when carefully done, have been shown to give fairly reliable *relative* statis-

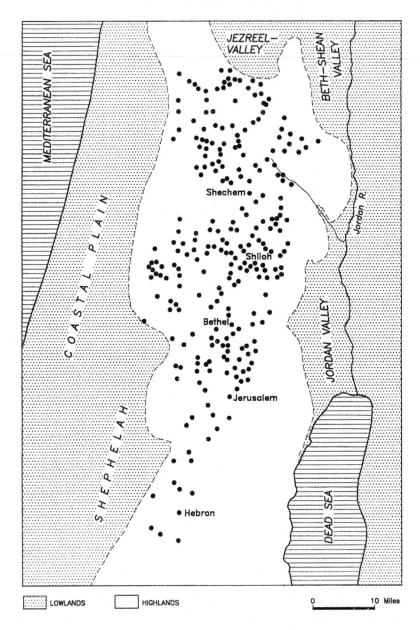

The "Manasseh" and "Ephraim" survey region of Finkelstein and Zertal
in the hill country north of Jerusalem
Israel Finkelstein and Neil Silberman, *The Bible Unearthed*

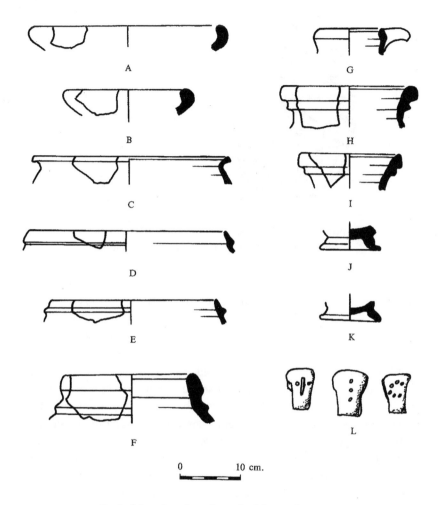

Typical Iron I pottery from the Manasseh survey
Israel Finkelstein and Nadav Na'aman, *From Nomadism to Monarchy*

tics — especially on period-by-period changes in settlement distribution. And these are among the archaeologists' most useful tools in dealing with long-term history and cultural change.

Before proceeding, let me answer a question that many readers may ask: "But how does pottery give a date for the successive settlements, since everything hinges on that?" The answer is actually rather simple. After

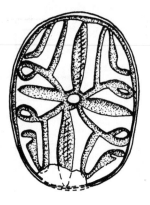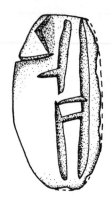

Egyptian scarab from Mount Ebal, dating exclusively to the
time of Ramses II or his 19th Dynasty successors
Tel Aviv 13-14:2

more than a hundred years of analyzing the common pottery of ancient
Palestine, we are now confident that we can date most forms, even small
fragments, within about a century or so. That is because we often find certain individual forms, and particularly groups of related forms or an "assemblage," in a *context* that can be dated. Sometimes the "peg" on which
we hang the chronology consists of associated Egyptian scarabs; evidence
of destructions known from ancient texts that can be astronomically dated
by references to related celestial events; later, by coins; and increasingly by
scientific means of dating such as Carbon 14 analysis. Thus the chronology
of the Iron I villages we are discussing is not really controversial. There are
scarcely any differences of more than fifty years among experts, and such
"historical dead reckoning" is sufficient for our purposes here.

A Region-by-Region Summary

Let us now turn to the survey data, not only that from the West Bank, but also
from recent surveys within Israel itself, as for instance surveys of Galilee, the
coastal plain, and the northern Negev. What we shall be looking for are particularly the following: (1) evidence for cultural *changes* from the 13th into the
11th century B.C.; (2) evidence for the distinctive "lifestyle" that emerges in
Canaan in this period and its probable origin; (3) evidence bearing upon the

question of the "ethnicity" of the inhabitants. In short, who were the "early Israelites," and where did they come from? (We already know when.)

Settlement Distribution and Demography

For the sake of convenience, let me give some of the basic data from recent
Israeli surveys in simple chart-form. This information is taken principally
from Finkelstein's *The Archaeology of the Israelite Settlement* (1988), sup-
plemented by Finkelstein and N. Na'aman's *From Nomadism to Monarchy:
Archaeological and Historical Aspects of Early Israel* (1994). By "Iron I" I
mean supposedly 12th-11th century Israelite sites.

Region	Number of Late Bronze Age and Iron I Sites		Estimated Population by 11th century B.C.?
Upper Galilee	8	23/40	2,300-4,000
Lower Galilee	5	25	2,500
Jezreel Valley	Many	?	?
N. Coastal Plain	—	—	—
Sharon Plain	?	10	2,500
Shephelah (foothills)	?	2	500
Manasseh	22	96	1,000-2,900
Ephraim	5/6	122	9,650
Jerusalem Area	8 ?	12-30	2,200-4,500
(Benjamin)	—	—	2,200
W. Jordan Valley	?	20	2,200
Judean Hills	7	18	1,250
Judean Desert	?	few	100
Beersheba Valley	?	2–3	150-200
Negev Desert	—	—	—
TOTALS	58	331-366	40,650-55,000

First we should note that the total number of sites found in these
surveys, not including the excavated sites, grew enormously from the Late
Bronze Age into the Iron I period — from 58 to around 350. An estimate of
total population of these sites by the 11th century B.C. in the second stage of
the supposed Israelite settlement, using Finkelstein's "correction factor" to

account for less than complete data, is around 50,000. In other publications, he gives an estimate of the 12th century B.C. "Israelite" population west of the Jordan as something like 21,000. The important thing to note here is the population growth from the "Canaanite" Late Bronze Age in the 13th century B.C. to the Iron I "Israelite" period by the 11th century B.C., especially in the *hill country*. Here are the figures:

Sites		Built-up Area	Est. Population
13th century B.C.	29	117	12,000
11th century B.C.	254	547	30,000-42,000

Stager's more recent (and more sophisticated) analysis of the survey data in 1998 yielded a somewhat different picture, although the all-important *relative* figures are comparable. These are Stager's estimates for the entire area of Canaan:

Sites		Built-up Area	Est. Population
13th century B.C.	88	500	50,000
12th-11th century B.C.	687	1,500	150,000

For the hill country alone, Stager gives these figures, which are only slightly higher than Finkelstein's:

Sites		
13th century B.C.	36	?
12th-11th century B.C.	319	?

Stager also notes that of the 687 12th-11th century B.C. sites, 633 (or 93%) are new foundations, usually small, unwalled villages. And such Iron I settlements are unusually dense in the areas of Manasseh and Ephraim, as shown already by the Israeli surveys. Stager does not give a population estimate for these areas. But since the bulk of the population was concentrated there, some 50,000 of his total of 150,000 would seem reasonable — only slightly higher than Finkelstein's 30,000-42,000.

The significant fact in all these figures is that in contrast to other areas of Canaan, the *hill country* — where most of the supposedly Israelite peoples settled and later developed into a nation-state — witnessed a population explosion in the 12th century B.C. As Stager puts it,

This extraordinary increase in population in Iron I cannot be explained only by natural population growth of the few Late Bronze Age city-states in the region: there must have been a major influx of people into the highlands in the twelfth and eleventh centuries BCE. . . . That many of these villages belonged to premonarchic Israel . . . is beyond doubt. (1998: 134, 135)

It may be helpful to say a few further words here about distribution and settlement type, which archaeologists always find among the most revealing ways to look at long-term cultural change. First, the overwhelming number of small villages that now dot the Iron I landscape of Canaan are not located along the coastal plains of Sharon and Judah, in the lowlands of the Shephelah, or in the major river valleys. In those places the prime areas, with their rich resources and large urban sites, remained largely Canaanite (or Phoenician) well into the Iron Age. And the Egyptian 19th Dynasty was still in political control until at least 1160 B.C. (above). The new Israelite settlements, by contrast, are almost all founded *de novo,* not on the ruins of destroyed Late Bronze Age sites, but in the sparsely populated hill country extending from Upper and Lower Galilee, into the hills of Samaria and Judah, and southward into the northern Negev. These areas constituted the frontier — the margins of urban Canaanite society. Why this pattern of settlement, unless a military confrontation was precisely what the highland colonizers wished to *avoid?* Here the peaceful infiltration and peasant revolt models of settlement fit the recent archaeological evidence much better than the old conquest model. There was no need for armed conflict, nor opportunity for conquest, in these areas, since they were largely devoid of Canaanite population.

A word also about the distinctive type of Iron I settlement in the hill country in general, although I shall reserve detailed discussion for later: Nearly all the settlements mapped in the Israeli surveys — and indeed all the Iron I excavated sites as well — are tiny villages, ranging from a fraction of an acre up to about four or five acres. (To give some idea of relative size, an acre is slightly smaller than a football field.) Not one of the supposed "early Israelite" settlements known thus far has anything whatsoever of an "urban" character, or even the characteristics of a small town. As we shall see presently, they are all agricultural villages or hamlets. It is not only their diminutive size that suggests this, but also their typical location on hilltops overlooking small but fertile intermountain valleys good for growing grain and also adjacent hillsides suitable for terracing for other crops such as olives, grapes, fruits, and vegetables. In addition, there are good grazing areas in the nearby marginal or steppe regions that are typically intermixed with the more arable hill country land of ancient Palestine.

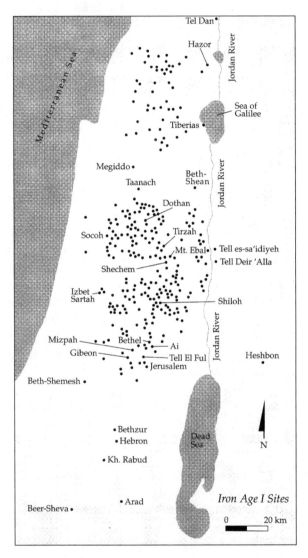

Excavated and surveyed early Israelite sites
Hershel Shanks et al., *The Rise of Ancient Israel*

CHAPTER 7

A Summary of the Material Culture
of the Iron I Assemblage

In the last chapter I introduced a basic working term that archaeologists use — an "assemblage." To refresh, by this I mean a group of contemporary types of material culture remains that are obviously related and tend to occur together so frequently that patterns emerge. These patterns may be seen first only at an individual site. But when the same pattern emerges at other sites, then throughout an entire region, a larger cultural assemblage may be described — one that cannot fail to have historical significance.

An assemblage may include any number of items: smaller artifacts such as pottery, stone or metal tools, and art objects. It may also embrace larger configurations of things such as house-forms, town plans, fortifications, burials, water works, industrial installations, and the like. Also considered are less specific but nonetheless tangible environmental factors such as geography, soil and water resources, and climate. Looking at all these interrelated physical remains, archaeologists may be able (as one of my colleagues puts it) to "write history from things" — even without texts. Thus we have available to us: (1) artifacts, (2) ecofacts, and (3) textual facts. What do we make of them?

Archaeologists begin by assuming that the human thought and behavior that leads to the creation of these assemblages is also "patterned" (in other words, it is part of culture). Thus there must be a relationship between the two — between thought and thing. As it is often put, "artifacts are the material correlates of behavior." In attempting to "read" these assemblages like texts so as to reconstruct past lifeways, or extinct social systems, many archaeologists have borrowed the concept of "systems" from the life sciences. The basic tenet of what is called General Systems Theory (GST) is that all living organisms are made up of highly complex systems, which are in turn composed of various subsystems. Thus the human body, for example, functions through the interrelated activities of a respiratory, circulatory, alimentary, nervous, and other subsystems. A second concept of GST is that of "equilibrium." When all the subsystems are in dynamic balance, the organism is healthy; but when one of them fails, disequilibrium results. And if several subsystems fail, there begins a downward spiral that leads to disintegration and ultimately to the death of the organism.

There are always some uncertainties in transferring models from the scientific to the social world. Nevertheless, many of us find GST useful, at least for analyzing archaeological assemblages in terms of their implications for inferring past social systems. I shall take that approach in the following summary of the Iron I village assemblage. The "subsystems" that I find most useful are the following (keep in mind that all these factors are interrelated, so the order is somewhat arbitrary):

1. House-plan and village layout
2. Subsistence, economy
3. Social structure
4. Political organization
5. Technology
6. Art, ideology, religion
7. External relations

In fact, one might begin with even more basic factors such as site type and distribution, as well as demography. But we have already mentioned these in dealing with the surface surveys that have produced most of the relevant data. Now we will proceed to integrate both survey and excavated data, examining in this chapter the first six of these seven factors.

House-plan and Village Layout

Closely related to site type and distribution are the distinctive plans of both houses and settlements. I have already introduced the typical pillar-courtyard or four-room house. Let me now expand the picture by noting

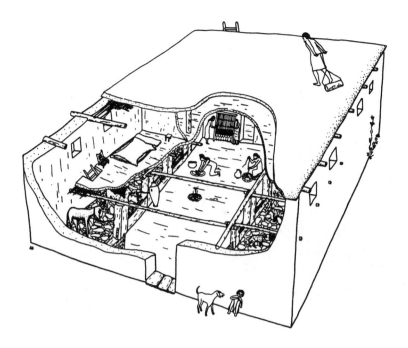

Reconstruction of a typical 12th-11th century-B.C. "Israelite house"
Abbas Alizadeh

that these houses have long been known in some parts of western Palestine and are attested as well in eastern Palestine in the early Iron Age. Many scholars have considered them to be "type-fossils" of ancient Israel — that is, uniquely characteristic and thus a reliable ethnic indicator. They have been called four-room houses because the plan of the ground floor features a large open courtyard around which are grouped three banks of adjoining rooms. Stone pillars set the rooms off from the central courtyard and also supported the second story.

The courtyards often feature a deep cistern cut into the bedrock, clay ovens and hearths for cooking, and space for storage or simple industrial installations. The living surfaces here are of tamped clay. The side rooms, often with pillars for tethering animals and cobbled floors that could have been more easily "mucked out," are best interpreted as stables. Excavations at Raddana and elsewhere suggest that these houses originally had only two banks of rooms, though after a time most were built with three. The

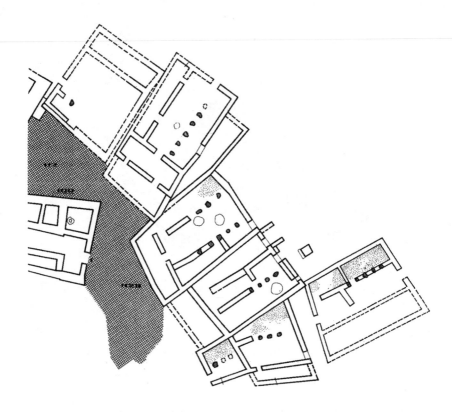

A cluster of pillar-courtyard houses from Str. II
at Tel Masos (11th century B.C.)
Fritz and Kempinski, Tel Masos.

several rooms of the upper story could easily have accommodated up to
two dozen people, with ample space for eating, sleeping, and other domestic activities. And the flat roof would have been an ideal area for drying
foodstuffs or for additional storage.

It is obvious that these pillar-courtyard houses, which for the most
part first appear in the early Iron Age, would have been ideal farmhouses
for a rural population with an agricultural economy and society. They are
spacious enough (with up to two thousand square feet of living and working space) to have served a typical large, multi-generational farm family,
together with their several animals. There is enough room for water and

stored foodstuffs and supplies to last through an entire season. Even the stabling of the animals — for most families probably a donkey, a cow or two, and a few sheep and goats — is practical: they are well protected, close at hand, their dung is readily available to mix with straw for fuel, and even the heat radiating from their bodies is useful. These are efficient, self-contained units, reflecting what economists would call the "domestic mode of production." Almost identical farmhouses are still in use in less developed Middle Eastern countries today. To the importance of these facts I shall return presently.

Very stereotypical examples of such houses are found at almost every Israelite Iron I site. And they persist throughout the Iron II period until the end of the Monarchy, even at sites by then highly urbanized, like "town-houses" based on a rural model.

This distinctive house-form has no real predecessors in the long settlement history of Canaan and appears suddenly on the 13th/12th century B.C. horizon, even sporadically in Transjordan. It seems to reflect a preference (or nostalgia) for a rural society and economy, and it also reflects the typical Israelite ideal of the "good life," based on close-knit families and communal values, as we can discern it from the later biblical texts. In short, the ubiquitous house-form, which archaeologists everywhere agree is useful in determining a culture's ethnicity, may be one of our best clues to the lifestyle, and even the origins, of the Iron I settlers. Unique houses; unique peoples? Yes. These really *are* Israelite houses.

More significant, however, than the individual house-plan is the *grouping* of two or three such typical houses, with common walls and shared courtyards, to form a larger complex, or what may be called a "family compound." The compounds are then typically grouped into larger "clusters," several clusters then forming the plan of the village as a whole. There are also open areas between each cluster, which would have been used for penning up animals, cultivating gardens, storage, dumping rubbish, or simple industrial operations like working stone tools or making pottery. All these features are best understood as reflecting the lifestyle of close-knit, independent, self-sufficient families in small rural villages.

In 1985, Lawrence Stager utilized typical Iron I house-plans and village layouts to make an ingenious connection between the "facts on the ground" and scattered references to family and social structure as well as to village life in the books of Joshua, Judges, and Samuel. The suggested equivalencies fit the actual evidence of house-form and village layout from

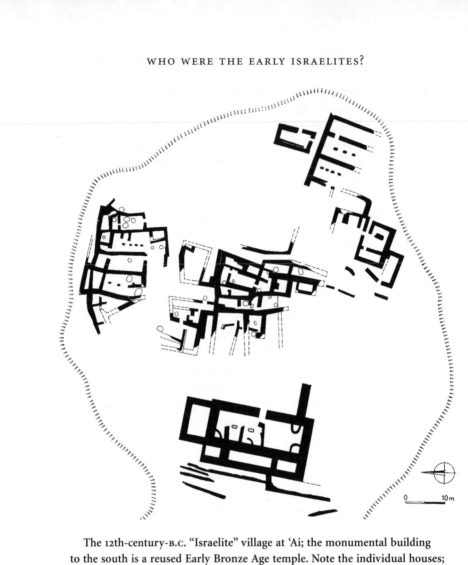

The 12th-century-B.C. "Israelite" village at 'Ai; the monumental building
to the south is a reused Early Bronze Age temple. Note the individual houses;
"clusters"; and larger compound.
Aharon Kempinski and Ronny Reich, eds., *The Architecture of Ancient Israel*

our Iron I sites astonishingly well. Let me set forth the evidence (slightly
modified from Stager's scheme) in simple chart form.

Socioeconomic Terms from the Hebrew Bible
with Suggested Archaeological Correlates

Hebrew term	Meaning	Archaeological evidence
geber	The "individual," in a nuclear family	Individual house
bet'ab	The "house of the Father"; a multi-generational family	Family compound of several "pillar-courtyard" houses
mishpaha	The extended family, or "clan"	The cluster of several compounds, the whole village
shebet	The "tribe"	Regional groups of villages
benei-yisrael	All the tribes, or "sons of Israel"	The entire network of hill country settlements

Stager's precocious, brilliant article was entitled "The Archaeology of the Family in Ancient Israel," and it remains one of our best analyses of both texts and artifacts in the task of identifying "early Israel."

Subsistence and Economy

What actual evidence do we have, however, that our "rural villages" of Iron I were really agricultural communities? Here the archaeological evidence, both from surveys and excavated sites, is abundant and conclusive.

1. *Food remains.* Archaeologists now routinely do what is called "paleo-ethnobotany," that is, they do extensive sampling using fine sieves and flotation devices to retrieve even minute remains of the plants that were once used as foodstuffs. As a result, we now know that the Iron I villages produced large quantities of grains such as wheat and barley, cereals and legumes, and produce typical of modern truck farms. Statistical studies have shown that many villages such as 'Izbet Sartah and Shiloh (both discussed earlier) were capable of producing a substantial surplus of these agricultural products. To me this evidence indicates that the inhabitants were farmers and stockbreeders who had long previous experience with the problems of local agriculture in Canaan. They could thus adapt fairly quickly to the adverse conditions of the hill country frontier — especially

when aided by newer technologies (see below). Pastoral nomads settling down suddenly in these areas would have faced daunting challenges. They might even have starved the first winter.

2. *Animal bones.* Similar sampling has recovered large quantities of animal bones, obviously evidence of the sort of small-scale stockbreeding that is typical of ancient (and modern) agro-pastoral economies. Most of the animals bred and herded in the Iron I villages were sheep and goats (between 45 and 80%), as in Arab villages today. But cattle, oxen, and donkeys are also well attested, obviously useful as the traction and plough animals that are required in farmsteads and agricultural villages — and hardly evidence of an urban or industrial way of life. To this evidence, we must add the fact that much of the ground floor of the typical pillar-courtyard house was given over to use as stables.

One animal species is conspicuously absent in our Iron I villages: the pig. Although not nearly as common as sheep and goats at Bronze Age sites, pigs are well attested then. They are also common at Iron I coastal sites that are known to be Philistine. But recent statistical analyses of animal bones retrieved from our Iron I Israelite sites show that pig bones typically constitute only a fraction of 1% or are entirely absent. A number of scholars who are otherwise skeptical about determining ethnic identity from material culture remains in this case acknowledge the obvious: that here we seem to have at least one ethnic trait of later, biblical Israel that can safely be projected back to its earliest days.

3. *Storage areas and facilities.* The typical Iron I house also features ample storage space of the sort that would be essential in a self-sufficient farming community. Some of this was in the back room of the ground floor; much of the rest was provided by the numerous large collar-rim storejars (discussed above) usually found in these dwellings. They constitute up to 75% of all vessels found in some rooms; remains of grapes, raisins, wine, grains, and olive oil have been retrieved from them. Urban sites show little evidence of such storage space and facilities, since most people there bought or traded for their food supplies day by day as needed. The collar-rim jars in particular are conspicuously absent at most urban sites. The common silos and cisterns discussed below also provided for storage.

4. *Tools.* Specifically agricultural implements are also found in our Iron I villages. Among the most common iron items in the early "Iron Age" are large heavy plow points of the sort that Arab farmers used until recently for dragging an iron-shod wooden plough behind a team of oxen or

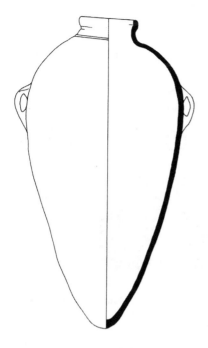

A typical Iron I "collar-rim" storejar, from Shiloh Str. V
Israel Finkelstein, *Shiloh*

donkeys. An iron pick from the village of Har Adir in Galilee is, surprisingly, the earliest known example of true steel, or deliberately carburized iron. In addition, we have small bronze adzes, daggers, knives, awls, and so on. Flint-bladed sickles are still in use, as well as other simple tools.

5. *Cottage industries.* I have already noted that the Iron I economy and society is a good example of what economic anthropologists would call the "domestic mode of production" — that is, a family-based system, which of course was common in the pre-industrial societies of the ancient world generally. We have good archaeological evidence of such cottage industries in our Iron I villages. There are archaeological remains of household facilities for making stone and flint tools, potters' workshops, olive and grape processing installations, and evidence of primitive looms for weaving textiles. All this shows that the typical village family produced most of what it owned, used, and consumed, rather than relying on commercial facilities.

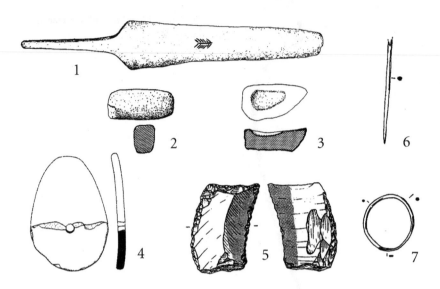

(1) Bronze dagger, Giloh; (2) Stone pestle, Mount Ebal; (3) Stone mortar, Mount Ebal; (4) Ceramic "polisher," Shiloh, Str. II; (5) Flint blade, Shiloh, Str. V; (6) Bronze needle, 'Izbet Sartah, Str. II; (7) Bronze bracelet, 'Izbet Sartah, Str. II

Israel Finkelstein and Nadav Na'aman, *From Nomadism to Monarchy* (1); *Tel Aviv* 13-14:2 (2, 3); Israel Finkelstein, *Shiloh* (4, 5); Israel Finkelstein, *'Izbet Sartah* (6, 7)

Social Structure

The economy and society that I have described thus far in our Iron I villages may certainly be characterized as rural, family-based, and undoubtedly agricultural. Judging from those facts, we may safely infer several qualities of the resultant lifestyle: "simple"; "self-sufficient"; perhaps "egalitarian," or better, "communitarian." Only the term "egalitarian" would be controversial for those taking a sociological approach to early Israel, as I am doing here.

The first full-scale modern sociological analysis of early Israel was that of Norman Gottwald, one of the architects of the peasant revolt model, in his monumental *Tribes of Yahweh* (1979) discussed above. Gottwald's emphasis throughout on social revolution led him to see early Israelite society as egalitarian, or lacking any social stratification, in contrast to the preceding stratified society of Canaanite overlords. Thus his subtitle: *A*

Sociology of the Religion of Liberated Israel. Critics pointed out early on his assumption of the Marxist ideal of a "classless society." Not only has such an ideal now turned out to be a cruel illusion, but it is to be doubted whether any society known to us throughout human history has been truly egalitarian. Even tribal societies, as sociologists will readily tell us, have sheikhs. In theory all are equal, but some are more equal than others, as the saying goes. To his credit, in more recent years (since 1985) Gottwald has abandoned his egalitarian terminology — indeed much of his peasants' revolt model — in favor of a "communitarian model of production" and an "agrarian social revolution." Here I could not be more in agreement, as I shall show in detail below. That is exactly what the more recent archaeological data (not available when Gottwald first wrote in 1979) implies. And I shall amplify the term "agrarian," which Gottwald mentions only in passing.

Another way of describing early Israelite society might be to characterize it as "bourgeois" — that is, as a middle class society that represents neither the aristocracy nor the proletariat (working class). But again this language carries too much Marxist baggage, and in any case it does little to help us to comprehend the reality of early Israel. "Bourgeois" is ultimately no more useful a term than "peasant."

Other biblical scholars have also commented on early Israelite social structure, both before and after Gottwald. But either they wrote without utilizing the now-definitive archaeological data, or else they belong to the revisionist camp for whom there *was* no early Israel. I shall acknowledge these scholars in my conclusion.

Political Organization

Closely related to social structure is political organization, since politics is in one sense the art of communal living. Traditionally anthropologists and others who have dealt with ancient political organization have analyzed the phenomena in terms of an evolutionary scheme that saw all early societies as passing through similar stages: those of band, tribe, chiefdom, and state. Not only was this supposedly an inevitable process of development, but a progressive and beneficial one as well.

Today such a scheme seems too mechanistic and deterministic to explain many case studies. There are simply too many exceptions to the rule.

Early Israel is one such exception in my opinion. It is unlikely that any of Israel's ancestors roved around the Mediterranean world in bands, at least after the Stone Age. Many scholars, however, have portrayed early Israel in Canaan as representative of the second presumed evolutionary stage, the tribe. Certainly the most ambitious effort was that of Gottwald in *Tribes of Yahweh*. Yet after an exhaustive analysis, he found it difficult even to define the term "tribe." Certainly the vast anthropological and ethnographic literature on tribes is bewildering. There are, however, certain elements that are common to most definitions. To wit, tribes are social entities that are:

1. Kin-based, usually claiming to be derived from a real or imaginary (and usually eponymous) ancestor.
2. Acephalous ("headless"), lacking highly differentiated social strata or centralized power (apart from local chieftains whose office is not necessarily hereditary).
3. Pre-state in terms of organization, or "anti-state," and thus autonomous.

There are obviously hundreds of such tribes known, past and present. And the dominant biblical tradition does indeed portray Israel in premonarchic times as having tribal origins — what has been called the "nomadic ideal." The Patriarchs, Israel's ancestors, are typical Amorite/Canaanite pastoral nomads, tribally organized. And early Israel is depicted as organized into twelve tribes with eponymous ancestors (the sons and grandsons of Jacob), already before the settlement in Canaan — tribes that prevailed as such until the emergence of the Monarchy. Even later the nomadic ideal persisted. When the northern tribes rebelled and seceded at the death of Solomon, according to 1 Kings 12, the rallying-cry was "To your tents, O Israel!" But is all this historical memory, or simply part of an origin-myth — that is, romantic fiction? One aspect of the problem that has bedeviled all observers is the tendency to confuse "tribal" with "nomadic." To do that assumes that all tribally organized societies are nonsedentary, specifically in this case pastoral-nomadic, at least in origin. But that is a fallacy. "Tribalism" is a particular form of *social* organization that may flourish especially among migratory peoples. But it can also be found among fully urbanized peoples, even in modern tribal states in the Middle East such as Saudi Arabia. The essential feature is a kin-based social system, rather than one that we may call "entrepreneurial." I shall argue that early Israel was indeed such a tribal society, but that both the later biblical memory and certain archaeological views of pastoral-nomadic origins (Israel Finkelstein's, for example) are not supported by the evidence.

Technology

Many scholars, especially cultural anthropologists who specialize in material and cultural remains, view technology as one of the so-called "prime movers" in cultural change. While I do not wish for a moment to overlook or to minimize the crucial significance of ideological factors (including religion), technology often does play a key role, especially when it is innovative. And there are several new technologies that do appear on the Late Bronze/Iron Age horizon — most of them, I shall argue, having to do with a new agricultural society, economy, and ideology.

1. *Terraces.* Terrace agriculture has had a long history throughout the Mediterranean world. It is still widely practiced in the hilly regions extending from Spain through southern Italy and Greece into the Middle East. Terracing is a highly specialized and efficient technology that enables even rocky slopes to be brought under cultivation, and it is especially well suited to small-scale farming on family plots. Building terraces is very labor-intensive, and keeping them up requires unrelenting attention (for which a farm family is well suited). But constructing terraces accomplishes several things. (1) It clears the hillsides of stones that would impede a simple plough. (2) At the same time, it removes the need to transport troublesome stones, by utilizing them on the spot to demarcate narrow plots suitable for an ox-or donkey-drawn plough. (3) More important, terraces create a system of stepped retaining walls down the slope that retain rainfall and allow it to percolate, as well as preventing erosion of topsoil.

A crucial role for terrace agriculture in the emergent Iron I hill country economy would seem to be obvious, but its importance has been debated. I have argued that much of the settlement area in the West Bank suitable for agriculture lies precisely in the hilly regions where the ubiquitous terraces seen today must have had a long history. I have even suggested, along with several other scholars, that the first use of these terraces coincides with our early "Israelite" settlements and was one factor in their emergence. Finkelstein, however, disputes both points. He contends (1996) (1) that the earliest Iron I sites are on the semi-arid eastern fringes of the

Remains of ancient hillside terrace systems south of Jerusalem
William G. Dever

central ridge, where terracing would not have been useful or even possible. (2) In the second place, he says, we cannot date ancient terrace systems precisely, and some go far back into the Bronze Age.

Yet these arguments are rather easily refuted using Finkelstein's own data. (1) The "marginal" settlements of the Israeli surveys are all known from surface surveys alone. Thus it is impossible to ascertain whether they were permanent agricultural settlements or simply pastoral-nomadic encampments. The rugged terrain and the relative lack of rainfall here suggest the latter to me. In any case, the fact is that all of the *excavated* hill country settlements — such as Shiloh, 'Ai, Bethel, Raddana, Giloh, and 'Izbet Sartah — are located in precisely those regions where terraces have long been essential to agriculture (and indeed remained in use until the recent introduction of modern agribusiness). (2) As for the question of dating terraces, three points are essential. (a) Several systematic attempts have been made to date the Iron I terrace systems, and they all point to a date in the 12th-11th century B.C., even though the ceramic evidence is admittedly scant and the terraces were obviously reused for centuries. (b) There are, of course, earlier isolated terraces; but the only large-scale integrated *sys-*

tems of terraces are found in the vicinity of our Iron I hill country villages, and their introduction is best explained as being contemporary with and connected to this first intensive colonization of the region. Indeed, it would have been impossible for these agriculturally based villages to survive without developing terrace systems sooner or later, and preferably sooner. (c) Finally, Finkelstein dates his own site of 'Izbet Sartah with its terraces among the earliest foundations, in the late 13th century B.C.; and yet it is the farthest west of all our known "early Israelite" settlements. *What* "east to west movement"? (More on that below.)

In reviewing Finkelstein's arguments about terraces, I cannot escape the impression that he is too attached to his theory of pastoral-nomadic origins to see the point of his own data. Consequently he has skewed the evidence for both the relative dating of the sites and for the origins of the settlers. Far more sophisticated is the treatment of Stager in his "Archaeology of the Family" noted above (which Finkelstein does not cite), treating not only the archaeological evidence for Iron Age terracing, but also the biblical and other textual evidence.

2. *Silos.* I have already alluded to the role of silos in the storage of foodstuffs. Here there is little controversy. Not only were silos essential to the Iron I agricultural economy in the isolated hill country, but it is also generally agreed that they began to proliferate only at this time. Silos are relatively rare at Bronze Age sites, but nearly every one of the sites in question has produced dozens of them, often grouped closely together. One house at 'Izbet Sartah, for example, was surrounded by 43 silos. The evidence of silos alone would be enough to confirm that these are self-sufficient agricultural villages where the uncertainties of rural life — drought, noxious pests, poor yields — would have necessitated large-scale storage facilities. Not only has grain been found in these stone-lined silos, but experiments in replicating them have shown that they could have been remarkably efficient, even in preventing spoilage by rodents or rot. As for capacity, calculations by experts in food production have demonstrated that the projected 110 silos at 'Izbet Sartah could have stored 54 tons of wheat and 21 tons of barley each year, harvested from some 250 acres. That would be nearly twice the amount required to feed the estimated population of 100, leaving a surplus for trade in good years. These were *very* efficient farmers, not recently settled nomads as Finkelstein proposes.

3. *Cisterns.* However attractive the hill country frontier may have been to settlers wanting to relocate in Iron I, there was one serious draw-

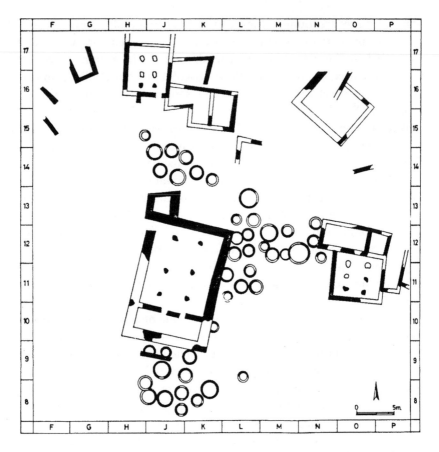

Stone-lined silos surrounding an 11th-century-B.C. house at 'Izbet Sartah
Israel Finkelstein, *'Izbet Sartah*

back: a shortage of water. There are no perennial rivers or even streams anywhere in the upland regions of Palestine, only springs here and there. To be sure, there is ample rainfall in good years, even more than along the coastal plain and in the lowland river valleys. (For example, Jerusalem gets an average of 25 inches of rain a year — more than London.) But it all falls from October through April; and summers are invariably hot and extremely dry, with rainfall almost unknown. Furthermore, cycles of good and drought years are typical, with as many as one in five years a disaster. Thus the ability to store water was essential to any large-scale attempt to settle the hill country. The settlers overcame this problem by developing

116

efficient cisterns, cut deep into the bedrock and usually lime-plastered to waterproof them. It was this innovation, as much as any, that made intensive occupation possible in Iron I. Finkelstein calls this argument, too, a "shaky pillar," pointing out that we now have lime-plastered cisterns that can be dated much earlier. He is correct. At Gezer we excavated several such cisterns from the Middle Bronze Age, *ca.* 1600 B.C. Lime-plaster technology had been around for a long time by the early Iron Age. But that is not the point here. It is only in the Iron Age, when the dense settlement of the hill country began, that we encounter the first *large-scale, intensive* use of cisterns, many (though not all) lime-plastered. Like terraces, cisterns were essential in most regions, not merely "byproducts" as Finkelstein maintains. (He adapts Zertal's questionable theory that the large collar-rim storejars were really for transporting water by donkey from nearby or distant springs; unfortunately, two of these jars full of water would have weighed something like six hundred pounds!) Until recently, every Arab house in West Bank villages had just such a cistern in the courtyard, and there were many more on the outskirts of villages and in the nearby fields. When I lived and worked in these villages in 1968-71, we sometimes had to use cistern water (thereby developing some very interesting ailments).

4. *Iron.* One would suppose that iron technology would have been a primary factor in the changes accompanying the advent of the Iron Age in ancient Palestine (*ca.* 1200-600 B.C.). But the fact is that iron implements were introduced only gradually in the 12th-11th centuries B.C., and they did not become common before about the 10th century B.C. The name "Iron Age" — following "Bronze Age," of course — was introduced nearly one hundred years ago, and it is somewhat arbitrary. But we archaeologists seem to be stuck with it.

There are known sources of raw iron in both eastern and western Palestine, but the spread of iron technology was slow and limited for several reasons. First, smelting iron requires less wood fuel than producing copper and bronze, but it is very labor intensive. Thus the gradual spread of iron may have to do with the fact that by the "Iron Age" the once heavily wooded central hill country was beginning to be deforested, a process only accelerated by new settlements. Second, although iron succeeds bronze in our "evolutionary" archaeological sequence, it is not necessarily a superior metal. Iron tools may be strong, but they are brittle and break more easily than bronze. Furthermore iron rusts badly, whereas bronze may last almost indefinitely. For these and many other reasons, the introduction of iron after *ca.* 1200 B.C. did not constitute a technological "revolution." For instance, several studies have yielded a total of fewer than 30 iron implements in the Iron I period (12th-11th centuries). And they have also shown that the ratio of bronze to iron in this period was about four to one. The later biblical writers correctly remember the scarcity of iron in recounting how the Philistines had a monopoly on ironworking, and only Saul and his son Jonathan had iron swords and spears (1 Sam. 13:19-23). It is doubtful today that there was any such monopoly (much less that the Philistines "invented" iron), but the biblical story does appear to have some basis in fact.

It may be significant that the few iron implements that we have from our hill country Israelite sites are all simple, utilitarian tools — a number of them plough points (as noted above in dealing with plough agriculture). Not one is a weapon of any type. Once again, peaceful infiltration or symbiosis models appear to fit the available archaeological evidence much better than the conquest model does. The Iron I settlers were farmers, not conquerors.

5. *Pottery.* Archaeologists seem to be obsessed with pottery and with ceramic analyses of all sorts — and with good reason. As one scholar, Robert Ehrich, has observed:

> Pottery is our most sensitive medium for perceiving shared aesthetic traditions, in the sense that they define ethnic groups, for recognizing culture contact and culture change, and for following migration and trade patterns. (1965: vii, viii)

We described above how pottery helps to fix the chronology of our Iron I hill country sites. But let us look now at how the pottery of the settlers may help us to determine their origins and their cultural distinctiveness, if they have any. Several facts are pertinent.

1. First, studies by ceramics specialists (among them my own students) have demonstrated that despite similarities in the basic forms of Late Bronze Age and Iron I pottery, the potting techniques were often different. In particular, Iron I pottery generally reveals fewer wheel-forming techniques, except in its finishing. The shift to hand-made vessels would seem to indicate a change from large-scale industrial production to cottage industry. Each family, or perhaps a village potter or two, would have made locally all the pottery that was required — a fairly simple repertoire, as we shall see.

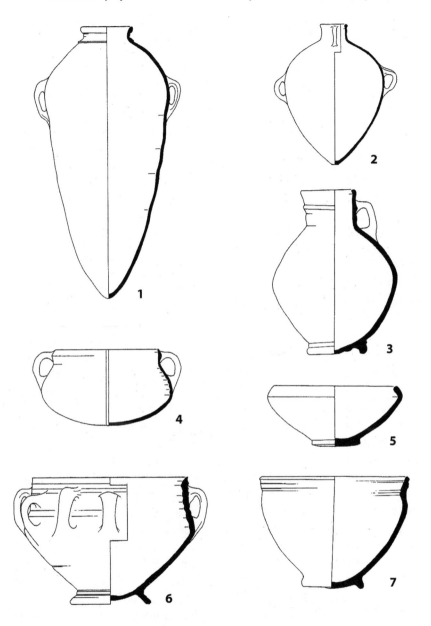

Typical 12th-century-B.C. pottery from Shiloh, Str. V
Israel Finkelstein, *Shiloh*

2. The ceramic repertoire of our Iron I villages shows many overall continuities with that of the Late Bronze Age II, but it contains far fewer individual forms. Shiloh is perhaps the best-published site thus far. The large collection of Stratum V pottery consists of only the following types:

Type	Number	Percentage	Number
Collar-rim storejars	24	40	1
Storejars	9	15	2
Jugs	10	17	3
Juglets	1	2	
Kraters (large bowls)	5	8	6, 7
Bowls	3	5	5
Cooking pots	6	10	4
Other	2	3	

The percentages at Shiloh may be skewed somewhat by the fact that much of the complete or restorable pottery came from what appear to have been storage areas, as Finkelstein notes. At other Iron I villages, however, storejars and cooking pots also predominate. At Giloh, for instance, storejars and cooking pots made up 76% of the findings. The ceramic data, therefore, strongly suggest a utilitarian ceramic repertoire that is more characteristic of rural than of urban sites, and one that is also better adopted to an agricultural economy based on domestic production.

3. Another piece of evidence pointing to a simplified ceramic repertoire in the Iron I villages is the near-total absence of any imported wares. This stands in sharp contrast to the typical urban repertoire of Late Bronze Age Canaanite sites, where luxury imports from Cyprus and the Greek mainland are common. By early Iron I, imports virtually cease. At 'Izbet Sartah, for example, there is one fragment of a "Late Mycenaean IIIB" stirrup jar, probably imported from Cyprus and dating to the late 13th century B.C. (It might have come to the site via contact with local Philistines at nearby Aphek, some of whom are known to have migrated from Cyprus.) And farther inland there are no Iron I occurrences of imported Cypriote or Greek pottery whatsoever. Also conspicuously absent are examples of the exotic Philistine bichrome (that is, two-colored) pottery that is widespread all along the coast in the 12th century B.C., brought to the Levant by migrating "Sea Peoples" and ultimately of Mycenaean Greek origin. The absence of Philistine pottery at our Iron I village sites underscores the ba-

sic accuracy of biblical accounts that detail the hostility between these two contemporary peoples — both newcomers in a sense, vying for a foothold in Canaan.

4. Although potting techniques and the relative percentages of ceramic forms may change from Late Bronze II into Iron I, virtually all of the individual forms that we do have exhibit a strong, and I would say direct, continuity. Thus our early Israelites look ceramically just like Canaanites. This assertion will be startling to many, and even some specialists consider it controversial. So to make my point, let me illustrate by juxtaposing typical 13th and 12th century examples of several basic forms (pp. 122, 123).

Even a non-specialist can see that the forms in each column are closely related. Indeed, the Iron I forms in each case are clearly *derived from* the Late Bronze Age forms. They exhibit only the typological developments (or changes in shape) that we would expect, and in fact can even predict. Note how the storejars change only slightly in the profile of the rim. The kraters (or large two-handled bowls) are almost identical, but may have a red "slip" or paint-like surface decoration. The large to medium-sized bowls are the same, except for a rim that is somewhat more bulbous. But the cooking pots betray the continuities better than other forms: the two types are almost identical, except for the slight lengthening of the everted, flanged rim on the latter. This is a continuous trend that we can easily chart from the 15th through the 8th centuries B.C.

I would argue that such direct, long-term continuities between earlier Canaanite pottery and later Iron I Israelite pottery, readily documented now, cannot be the result of coincidence. Nor can they be explained by continuing to regard the early Israelites as foreigners, newcomers to Canaan from Transjordan and ultimately from Egypt. To defend the latter view, one would have to argue that (1) these intruders brought with them no pottery traditions whatsoever, and (2) that upon arriving they immediately adopted the local pottery repertoire and replicated it exactly. That would be astounding, and also unprecedented in my experience. But such speculations lead us now to the most intriguing aspect of the pottery of this period. Can ceramic analysis enable us to identify our hill country settlers *ethnically* and to determine their origins?

5. No issue in the current study of the early history of the Israelite peoples is as controversial as the above question. Debates rage among specialists, accompanied by acrimonious name-calling, and lay people by now are thoroughly confused, perhaps even a bit disgusted. What is going on here?

13TH CENTURY B.C.   12TH CENTURY B.C.

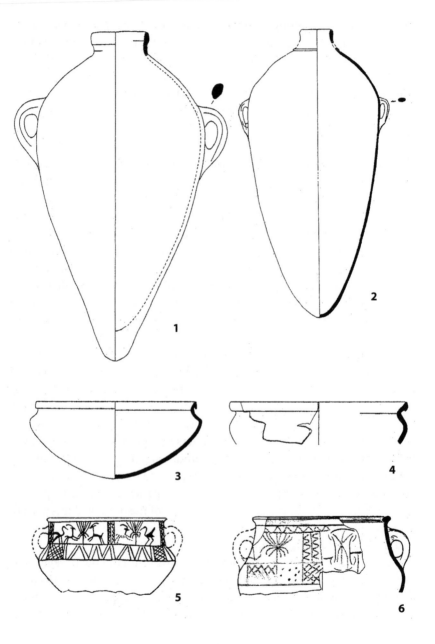

13TH CENTURY B.C.   **12TH CENTURY B.C.**

(1) Gezer, Str. XV; (2) 'Izbet Sartah, Str. III; (3) Gezer, Str. XV;
(4) 'Izbet Sartah, Str. III; (5) Lachish, Fosse Temple III; (6) 'Izbet Sartah, Str. III;
(7) Gezer, Str. XV; (8) 'Izbet Sartah, Str. III; (9) Gezer, Str. XV; (10) Shiloh, Str. V;
(11) Lachish, Fosse Temple III; (12) 'Izbet Sartah, Str. III;
(13) Megiddo, Str. VIII; (14) 'Izbet Sartah, Str. III

Gezer (1, 3, 7, 9); Israel Finkelstein, *'Izbet Sartah* (2, 4, 6, 8, 12, 14);
Lachish (5, 11); Israel Finkelstein, *Shiloh* (10); Megiddo (13)

Amihai Mazar was one of the first modern scholars to analyze the supposed "Israelite pottery" of Iron I, although Albright had attempted some characterizations as far back as the 1920s, as had the Israeli archaeologist Yohanan Aharoni in the 1950s. Mazar demonstrated that most of the pottery of Giloh, which he identified with biblical Ba'al-perazim (2 Sam. 5:20), derived directly from the typical repertoire of the Late Bronze Age in the 13th century B.C. — that is, it was "transitional." Mazar showed further that the Giloh pottery was typical of that known at other supposedly "Israelite" sites at the time he was writing (1981). Mazar's notion of Late Bronze–Iron I ceramic continuity was further developed in 1985 by another Israeli archaeologist, Aharon Kempinski (published, unfortunately, only in Hebrew).

Finkelstein was the first to offer a comprehensive analysis of this pottery, first in treating the survey pottery in his *Archaeology of the Israelite Settlement* (1988); then in publishing the large 12th century B.C. *corpus* from Shiloh (1993); and most recently in a general article opposing the view that I restate here (1998). In 1988, even though he acknowledged that this pottery was Israelite and indicated local, indigenous Canaanite origins, he stated categorically:

> Although it is possible to point to a certain degree of continuity in a few types, the ceramic assemblage of the Israelite Settlement types, taken as a whole, stand in sharp contrast to the repertoire of the Canaanite centers. (1988: 274)

Those few similarities that do exist, Finkelstein argued, should be explained by the fact that his sedentarized nomads "lacking an established ceramic culture would, when undergoing sedentarization, be likely to absorb traditions from the well-developed cultures in their vicinity" (1988: 275). However, when one examines Finkelstein's arguments for "sharp differences" between Late Bronze II and Iron I ceramics, it turns out that the only real distinction he can make is in the differing *percentages* of vessel types. That is, there are more kinds of pottery, occurring in different proportions, at the Late Bronze Age (and also early Iron Age) urban Canaanite sites. I had already noted the same phenomenon in pointing out, for instance, that large storejars are statistically much more common in the Iron I hill country sites. But this, too, misses the point: such differences have to do largely with the contrast between urban and rural lifestyles. The actual vessel types are identical or have the same ancestry. The "urban-rural" phenomenon was noted in 1989 by Gloria London, an expert on ceramic technology, although the distinction is not as absolute as she then thought. (For example, collar-rim storejars now occur at a few urban, possibly Canaanite sites such as Megiddo.)

Finkelstein continues to ignore my critique of his ceramic arguments. In one of his latest statements, however, he reveals his own ambiguity: "Except for a few rare vessels, there are no special features in the pottery of the Iron I highland sites, neither in the *assemblages* as a whole nor in *specific types*" (1996: 204; emphasis mine). The first point contradicts his own data and former conclusions; and the latter is precisely *my* point!

Again, it seems to me that Finkelstein's reluctance to use pottery as an ethnic indicator or clue to origins is due to the fact that he senses that ceramic analysis would undermine his resedentarized nomads theory. Indeed, he usually couples his rejection of the continuity argument with a rejection of the related argument I make that our early Israelites came from the Canaanite lowlands (below). Yet Finkelstein still insists, as he has all along — and rightly so — on "indigenous origins." Does he suppose that the hill country settlers invented their pottery tradition entirely on their own, and by coincidence it closely resembles that of the Late Bronze Age Canaanite repertoire? His *idée fixe* prevents him from seeing the implications of his own data. The fact is that it is the pottery of the Iron I hill country colonists that is our best clue to their origins. The continuity shows that they emerged from within Late Bronze Age Canaanite society. The only question is *where,* and to that question I will turn directly.

Aesthetics, Ideology, and Religion

Now we come to categories of culture and society that are often more intangible and may therefore seem "invisible" to the archaeologist, no matter how intently he or she is looking. Let us look first at aesthetics, as reflected in artistic production. That should be easy: there is almost none. Biblical scholars have often insisted that there is, in fact, no such thing as native "Israelite art" — presumably because the Second Commandment preventing the representation of almost any image was consistently honored. But they are wrong on both counts, as the recent work of a German biblicist and art historian, Sylvia Schroer, has shown: *In Israel There Was Art* (*In Is-*

rael Gab es Bilder; 1987). During the Israelite Monarchy (10th-7th centuries B.C.) we now have a relatively rich artistic tradition, even if partly borrowed from Phoenicia and elsewhere. Thus well attested are carved ivories, gem seals, jewelry, terra cotta offering stands, figurines, worked stone and alabaster, decorated pottery, architecture, and even occasional wall paintings. Only monumental sculpture is missing.

When we come to the Iron I or settlement period, however, it is precisely this later and indisputably "Israelite" art that is almost entirely missing. Even more striking is the near-total absence of any of the even richer, local Late Bronze Age artistic traditions. All we have in Iron I are a few crude seals featuring primitive stick-figures; a handful of terra cotta offering stands; and some pottery shards or vessels with impressed decoration and sometimes an animal or human figure in bas relief. A notable exception is the fine bronze figurine from the "Bull Site" of Mazar. Otherwise the aesthetic tradition of early Israel was barren indeed. Yet that would suit the simple, isolated agrarian society that I have already characterized on other grounds. Whatever genius these hill country folk may have had, it lay in other areas.

Related to aesthetics generally would be certain specific practices that might have left more tangible symbols, perhaps readily detectable to archaeologists. Among these would be burial practices, which archaeologists everywhere regard as potentially eloquent on such matters as social status and, particularly, beliefs about the afterlife. Unfortunately, neither a cemetery nor even an isolated burial has ever been found that is connected with the hill country villages or any other supposed early Israelite site. It is as though a lot of people lived in the 12th-11th centuries B.C., but no one ever died. One large 13th-12th century B.C. cave-tomb was discovered at Dothan with numerous burials and pots. It is unpublished, but my examination of the material does not suggest that it will be particularly helpful, even if it were Israelite.

Curiously enough, religion and cult — which Mendenhall, Gottwald, and many other biblicists have taken as a crucial factor in the "social revolution" that produced early Israel — is virtually unattested archaeologically. The temples and their elaborate paraphernalia that are so typical of Late Bronze Age Canaanite society simply disappear by the end of the 13th century B.C. The only surviving example is the reused "fortress-temple" excavated at Shechem, which Wright connected with the early Israelite covenant-renewal ceremonies described in Joshua 24 and Judges 9. Wright

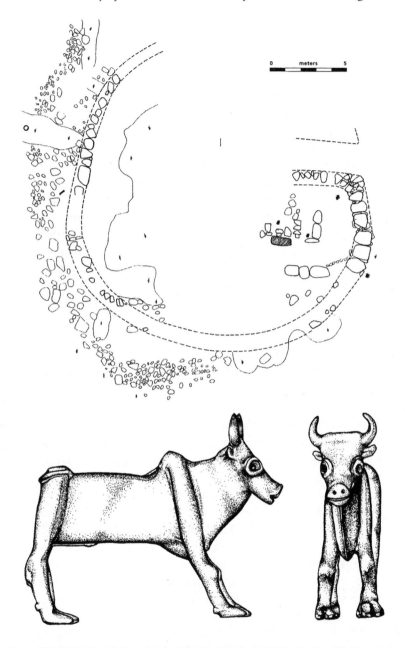

Plan of "Bull Site" and the principal find, a bronze bull figurine; 12th century B.C.
Biblical Archaeology Review 9:5

made much of the story of the change of name from "Temple of *Ba'al* of the Covenant" to "Temple of the God *(El)* of the Covenant" (Judg. 9:46). But such a direct connection between biblical texts and an actual archaeological artifact would be exceptional, and so scholars remain skeptical about the "temple" at Shechem. Apart from that possible occurrence of an Israelite shrine or a temple in Iron I, the only evidence we have is Mazar's "Bull Site" (above). And there the bronze bull figurine is almost certainly to be associated with El, the well-known principal male deity of the Canaanite pantheon, whose main title was "Bull El."

Thus our only material evidence of early Israelite beliefs and cultic practices provides additional, corroborative evidence for continuity with Canaanite religion — nothing whatsoever here that is new or revolutionary. Of course, traditionalists may protest that the biblical tradition envisions an old Yahwistic belief and a pre-Israelite Mosaic covenant that were unique, as well as continuative. But the biblical texts are centuries later. Even so, the writers tacitly acknowledge (and oppose) Canaanite religious influence, especially throughout the period of the judges. And they also admit that their portrait of Israelite religion even much later is more ideal than reality. Some biblical scholars, including my own teachers and others in the Albright tradition, would date several poems like the "Blessing of Jacob" (Gen. 49), the "Song of the Sea" (Exod. 15), or the "Song of Deborah" (Judg. 5) to the 12th or 11th century B.C. Most scholars, however, regard these archaic poems as perhaps part of an older oral tradition, but reduced to writing only in the 8th-7th centuries B.C. Thus they cannot be considered "contemporary sources." Today few biblical scholars and no archaeologists would dare to characterize early Israelite religion as rigidly monotheistic, much less unique.

The deity called Yahweh is attested as early as the 13th century B.C. in Egyptian texts that place him among the Shasu-bedouin of southern Transjordan — where some biblical texts also locate the origins of his cult. But *archaeologically* Yahweh is as invisible in Iron I villages as he was said to be later in biblical Israel (see below on Moses, pp. 234ff.).

The apparent silence of the archaeological record may be misleading, however, because we lack any written texts, and these would be necessary to characterize early Israelite ideology in any depth. The only two "texts" that we have thus far are the one broken name on the Raddana jarhandle and the 'Izbet Sartah abecedary, both discussed above.

CHAPTER 8

Previous Attempts at a Synthesis of Textual and Artifactual Data on Early Israel

Before attempting my own synthesis of the data that I have now surveyed in some detail, both textual and archaeological, let me summarize previous views to give some background. Let us begin by looking at past biblical scholarship.

Older Israeli Biblical Scholarship

Kaufmann

One of the predecessors of modern Israeli biblical scholarship was Yehezkel Kaufmann. His monumental eight-volume *History of Israelite Religion* began to appear in 1937, but it was published only in Hebrew (a one-volume English version came out in 1960). Kaufmann, a traditional, almost Orthodox Jew, took as his starting point the assertion that "Israelite religion was an original creation of the people of Israel. It was absolutely different from anything the pagan world ever knew" (1960: 2). For him, then, the Hebrew Bible's story of Israel's divine calling and unique origin is literally true. To write a history of Israel from early times, one need only paraphrase the Bible. Another early Israeli scholar who may be mentioned here is Shmuel Yeivin, who in 1971 published an idiosyncratic little work entitled *The Israelite Conquest of Canaan*, only a historical curiosity today.

The "German School"

The giants of the German school were fully of the stature of Albright and Mazar and their contemporaries.

Alt

We have already discussed the views of Albrecht Alt in connection with the peaceful infiltration or internal immigration model that he pioneered in the 1920s.

Noth

Alt's pupil Martin Noth, equally distinguished, developed in the 1930s a model for Israel during the period of the judges that until recently held a great deal of sway. Noth interpreted the biblical stories of a twelve-tribe league in the light of later Greek tribal confederations known as amphictyonies. These were "sacral unions" bound loosely together for the common good, and maintained through periodic covenant-renewal ceremonies at a central sanctuary. Noth's amphictyony theory accounted for the Bible's tribal memories, as well as for certain of the early institutions in the Bible regarding centers like Shiloh and Shechem. For those reasons it remained very influential into the 1960s. But today it has largely been abandoned because of a lack of agreement on interpreting the biblical texts on which it rests, and because there never was any archaeological support for such an amphictyony.

Weippert

A younger German biblical scholar, Manfred Weippert, published *The Settlement of the Israelite Tribes in Palestine* in 1971. Weippert, with typical German thoroughness, surveyed all the archaeological evidence available to him up to about 1970. But essentially he restated the theories of Alt and Noth. As he put it, "the ancestors of the later Israelites were full nomads of the Middle and Late Bronze Ages," comparable to present-day Bedouin.

This was similar in some ways to Mendenhall's and Gottwald's views. But Weippert vigorously denied the latter's basic *'Apiru* = "Hebrew" equation. And his view of pastoral nomadism was perhaps more nuanced. But ultimately his conclusion was not especially original in rejecting the "American school":

> The 'subjective' methods of the 'school' of Alt seem to me to provide a 'more objective' picture and one which corresponds better with the sources than do those of his critics. . . . Albright and his followers all too often attribute to their material more than it can bear. . . . (1971: 145)

The "American School": Biblicists

We dealt in Chapter 4 with the famous triumvirate of Albright, Bright, and Wright, the leading advocates of the conquest model, as well as with their critics Mendenhall and Gottwald. By the 1980s, however, there were other American biblical scholars with new opinions about the origins of Israel.

Halpern

Baruch Halpern, a young scholar trained at Harvard in the Albrightian tradition, produced in 1983 a work of enormous erudition, *The Emergence of Israel in Canaan*. Halpern's work explicitly rejected his teachers' conquest model, as well as those of Mendenhall and Gottwald. Yet Halpern, a scholar well known for his often brilliant and radically innovative views, was surprisingly conservative in his own conclusions. As for the difficulties in the biblical materials, he concluded that "the simplest way to explain this is to invoke the traditions of a Hebrew or Israelite invasion following on the heels of occasional penetration" (1983: 90). The impetus for this was that

> over the course of the 13th and 12th centuries, an ethnic consciousness and solidarity dawned on this Israel. No later than the 12th century, the time of the song of Deborah (Judg. 5:13-18), a full-blown confederacy of tribes existed. (1983: 91)

More recently, in a Smithsonian Institution seminar in 1991 (in which I also gave a paper on early Israel), Halpern addressed issues of origins more directly. He argued that the Exodus story, like Homer's *Odyssey*, "reflects a healthy admixture of fancy with whatever is being recalled." But what exactly is being recalled? Halpern argues that it is reasonable to believe that behind the biblical story of oppression in Egypt and eventual liberation there lie some historical events. He argues the same for the route through Transjordan — with a twist, however. In his view the wanderers were related to the Aramaeans, Israel's West Semitic first cousins, who we know were also beginning to become sedentary at this time. Early Israel was thus a mixture of those who shared an Exodus tradition — perhaps pastoralists for some time — and those who did not — that is, other peoples from somewhere within Greater Canaan. Exactly how these two groups came into contact and formed a common way of life, we shall never know. But the resultant culture in the highlands of Canaan in the Iron I period "was receptive to the notion that the Israelites were immigrants in the land, whose property had been converted into livestock in the 13th and 12th centuries B.C." (1992: 106). Halpern concludes that "much of the Exodus story is typologically true" — in other words, it is a metaphor for liberation. I find Halpern's scenario provocative, and I shall return to it at the end of this book.

Chaney

In 1983, the same year that Halpern's book appeared, several biblical scholars collaborated in a volume of essays in the "Social World of Biblical Antiquity" series — in itself evidence of a growing interest in the sociological school pioneered by Mendenhall and Gottwald. Indeed, both scholars have essays in this volume (Mendenhall's a vitriolic attack on Gottwald), entitled *Palestine in Transition: The Emergence of Ancient Israel*. The most innovative essay is that by Marvin L. Chaney, on "ancient Palestinian peasant movements."

Chaney rejected both the older conquest and peaceful infiltration models, and was especially critical of Weippert's version of the latter. He was much more sympathetic to the idea of social revolution posited by Mendenhall and Gottwald, but without their assumption of Yahwistic religion as a crucial factor. For Chaney, the operative ideology was more eco-

nomic, that of landless peasants seeking to abolish the abusive land poli-
cies of Canaanite society. Thus he saw the earliest "Israelites" in the
tradition of the rebellious "'Apiru" of the Amarna letters in the 14th century B.C. (as did Mendenhall, Gottwald, and others). Chaney, however,
added to the "revolt" model the new notions of "frontier" (later commonly
adopted) and "agrarian." He concluded:

> While it remains a working hypothesis, a model of peasant and frontier
> revolt has been found to accommodate and illuminate the data provided
> by the Amarna archive, Syro-Palestinian archaeology, and the biblical
> traditions, and to do so within parameters defined by the comparative
> study of agrarian societies by social scientists. (1983: 72)

At the time Chaney's discussion was regarded as innovative; and it was, in
the very best sense.

Coote and Whitelam

Just four years later, writing in the same series, Robert B. Coote and
Keith W. Whitelam, both biblical scholars with no archaeological experience, published an even more innovative work, *The Emergence of Early Israel in Historical Perspective.* What was striking about this work was the
way it viewed the Late Bronze/Iron I transition within the much longer
settlement-history of ancient Palestine. Coote and Whitelam took as their
point of departure the French historian Fernand Braudel and others of
what is known as the *Annales* school. They saw long-term history *(la
longue durée)* not so much in terms of episodic events or the public deeds
of Great Men; these they saw as merely "froth on the waves." They looked
rather at history as the result of cultural adaptation to the "deeper swells"
of changing natural conditions over the millennia. And they applied this to
the history of Bronze Age Palestine from the mid-3rd millennium B.C. onward, as well as to the specific task of rewriting early Israel's history in the
Iron Age.

Using primarily the archaeological data as they understood it, Coote
and Whitelam gave only a supporting role to the biblical texts. They characterized early Israel as a highland and steppe group, originating within
Canaan largely in response to the decline of trade and the deterioration of

the urban Canaanite culture of the end of the Bronze Age around 1200 B.C. When one looks back at how few reliable archaeological data were available to them, and takes into account the fact that these authors were by no means specialists in archaeology, theirs was a refreshing and remarkably precocious work. (My own copy is heavily annotated and well worn.) At the end of their book Coote and Whitelam state:

> The investigation into the history of Israel, particularly its emergence, has reached an exciting stage. Our understanding of the period promises to be profoundly affected by the results of new archaeological work, especially the regional surveys still in their early stages. . . . The study of the history of Israel is becoming such a complex task that, like recent archaeological digs, it requires the co-operation of a team of experts drawn from many disciplines. The dialogue is only just beginning and it promises to be a most exciting phase in the history of scholarship. (1987: 177)

This conclusion points in precisely the right direction; but unfortunately the dialogue its authors envisioned has yet to materialize.

Coote

In 1990, Coote attempted to expand his programmatic work with Whitelam into a larger history, *Early Israel: A New Horizon*. This solo work does not seem to have won much of a following, although it is a vigorous, concise, and exceptionally clear statement. And it was able to make use of the first full reports of the Israeli surveys, among them Finkelstein's landmark *Archaeology of the Israelite Settlement* (1988). Coote's bold hypothesis was that early Israel was at first a tribal confederation, perhaps even a paramilitary coalition, promoted by Egypt to prop up its declining empire there. Later, these peoples withdrew to the highlands and became village farmers, although they were still subsidized for a time by the Egyptian authorities. Virtually no one has taken up this scenario. But Coote's fundamental contention that the early Israelites were essentially Canaanites is now widely accepted (as we will see below). Regarding the origin of the highland settlers, I could not agree more with Coote's conclusion, based on his understanding of the archaeological evidence:

The evidence shows just what would be expected: the transfer of subsistence farming from the lowland frontier to the highland frontier. People who subsisted on dry farming in the lowlands moved to the highlands and did the same thing. Moreover, these village communities show cultural continuity with the lowlands, except in the areas of adaptation to highland conditions. (1990: 127)

As we shall see, Coote foreshadowed the later "symbiosis" model held by a number of archaeologists.

Ahlström

An adopted American biblical scholar, trained in Sweden, Gösta W. Ahlström, attempted a semi-popular synthesis in 1986, giving it a title similar to mine here: *Who Were the Israelites?* Ahlström, considered by many somewhat eccentric, didn't seem to know. But his basic thesis was that the term "Israel" had originally designated not a particular ethnic group, but rather a geographical region, specifically the hill country of Canaan. He derived this notion not so much from the archaeological data (not then well known) but from the mention of "Israel" on the famous "Victory Stele" of Pharaoh Merneptah, *ca.* 1210 B.C. Later, the people who dwelled in those highlands came to be called "Israelites." Ahlström sought the origin of the "hill country pioneers" among the lowland population of Canaan, displaced by the upheavals of the end of the Bronze Age. He thought that some "'Apiru-like" people may have been part of this group. However, he declined to use the term "Israelite" for *any* of these peoples prior to the Israelite Monarchy (10th century B.C.).

"Histories of Israel"

Thus far I have presented in brief the views of several biblical scholars writing in the 1970s and 1980s specifically on the topic of early Israel. There were, however, several new overall histories of ancient Israel written in this period. Siegfried Herrmann's brief *A History of Israel in Old Testament Times* (1973) does not advance beyond Alt and Noth, and of course was published before Gottwald's epochal study had appeared. Furthermore,

Herrmann repeats the tired notion, originating with German biblicists, that archaeology is "mute," what he calls "dumb archaeology" (1973: 36). (In my opinion archaeology is *not* mute; but some historians are deaf!)

Another European history of Israel was that of the Italian scholar J. Alberto Soggin in 1985, *A History of Ancient Israel from the Beginnings to the Bar Kochba Revolt, A.D. 135.* Soggin (with whom I worked at Shechem in the 1960s) takes a much more positive view of archaeology. But he thinks that the real history of Israel, as far as adequate sources go, begins only in the 10th century B.C., in the period of the biblical United Monarchy. Thus he does not treat the topic of origins at all.

The most widely used history of ancient Israel in the English-speaking world today is that of J. Maxwell Miller and John H. Hayes, *A History of Ancient Israel and Judah* (1986). Its extensive and generally competent use of archaeological data reflects the fact that Miller has had considerable field experience, notably from his own surveys in Jordan. Nevertheless, in closing their chapter on "The Question of Origins," Miller and Hayes, after surveying various hypotheses, conclude:

> We are cautious about saying anything. The evidence, or lack of evidence, is such that a confident treatment of the origins of Israel and Judah in terms of critical historiography is, in our opinion, simply impossible. This is one of those places where the historian must be willing to concede that anything said is largely guesswork. (1986: 78)

(This makes me recall an annual meeting of the Society of Biblical Literature, at which a seminar was organized to celebrate the appearance of this book and to discuss it. I sat quietly in the back of the room, the only archaeologist present, with mounting frustration, hearing one learned biblicist after another explain why a "history of ancient Israel" could no longer be written. Finally, I could keep silent no longer. I rose to my feet and protested loudly to my old friend Miller: "If you biblical scholars are no longer able or willing to write the history of Israel, then we archaeologists will do it!" People turned their heads and looked at me as though I had landed from the moon.)

And yet Miller, despite his earlier skepticism, did return to the subject of Israelite origins in revising a chapter originally written by Joseph Callaway for the excellent semi-popular handbook published in 1999 as *Ancient Israel from Abraham to the Roman Destruction of the Temple* (edited by Hershel Shanks). The differences in the two treatments only nine years apart are striking (and illustrate that scholarship *does* make progress). After giving an excellent survey of older data and theories, Miller begins with sources concerning tribal groups in Joshua and Judges, where a "historical memory is deeply embedded." As Miller (cf. Callaway, 1985) puts it:

> In any case, earliest Israel was probably a loose confederation of tribes and clans that "emerged" gradually from the pluralistic population of the land. Accordingly, Israel's ancestors would have been of diverse origins. Some may have been immigrants from Transjordan, possibly even from Egypt. But basically Israel seems to have emerged from the melting pot of peoples already in the land of Canaan at the beginning of the Iron Age. Accordingly, their lifestyle and material culture were essentially "Canaanite." (1999: 82)

If readers think that they perceive a growing consensus here, they are right.

The Biblical Revisionists

Before leaving "biblical histories of early Israel," we must turn to several non-histories proposed recently by a small but vocal (and contentious) group of European biblical scholars. They often call themselves revisionists; others describe them as minimalists. I have suggested that they are more accurately nihilists — for when they are finished rewriting Israel's history, early or late, there is nothing left that most of us would recognize as history. That is as they would have it, however, for their fundamental conclusion (or is it a preconception?) is that one can no longer write a history of ancient Israel, at least not one based on the biblical texts.

Scholars have been generally skeptical in this matter, of course, since the beginning of modern critical biblical studies more than a century and a half ago. But even the most radical have never suggested discarding the biblical texts altogether, which is just what I have charged the revisionists with doing in several recent publications (especially in *What Did the Biblical Writers Know and When Did They Know It?*, 2001).

Davies

The public is only now getting wind of this controversy over whether the Bible is historically true, but the fuss actually began in 1992 with the publication of the University of Sheffield's Philip R. Davies, *In Search of "Ancient Israel."* To make a long story short, Davies never found any of three "Israels" that he distinguished: (1) the "historical" Israel of the people of Iron Age Palestine; (2) the biblical or "literary" Israel; and (3) the "ancient Israel" created by modern scholars out of the first two. According to Davies the latter two are nothing more than social constructs — that is, fiction. The historical Israel might in theory be reconstructable; but the limitations of archaeology, our only reliable source, prevent that. Davies does not even cite the standard handbook, Mazar's *Archaeology of the Land of the Bible,* except to say in a footnote that it is irrelevant for not dealing with Davies' own concept of the "Persian" Bible and its invention of ancient Israel. Thus for him there is, practically speaking, no early Israel about which we can know anything. (When I have pointed this out, he has protested; but he has not been able to come up with anything that I would call even a minimalist history, nor can he with his methodology.)

Whitelam

Davies' little book, which many thought amusing but harmless (just the work of another British eccentric), was followed by a number of articles by other revisionists, many published by the Sheffield Academic Press. Then in 1996 Keith W. Whitelam of the University of Stirling in Scotland (now at Sheffield) published a much more radical and provocative statement: *The Invention of Ancient Israel: The Silencing of Palestinian History.* In this manifesto, the overtly ideological and political agenda of the revisionists was made explicit. Not only had modern scholars, especially pious Christians and Zionist Israelis, "invented" their Israels, but in the process they had dispossessed the Palestinians, the real native people of the region, of their history. The following are typical of Whitelam's assertions:

> The 'ancient Israel' of biblical studies is a scholarly construct based upon a misreading of the biblical tradition and divorced from historical reality. (1996: 3)

> Biblical scholarship is not just involved in 'retrojective imperialism,' it has collaborated in an act of dispossession . . . has silenced the history of the indigenous peoples of Palestine in the early Iron Age. (1996: 222)

In Whitelam's scenario, the "Palestinians" are the ones whose identity is in question. But even those sympathetic with his anti-Israel rhetoric have pointed out that the Palestinians of the present conflict were not *present* in ancient Palestine. They did not emerge as a "people" at all until relatively modern times. Not only is this bad historical method, it is dishonest scholarship. And it unnecessarily drags politics into Near Eastern archaeology, an inflammatory enough discipline as it is. Archaeologists have been writing his called-for "history of Palestine" for a hundred years — the history of all its peoples, from those of the Lower Paleolithic to Ottoman times. Whitelam should have recalled his own 1987 work with Robert Coote, in which he seemed to know a great deal more about archaeology.

(That same year Whitelam wrote an article for the Sheffield *Journal for the Study of the Old Testament* on "the realignment and transformation of Late Bronze–Iron Age Palestine." It was so full of caricatures of modern archaeological theory and results that I felt compelled to answer it in the same journal. I asserted that biblicists dabbling in archaeology, as well as archaeologists dabbling in biblical studies, are indulging in monologues — thus inhibiting the dialogue we so badly need.)

Lemche

Copenhagen became the other university center of the revisionist movement. There the biblical scholar Niels Peter Lemche published a provocative but widely admired work in 1985, *Early Israel: Anthropological and Historical Studies on the Israelite Society Before the Monarchy.* The book was very innovative. I recall being disturbed yet excited upon reading it; and later I was pleased when Lemche and I became colleagues.

Then in the early 1990s he began to espouse more radical views. Now the Hebrew Bible was no longer a document from the Iron Age, or the period of the Monarchy, but was composed (not just edited) almost entirely in the Hellenistic era, the 2nd century B.C. Thus it could not possibly serve as an adequate source for a history of ancient Israel in the Iron Age. Rather the Hebrew Bible is a product of its own times, in effect a piece of "pious propaganda" stemming from the identity crisis of Jews living in Hellenistic Palestine. They made up a fictitious Israel to give themselves a legitimate history. Like Whitelam, Lemche now argued that the story of ancient Israel in the Bible was a myth.

By 1998 Lemche had produced his own revisionist history, almost diametrically opposed to his 1985 work (which he now repudiates): *The Israelites in History and Tradition*. Since the Hebrew Bible was no longer a proper source, and archaeology could make up for that deficiency only sporadically, Lemche's was a minimalist, if not a nihilist, history. Here are some typical statements:

> The Israel(s) of the Old Testament showed itself to be a product of a literary imagination. Its history was not one of the real world, but in its organization was directed by the requirements of the two foundation myths, the first of the Exodus, and the second of the Babylonian exile. Whether or not parts of this history really happened in the 'real' world is to the mind that formed this history immaterial. (1998: 129)

> The only thing that remains is the tradition of two tiny states of Palestine in the Iron Age, which were long after their disappearance chosen as the basis of a history of a new nation to be established on the soil of Palestine in the postexilic period. (1998: 155)

> At the end we have a situation where Israel is not Israel, Jerusalem is not Jerusalem, and David not David. No matter how we twist the factual remains from ancient Palestine, we cannot have a biblical Israel that is at the same time the Israel of the Iron Age. (1998: 166)

Is it any wonder that I regard Lemche, too, as a nihilist, only capable of producing a non-history of ancient Israel? He has reacted sharply to my several critiques, but he has never taken them seriously, much less attempted to answer them. (Most recently he has dismissed me as a "Zionist," yet at the same time implied that my persistent restatements of my position contrary to his are an example of "Nazi"-like propaganda.)

Thompson

Perhaps the most extreme of the revisionists is Thomas Thompson, an American now teaching with Lemche at Copenhagen. In 1974 he wrote a book on the *Historicity of the Patriarchal Narratives* that helped to undermine Albright's "positivist" synthesis; it was poorly received at the time but has since come to be regarded as a turning point. Then in 1992 he published *Early History of the Israelite People from the Written and Archaeological Sources.* This massive work was an attempt to produce the "secular history of Palestine" that the revisionists and many others (myself included) had been calling for. Unfortunately, it was a caricature, not a history that any archaeologist would have even recognized. And within five years Thompson himself had repudiated it, stating that only his late, Hellenistic dating of the Hebrew Bible could be salvaged. Thus he published two years later his revisionist treatment of ancient Israel: *The Mythic Past: Biblical Archaeology and the Myth of Israel.* Despite its subtitle, this work has next to nothing to do with real archaeology. More significantly, Thompson caricatures not only archaeologists and nearly all biblical scholars, but the Hebrew Bible as well. His conclusion is that

> The history of Iron Age Palestine today knows of Israel only as a small highland patronage lying north of Jerusalem and south of the Jezreel Valley. Nor has Yahweh, the deity dominant in the cult of that Israel's people, much to do with the Bible's understanding of God. (1999: xv)

Thompson goes on to observe that "it may perhaps appear strange that so much of the Bible deals with the origin traditions of a people who never existed as such" (1999: 34).

It should be no surprise that Thompson's supposed presentation of the "real" Israel contains in its 412 pages only seven pages on the period of the Monarchy (9th-6th centuries B.C.); and on the settlement period a total of less than four pages. And nowhere does Thompson deign even to *use* the term "Israel" for the peoples in question. Instead he speaks of the "population of Syria's southern, marginal fringe." And as for our topic here,

> The quest for origins is not an historical quest, but a theological and literary question, a question about meaning. To give it an historical form is

to attribute to it our own search for meaning. Biblical scholarship used to believe that we might understand the Bible if we could only get back to its origins. The question about origins, however, is not an answerable one. (1999: xv)

A 1997 collection of essays, mostly by European revisionists, entitled *Can a "History of Israel" Be Written?*, poses the question but offers few answers. Among the authors there are many biblical scholars but no archaeologists. The editor calls for a "genuine dialogue"; but this, like so much of revisionist discourse, is a monologue, and a tiresome one at that. It shows little awareness of the archaeological revolution outlined here, and it does nothing whatsoever to enlighten us on any early Israel.

To many readers, the revisionist attempt to read ancient Israel out of history may seem too absurd for words. But their approach to understanding the past is not uncommon these days. There is a large and influential school of academic "historians" who hold, following French postmodernist philosopher Michel Foucault, that "all history-writing is fiction."

The fundamental assumption of postmodernism is that no objective knowledge is possible, especially of a past that is only attested by texts. In the postmodern view, texts are all simply "social constructs" that must be deconstructed (in other words, analyzed in terms of the way language is used in them rather than in terms of what their authors intended to communicate). And of course since no knowledge of objective truth is possible, texts can mean anything that we want or need them to mean. Postmodernism is particularly skeptical of "metanarratives" — that is, texts that make sweeping, universal claims to knowledge of a superior order. Obviously the Bible is one such metanarrative; indeed, it is the dominant one in the Western cultural tradition. Thus it is not only proper to demythologize the Bible and to unmask its pretense to truth; it is also necessary. Keith Windschuttle, whose book *The Killing of History: How Literary Critics and Social Theorists Are Murdering Our Past* was mentioned in this book's Introduction, argues that history belongs to the whole of humanity, not just to the Western cultural community. He puts it this way:

The attempt by cultural relativism and postmodernism to eliminate the metanarrative from history — that is, to eliminate the narrative of what really happened irrespective of whether the participants were aware of it or not — would deprive us all, no matter what culture we inhabit, of genuine knowledge of our past. (1996: 281)

But since they have adopted precisely this philosophy of history and knowledge, it should not surprise us when the biblical revisionists claim that the Bible's ancient Israel is invented.

However, for those of us who disagree, questions remain. What *did* happen in Canaan on the Late Bronze-Iron I horizon as new peoples emerged? *Was* there any early Israel? And can we, with our modern critical methods, improve on the understanding of the Bible's writers and editors?

Israeli and American Archaeologists

I turn now from representative biblical scholars, who specialize in texts, to archaeologists, who "write history from things."

Lapp

Paul W. Lapp was a student first of Albright and then of Wright. When he died in 1970 at the age of 37, he was considered America's most brilliant (if somewhat erratic) young biblical and Syro-Palestinian archaeologist. In 1967 he published a site-by-site survey of the archaeological evidence on the Late Bronze/Iron I horizon. Unfortunately, it appeared in an obscure church-related journal, and it was never widely read. Because of Lapp's authority as the ranking American archaeologist of his time, however, his article did have some impact on biblicists. By and large Lapp supported the "conquest" model of his mentors. Thus he declared that

> The stratigraphic evidence . . . outside the coastal cities and the Plain of Jezreel, points strongly to the thoroughgoing destruction of nearly all important cities in the last half of the 13th century. (1967: 295)

Needless to say, no reputable archaeologist would make such a statement today. The "destruction horizon" is much more complex.

Benjamin Mazar

The late Benjamin Mazar, until his death at 92, was the doyen of modern Israeli biblical historians, a man of immense learning in many fields, including topography and archaeology. He was Israel's Albright. His method, like Albright's, was to bring together data from a vast array of sources, usually in a masterful historical synthesis. His approach was conservative in the proper sense, yet not as conservative as Albright's. Some of Mazar's seminal early articles appeared only in Hebrew, but a 1981 translation of one of them makes his views clear to the English-speaking world. In dealing with the early Israelite settlement in the hill country, he concluded:

> The settlement of the Israelite tribes in the hill country appears from the first to have been governed by their sense of national-religious destiny and by their way of life as stockbreeders who ranged with their herds over Canaan and Transjordan. It is only gradually that the early Israelites adapted to the conditions of a settled life, to living in permanent villages, and to direct contact with their non-Israelite neighbors whose influence made itself felt in the establishment of their settlements and in their gradual transition to an economy based mainly on agriculture. The Israelite tribes and associated groups contracted alliances with these neighbors on the one hand, but they also fought them fiercely to secure life and property, for the right to settle surplus populations, in order to make subject the autochthonous inhabitants or absorb them into the Israelite tribal framework, and eventually to attain political supremacy. (1981: 78)

Mazar thus conceived of the Israelite conquest as a complex, dynamic process, extending over a relatively long period of time. In treating the textual evidence, he took a serious but not literal approach, mining the later tradition for historical details and memories. Above all, he stressed that early Israel was an amalgam of many different ethnic groups — "Hittites, Hivites, Jebusites," and others, as the Bible puts it.

Yadin

Yigael Yadin, later Israel's most distinguished archaeologist, had been a pupil of Mazar and continued his basic approach in many ways, although with more style and perhaps less substance. In Chapter 4 we looked at Yadin's views on Israelite origins based on his own 1956-1958 excavations at Hazor.

Aharoni

Yohanan Aharoni, another protégé of Mazar, made his chief contribution to the subject at hand with his 1957 doctoral dissertation *The Settlement of the Israelite Tribes in Upper Galilee,* published only in Hebrew (but abstracted in English in 1957). His later publications on the theme include a provocative semi-popular article in 1976, "Nothing Early and Nothing Late: Re-Writing Israel's Conquest"; and a chapter in his widely used handbook *The Land of the Bible* (1966, revised in 1979, after his death). Basically Aharoni followed Alt in advocating the overall process of infiltration. But he also believed that the sedentarizing Israelites destroyed a number of sites in the hill country on both sides of the Jordan. And in the north, especially in Upper Galilee, he envisioned a large-scale confrontation. Based on his survey in the 1950s, he isolated what he called "conquest pottery" (like the collar-rim jars), which he dated to the mid-13th century B.C. or even earlier. But he held that the conquest continued until at least 1150 B.C., when he thought that Hazor, for instance, was destroyed (a date over which he and Yadin quarreled bitterly). Despite Aharoni's pioneering emphasis on regional surveys and projects, both in the Beersheba Valley and in Galilee, his synthesis is obsolete today. It was made so principally by his own students in the school he founded, the Institute of Archaeology at Tel Aviv University (more on that below).

Fritz

We have already discussed the excavations at Tel Masos, near Beersheba. The German scholar who co-directed these excavations is a leading biblicist, atypical because of his long archaeological field experience in Israel (which goes back to the 1960s). On the basis of the evidence, such as I have summarized here, Volkmar Fritz developed a distinctive version of previous indigenous origins theories (such as peasant revolt and internal immigration) that is sometimes called a "symbiosis" model. He noted elements of continuity with Late Bronze Age Canaanite culture, as in pottery and metalworking, and even in the pillar-courtyard houses, which he thought derived from earlier local and even some Egyptian courtyard houses. On the other hand, the Iron I adaptation of house-form and pottery at Tel Masos and elsewhere, as well as the newly-sedentarized lifestyle, indicated to Fritz that the Canaanite and Israelite peoples had the same origins and continued to live alongside one another in Iron I. Thus the notion of symbiosis. As Fritz put it:

> It is much more likely that there was an intensive cultural contact that can only have come about through a long period of co-existence. Before the establishment of the settlement in the 12th century, the settlers presumably lived for some generations in the vicinity of the Canaanite cities without entirely giving up their nomadic lifestyle. This means, however, that the founders of the settlement did not come directly from the steppes but had already penetrated the settled region in the 13th century or possibly even earlier and had entered into a form of symbiosis with the Canaanites. (1981: 69, 70)

Furthermore:

> The settlers were not simply pastoral nomads from the steppes. Rather, they had presumably lived for a long time as *semi-nomads* in the vicinity of the Canaanite cities, until they went over to the founding of new settlements and thus finally to a sedentary way of life after the far-reaching collapse of the Late Bronze Age city-states around 1200 B.C. The transition to the sedentary lifestyle was preceded by the adoption of the economic system belonging to this style of life. In this period of extensive cultural contact there was probably still a good deal of transhumance, which involved the herds being driven during the rainy season from the settled region to the pastures in the steppes. The "settlement" of the land therefore does not represent a seizure of the land from the outside. Instead, it is a development in the transition from the Late Bronze Age to the Iron Age. (1981: 71)

Fritz's model was not fully developed, nor did he label it explicitly a symbiosis model. But it has had considerable significance, and rightly so in my judgment.

Callaway

I have already noted Joseph Callaway in looking at his 1970s excavations at ʿAi, after which he turned more and more to archaeology as a primary source for writing the early history of Israel. In 1985 he published a larger treatment in which he basically supported Alt's immigration theory, but with an important exception: the Iron I hill country settlers had not been nomads, but settlers "with fixed cultural patterns of village life with the aid of two new subsistence strategies" (1985: 33). These strategies were terrace agriculture and the use of rock-cut cisterns. In Callaway's view, "the hill country settlers migrated to escape wars and violence, and they sought out in their remote and isolated mountain-top villages a place of refuge from the strife and disruption in the more fertile plains" (1985: 33). The *integrated* material culture and social organization of the Iron I villages in the hill country is evidence that the villagers

> were part of more general population movements in the entire land of Canaan by people whose background was in agriculturally-based sedentary village life rather than that of nomads or even semi-nomads. (1985: 43)

Kochavi

The same year Callaway's book was published, several Israeli archaeologists addressed the same issue. One was the veteran scholar of Tel Aviv University, Moshe Kochavi. Kochavi based his work on the Israeli surveys discussed above, but he stressed regional differences and the gradual process of settlement. For the hill country, Kochavi agreed with Finkelstein (and Zertal below) that the settlement reflects an east-to-west movement by pastoral nomads gradually settling down. And he concluded that it would be for future archaeologists to provide "the only really authentic source for this period" (1985: 58).

Amihai Mazar

In the same volume as Kochavi, *Biblical Archaeology Today: Proceedings of the International Congress on Biblical Archaeology* (1985), Amihai Mazar expanded his 1981 views, which I summarized above in introducing his excavations at Giloh. Mazar's chapter was an excellent summary of the archaeological evidence known up to that time — comprehensive, well balanced, judicious, free of ideology. Mazar concluded:

> Recent archaeological research increasingly stresses the Canaanite origin of various components of this material culture, such as details in architecture, pottery-making, artistic traditions and cult practices. Yet the Israelite material culture as a whole differs markedly from the previous and contemporary Canaanite culture. Various factors, such as the distribution of sites, their location and planning, the composition of the pottery assemblages, and the economic and social structure, are definitely non-Canaanite. Surveys and excavations thus reveal a material culture of a distinct character, which although inspired by Canaanite traditions, had an independent development of its own. (1985: 70)

Stager

Lawrence E. Stager, whose 1985 article "The Archaeology of the Family" I have already praised (and shall return to), also had a chapter in the 1985 volume. Here he covered much of the same ground as in his article, but now he emphasized the regional diversity of the Iron I villages, arguing that it would be simplistic to relate them all to the Israelites of the biblical tradition. Thus he opposed Finkelstein's pan-nomadic theory. Again he highlighted demography, pointing out that neither the supposed peasants nor the nomads of the Canaanite Late Bronze Age alone could have supplied enough people to account for the veritable population explosion in Iron I in the hill country (which indeed turns out to be the crucial fact). Stager ended, however, on a note of caution: "Without clear indications from texts, I seriously doubt whether any archaeologist can determine the ethnic identification of Iron I villagers through cultural remains alone" (1985: 86). I shall return presently to this issue, as well as to Stager's subsequent treatment of it.

Bunimovitz

In the extremely important collection of essays in the 1994 volume *From Nomadism to Monarchy: Archaeological and Historical Aspects of Early Israel*, a young Tel Aviv scholar, Shlomo Bunimovitz, accepted Finkelstein's resedentarized nomads model, based on long-term settlement history. But he nuanced it considerably, particularly the notion of shifting frontiers. Bunimovitz argued that

> Even though the frontier of the Late Bronze Age expanded into all the regions of Palestine, there were periods of ebb and flow, in accordance with the constant changes in the power of Egyptian government. The withdrawal of the shepherds/nomads (and other non-sedentary elements) from the lowlands in the beginning of Iron Age I, and their sedentarization in the highlands can also be explained in line with the shifting frontier model. (1994: 200)

Thus Bunimovitz agreed with the picture of pastoral nomads (and others) settling down in the hill country, but neither in Finkelstein's overwhelming and almost exclusive numbers nor moving from east to west. But before turning finally to Finkelstein's views, which are at the center of the controversy, let me introduce two somewhat "maverick" reconstructions.

Stiebing

In 1989 William H. Stiebing, trained as an archaeologist but mostly a popular writer, produced an idiosyncratic book entitled *Out of the Desert? Archaeology and the Exodus/Conquest Narratives*. In it he follows the various indigenous origins and frontier theories that had become widespread by that time. But he absolutely rejects Finkelstein's resedentarized nomads theory. In Stiebing's view, the biblical Israelites, while newcomers to part of Canaan, were peoples that had been set in motion by the upheavals all over the Mediterranean world, which brought the Bronze Age to an end beginning in the late 13th century B.C. He believes that a small-scale biblical Exodus probably did take place and led some group ultimately to Canaan. But his astonishing conclusion — merely asserted, not documented — is that *most* of the people who made up later "Israel" migrated from somewhere in the Mediterranean world because of a widespread drought that devastated the entire area between the 13th and the 10th century B.C. The "pan-Mediterranean drought theory," originated with the classicist Rhys Carpenter more than 40 years ago. But very few scholars would take it seriously today, and the theory is rarely even cited. There may have been periodic local droughts, but there is simply no archaeological or scientific evidence (pollen analyses, for example) that would support Stiebing's thesis. That, plus second-hand and often erroneous use of the archaeological data, has made his work almost invisible in the current discussion.

Redford

Donald B. Redford is also something of a maverick on the subject of ancient Israel, but he is one of the leading Egyptologists in the world. His 1992 book *Egypt, Canaan, and Israel in Ancient Times* is brilliant, polemical, and exasperating at times when it discusses subjects other than Egypt. It is also full of provocative insights. Redford often contemptuously dismisses the Bible and biblical scholars, along with virtually every theory of Israelite origins except his own. According to Redford, the early Israelites were simply a contingent of the Shasu Bedouin of southern Canaan, well known to us from 18th-19th Dynasty Egyptian records. There are several rather detailed descriptions of these Shasu, placing them principally on the semi-arid borders of Egyptian lands, particularly Moab, Edom, and into the Negev. In the Egyptian records they are regarded as seasonal, donkey-mounted pastoral nomads, but also as brigands — by and large a nuisance to the faraway Egyptian authorities. Several fascinating texts make reference to a deity "*Yhw* (in) the land of the Shasu," recalling the biblical tradition that also derives Moses' knowledge of Yahweh from the Land of Midian. Indeed, such texts are our earliest known reference to the Israelite Yahweh, and among the few anywhere outside the Bible. As Redford puts it:

> The Shasu settlement in the Palestinian highlands, or nascent Israel as we should undoubtedly call it, and whatever related group had begun to coalesce in the Judean hills to the south, led a life of such rustic simplicity at the outset that it has scarcely left an imprint on the archaeological record. When after the close of the thirteenth century B.C. they began to

develop village life, it is significant that in large part they mimicked settlement patterns and domestic architecture that were borrowed from
the Canaanite towns of the lowlands. (1992: 279)

Redford's association of the Shasu with our supposed Israelites has
been proposed by others, including some biblical scholars and a handful of
archaeologists. But most of these did not have the current archaeological
data at their disposal. Nor was Redford able to cite much of it when he
wrote (he does not mention Finkelstein's 1988 work, *Archaeology of the Israelite Settlement*). Nevertheless his Shasu theory should not be dismissed
out of hand (indeed, it has recently been endorsed by the notable Israeli
scholar Anson Rainey, who is well versed in matters Egyptological). Sometimes a non-specialist, unencumbered by any of the usual intellectual (and
in this case often theological) baggage, comes up with a refreshingly simple
solution to a vexing problem.

CHAPTER 9

Toward Another Synthesis on the Origins and Nature of Early Israel

I have reserved a critical treatment of Israel Finkelstein until last, even though in many ways it was he who initiated the current discussion on Israelite origins with his pioneering surveys and excavations in the 1980s and then with his later syntheses of the data. Finkelstein, by any account, has been the major spokesperson, and I take his views with utmost seriousness even though I often disagree with him. Our back-and-forth discussion dates from the early 1990s, when I began to write more explicitly on this subject and Finkelstein responded. For the most part it has been a good-humored debate, and I think a useful one. It may clarify matters to set forth briefly our agreements and disagreements.

We agree largely on the following (and for that matter, so do most archaeologists):

1. All older models are now obsolete; in future the archaeological data will prevail, even over textual sources, including the Hebrew Bible.
2. The recent Israeli surveys, plus a few excavations, provide the critical information.
3. All the current evidence points to a demographic surge in Iron I, especially in the hill country.
4. The highland settlers were not foreign invaders, but came mostly from somewhere within Canaanite society.
5. The overall settlement process was gradual, best understood within the framework of long-term, often cyclical patterns of Palestinian settlement-history *(la longue durée)*.

6. There are significant continuities with Late Bronze Age material culture, as in the pottery; and also continuities from Iron I into Iron II (the period of the Israelite Monarchy).

7. The unique culture that emerges in the 12-11th century B.C. is not homogeneous and reflects an ethnic mix.

8. Environment and technology were factors in cultural changes on this horizon.

There are, however, several critical points of disagreement between Finkelstein and myself:

1. The exact origins within Canaan. Finkelstein favors a large-scale resedentarization of local pastoral nomads (similar to Alt), while I see a much more varied origin, with fewer nomads and more sedentarized peoples from the lowlands.

2. Chronology. Finkelstein dates the settlement mostly to the late 12th and even the 11th century B.C. (except for 'Izbet Sartah), while I believe that it began in the 13th century B.C.

3. Pottery. I find much more continuity than Finkelstein does with the overall Late Bronze Age Canaanite repertoire, regarding the differences in relative percentages of types as less significant.

4. Technology. I see technologies like terrace-building and cistern-digging as both more systemic (that is, more part of a larger sociocultural pattern of innovation) and also more fundamental than Finkelstein sees them.

5. Ideology. I take a less materialistic, less deterministic approach, allowing a relatively greater role for sociological and ideological factors in cultural change (even though they are admittedly harder to specify archaeologically).

6. Ethnicity. I am much more optimistic than Finkelstein on the question of defining ethnicity in the archaeological record. In the end, Finkelstein is unable or unwilling to identify the hill country settlers; I believe that we can classify them as "proto-Israelites."

I have already dealt here and there with Finkelstein's evidence for the positions that he takes, which is difficult to evaluate since he has not disclosed until recently much of the relevant data. In addition, he has changed his mind on some key issues. Nevertheless, his basic thesis was implicit already in his *Archaeology of the Israelite Settlement* (1988) and has remained much the same since. One of his clearest summaries came in 1992, in a solicited response to a public lecture of mine with which he disagreed sharply. Again in 1996 he responded, in the same vein, to a review article of mine published in 1995. I had entitled it "Will the Real Israel Please Stand Up?" Finkelstein's title was "Ethnicity and Origin of the Iron I Settlers in the Highlands of Canaan: Can the Real Israel Stand Up?" His answer was "No," at least not before about the 9th century B.C., with the rise of an Israelite state. (And this from the man who quite literally "wrote the book" on the subject in 1988 — *Archaeology of the Israelite Settlement!*)

An Overview

In rereading everything that Finkelstein has written on the subject, three things in particular surprise me. (1) Nowhere does he give a succinct, quotable description of the entity he once characterized as "early Israel," like those of other scholars whom I have quoted above, all easily found. These are lacking even in his best summary, in a 1995 volume entitled *The Archaeology of Society in the Holy Land* (ed. Thomas E. Levy). (2) In discussions after 1995 (such as those in 1996, 1997, and 1998) he mostly repeats himself, sometimes word for word. (3) While Finkelstein pointedly rejects my several criticisms in all his publications, he "answers" only with *ad hominem* attacks, not with any real data, old or new. Not only does he frequently misrepresent my views (I was never a "Gottwaldian"), but he also thinks that I am a closet "biblical archaeologist" (never mind the fact that I was writing to oppose that approach when Finkelstein was still a schoolboy).

Polemics aside, let me try to summarize Finkelstein's main points on origins, both for the sake of the following argument and in the hope that I am representing his views fairly (see, for instance, his 1995 summary).

1. The long-term settlement history and demography of ancient Palestine are characterized by "oscillations," with alternating patterns of nomadization and sedentarization. In the hill country, for instance, there were three "waves of settlement" — in (a) Late Chalcolithic-Early Bronze I; (b) Middle Bronze II-III; and (c) the late 13th-11th centuries B.C. — separated by two "intervals of decline."

2. The Iron I horizon represents the third "wave" in this cyclical process, in which nomads who had been displaced by the destructions of the

end of the Middle Bronze Age and who had remained nomadic throughout the Late Bronze Age gradually became "resedentarized."

3. The clue to the ultimate Middle Bronze Age origins of the Iron I population group lies in close similarities in traits such as the lack of fortifications, domestic architecture, pottery, and mountain-top "cult places."

4. "There is absolutely no *undisputed* archaeological evidence for a *direct* shift of a significant population from the lowlands to the highlands in the Late Bronze-Iron I transition" (1995: 363; emphasis mine).

A Critical Look at the Evidence

Let us look at Finkelstein's major points one by one.

1. His basic premise about long-term cycles of settlement is correct, as I have often pointed out independently (contrary to his charge that I ignore this). And he and I agree entirely on at least one interval of nomadization on which I have worked extensively, the Early Bronze IV period, *ca.* 2300-2000 B.C. These cycles constitute such a well-known phenomenon that no defense of the argument is required.

2. Finkelstein's next point, while a reasonable assumption, remains almost entirely undocumented. Elsewhere he has put it this way:

> The breakdown of the political system of the Middle Bronze Age led to the nomadization of a significant part of the population of the highlands frontier; in the Late Bronze Age these pastoral groups lived in a close symbiotic relationship with the remaining urban centers. (1992: 68)

These assertions are stated straightforwardly as facts, but there is no evidence whatsoever for such nomadization in the Late Bronze Age. All we really know is that surveys and excavations have suggested a marked decline through Canaan in this period, from some 272 sites to 101, and from a population of 140,000 to 60,000 or 70,000. Using Finkelstein's own data, the hill country sites declined from 248 to 29, and the population (estimated as usual by built-up areas) may have declined from *ca.* 36,750 to *ca.* 11,750.

Some sort of displacement of the population following the Middle Bronze Age destructions *ca.* 1500 B.C. does seem to have taken place (they weren't all killed, after all). Even so, the refugees are invisible in the archaeological record. Finkelstein is apparently relying largely on the 1984 analysis of Rivka Gonen, who painted a picture of a depopulated Canaan, marked by a shift in Late Bronze from urban centers to scattered rural settlements. Why does Finkelstein not cite, however, the work of one of his own younger Tel Aviv students, Shlomo Bunimovitz, whose 1989 doctoral dissertation proffers a very different portrait? Bunimovitz writes as follows:

> Though it is true that many of the large urban centers which formed the backbone of settlement in Middle Bronze Age Canaan dramatically diminished in size, it should be emphasized that they remained urban in character. . . . The moderate Late Bronze Age cities controlled a much diminished rural sector. Indeed, during most of this period hardly any rural settlements existed in the highlands and in few other regions of the country. (1995: 324)

"Invisible nomads" indeed!

3. Let us look, however, more closely at these nomads. That there *were* pastoral nomads in the hill country in the Late Bronze Age, as in all other periods in Palestine, is beyond reasonable doubt, even without direct archaeological evidence. But by Finkelstein's own estimates, the pastoral-nomadic element of the population of Palestine in all periods up until recently has been about 10% of the total (or a maximum of 15%), which is universally accepted. Thus we should add to the 12,000 people in the hill country in the Late Bronze Age (again, Finkelstein's estimate) another 1,200-1,500 pastoral nomads, giving us a maximum of 13,500. Then keep in mind that Finkelstein's estimate of the hill country population by the 12th century B.C. works out to anywhere from *ca.* 12,800 to 17,000, and for the 11th century B.C. 30,200 to 42,700 (cf. 1988: 194; 323, 333).

Finkelstein himself was the first to document the "demographic explosion" in the hill country in Iron I, accepted now by all authorities. He has his facts straight, but his explanation is wrong, as simple arithmetic shows. As I pointed out in 1998, even if *all* 1,200-1,500 13th century B.C. pastoral nomads settled down in the 12th century B.C., there is no way that natural increase alone could account for a ten-fold growth in population in Iron I — not even if every family produced 50 surviving children! There must have been a very sizable population increment from somewhere else, and early on. Indeed, every other archaeologist thinks so; no one follows Finkelstein's almost exclusively resedentarized nomads theory. But Finkelstein has never replied to Bunimovitz's criticisms, to Stager's, or to mine.

Three other pieces of evidence are adduced by Finkelstein. He asserts that (a) most Iron I sites are to be found in the east; (b) the plan and design of the pillar-courtyard house was modeled on the Bedouin tent; and (c) in Iron I a number of cultural traits of the Middle Bronze Age reappeared. Let us consider each of these assertions in turn.

Location of Iron I Sites

Finkelstein states that in his southern Samaria ("Ephraim") surveys "most of the early Iron Age I sites (75%-90%)" were located in the eastern part of the region, that is, "on the desert fringe and the eastern flank of the central range" (1988: 191; 1995: 357). However, he is not consistent geographically. Elsewhere he modifies this to include "regions adapted for grain-growing" (1992: 67). And in still another place he adds to this "early," presumably "nomadic," phase of settlement "the intermontane valleys of the central range, and flat areas, such as the Bethel plateau" (1992: 64). Why the irregularity?

Finkelstein is also inconsistent in his statistics. In one place (1988: 191) he says that 75%-90% of all the early Iron I sites are in the "desert fringe." But elsewhere (1988: 194) he claims that "early in Iron I most of the inhabitants were concentrated in the central range." Which is it? In either case, his principal stress on the marginal areas, however defined, is not so much on the environment itself — more suitable for herding and some dry-farming — but on the absence of any need for either terraces or cisterns. Thus he argues that the first Iron I settlers must have been pastoral nomads.

There are several problems with this argument, quite apart from Finkelstein's inability to specify his "pastoral nomadic zone" geographically and ecologically. First is a lack of evidence that the easternmost survey sites are indeed the earliest. This is the fulcrum of his entire argument; but though surface surveys have been conducted, few sites have actually been excavated. And as his own discussions tacitly admit, it is almost impossible to distinguish 12th from 11th century B.C. pottery on the basis of the few sherds that most survey sites produce. One should note that Finkelstein's original site distribution maps and demographic projects (published in 1988) do not separate these two phases. In subsequent discussions, his "Iron I" data turns out to be almost exclusively 11th century B.C., although he dates the first "wave" of settlement to the 12th century B.C. But if this is the case, then where is the 12th century evidence? Only in one map (1988: 189) does Finkelstein distinguish the two phases. But how, then, does he know that the pottery of his eastern sites is "earlier"? (Zertal made a similar "east-to-west" argument, and even published some cooking pot rims that can be assigned broadly to one century or another. But his statistics, too, can easily be refuted — as we will see below.)

Before proceeding, let me state for the reader what every archaeologist knows. Given a handful of worn, generally undiagnostic Iron I sherds, cooking pot rims alone can be reliably separated into rough "12th century" and "11th century B.C." groups. This is because these short-lived vessels change predictably and the changes can now be reasonably well dated from larger samples and whole vessels recovered in some quantity from excavated sites (such as Giloh, Shiloh, and 'Izbet Sartah). Finkelstein has conceded this point (1988: 190).

Furthermore, Finkelstein's frequent claim that 75%-90% of the "early" survey sites are on the "desert fringe" is not borne out by the later publication of his own database in 1997, in which all the diagnostic pottery is presented. In 1988, only ten sherds were published, without provenience; charts at that time simply listed the number of sherds of these "types" for each site. Even in 1988, Finkelstein had listed only fourteen sites in his "Desert Fringe" column of the Ephraim survey (1988: 186) — out of a total of 115. Unless I am missing something here, that amounts to about 12%, not 90% or even 75%. And how do we know that any of these fourteen are "early"?

Here a bit of detective work is required — which shows, incidentally, why non-specialists will have so much difficulty in trying to assess Finkelstein's theories about early Israel. I have taken the fourteen desert fringe sites listed in 1988, and then consulted the pottery now published in the 1997 final report. The information thus derived is most conveniently summarized in chart-form.

Site no.	Arabic name	"Iron I" sherds	Published (1988 fig.)	Comments
18-15/1	Kh. en-Marjam			
18-15/31	Kh. en-Najama	8		
18-15/44	Kh. Jib'it	14	8.303:5-7	Ud
18-16/6	Kh. Qarqafa	12	8.307:1-3	Ud
18-16/41	Kh. el-Marajim	14	8.317:2-4	No. 3 = 12th cent. cooking pot
18-16/50		3		
18-16/51	Kh. er-Rahaya	5	8.321:8, 9	No. 9-12th cent. cooking pot
18-16/54	esh-Sheikh Mazar	23	8.323:12-15	No. 14-12th cent. cooking pot
18-16/55		3	8.325:5	
18-17/42	'En Nabi Nun	1		
18-17/43	Kh. Yanun	9	8.339:1-3	No. 1 = early 12th cent. cooking pot
18-17/44		19		
18-17/51	Kh. el-Jarayish	11	8.342:10, 11	Ud
18-17/73	Kh. Tana et-Tahta	3		

Tabulated data on Iron I survey sites of the desert fringe; compiled from the 1997 final report volume. "Ud" = non-diagnostic; pottery dates are the present author's.

There are several important implications of the raw data here — none of which are explored by Finkelstein. Note first that, of all the 14 "desert fringe" sites now fully published, most have only a handful of sherds, and these are only described in the statistical tables as generic "Iron I" — that is, 12th-11th centuries B.C. generally. But Finkelstein's east-west/early-late scheme would require at least some of these Iron I sites to date from the 12th century B.C. The problem here is that only a very few experienced archaeologists will be qualified to examine the published pottery from these sites. (Having handled many thousands of Iron I sherds at Gezer over the years, and having studied virtually all the comparable ceramic material, I elect myself to the club.) And a close examination shows that most of the published sherds are non-diagnostic (thus "Ud"). Four sites have one clear 12th century B.C. cooking pot rim each, of the simple elongated flanged type well known from excavations of the early sites and phases of Shiloh and 'Izbet Sartah. One site, Kh. Yanun, has one cooking pot rim of the shorter, triangular type similar to Giloh, which is more common to the early 12th century B.C. The remainder of these 14 desert fringe sites are represented mainly by storejar rims, which Finkelstein agrees (1988: 276) cannot be separated into 12th or 13th century B.C. categories. Thus Finkelstein's only evidence for his sweeping assertion that 75%-90% of the 115 Iron I sites in Ephraim are located in the desert fringe, and that this proves that the first "wave" of settlement reflects pastoral nomads settling down, rests on four sites and four identifiable sherds! When that data is taken into consideration, Finkelstein's entire house of cards comes tumbling down. Yet the unwary biblical scholar or the non-specialist reader would never know the facts I have documented here.

A final point on the locations of some of the individual desert fringe sites: two photographs of Kh. Yanun — one of the four sites where there is evidence of some 12th century B.C. occupation — show clearly (1) that this is a *hilltop* site; (2) that it has *terrace-systems* all around; and (3) that it overlooks a *fertile valley* (1997: 330, 331). It hardly seems accurate to describe it as "desert fringe." The same is true for another early site, Kh. el-Marajim (1997: 782). Only Kh. er-Rahaya and esh-Sheikh Mazar appear to be situated at the head of a deep decline leading down to the steppe-zone (1997: 793; 796). One of Finkelstein's general Iron I sites, Kh. Marjama, was partially excavated in the 1970s by Amihai Mazar. Marjama is situated on a hilltop some eighteen miles north of Jerusalem, just east of the main road to Shechem. I have visited this site and know the region well firsthand. To call Marjama a desert fringe site is misleading; it is rather typical of many central ridge sites, with heavily terraced hillsides, located near a major spring, and adjacent to a very fertile valley. Incidentally, this ten-acre site, heavily fortified, was dated to the Monarchy by Mazar (*ca.* 10th century B.C. on), and he reports no Iron I remains at all. Finkelstein published no pottery in 1997; and his 1988 does not list any pottery collected. Why then claim Marjama as an Iron I site at all?

Site Plans and Pillar-Courtyard Houses

However, even Finkelstein admits that the above picture reflects only the situation in Ephraim, or southern Samaria, agreeing that in Manasseh, to the north, the settlers came from a "more sedentary" background (1995:

357). Finkelstein's other argument for south Samaria rests on the contentions (a) that the oval or circular plan of several early settlements reflects the socio-economic and cultural background of Bedouin tents drawn up in a circle, and (b) that the individual pillar-courtyard or four-room house derives from the typical Bedouin-like tent of pastoral nomads. Here, unfortunately, the arguments are even more speculative — indeed, entirely so.

First, the oval or circular plan. It resulted, of course, not from a town wall girdling the site, but rather from houses built side-by-side so as to form a sort of enclosed perimeter. Typical examples that Finkelstein cites are Beersheba and 'Izbet-Sartah III (plus, it seems, some of the hilltop villages found in the Israeli surveys). However, the Beersheba that Finkelstein cites (following Herzog; as in 1988: 243) is the village of Stratum VII, which dates to the late 11th or early 10th century B.C. The late 12th century-early 11th century B.C. level at Beersheba, the earliest occupation, would be Stratum IX, of which only storage pits and cisterns were found and no plan could be discerned.

As for Finkelstein's own site of 'Izbet-Sartah, which is indeed of crucial importance, I have already noted several objections to his interpretation. The plan published of Stratum III is largely conjectural and consists of only parts of some half-dozen adjacent structures (out of a projected 24 or so), of which some walls curve slightly. I would judge that no more than about 15% of the plan, as shown, was actually excavated. In answering this objection in 1992, Finkelstein claimed that 40% of the "peripheral wall" was uncovered (1992: 67). The reader can easily decide between us by looking at the illustration on page 81 above. The other reason why it is doubtful that 'Izbet-Sartah was a pastoral encampment is staff member Barukh Rosen's calculation from the zoological and botanical remains that the site produced a substantial agricultural surplus — unlikely for pastoral nomads. In fact, in the earliest stratum, Stratum III, cattle bones constituted 43% of the total, and the number *decreased* by Stratum II to 23%. Neither of these pieces of evidence looks like "nomads settling down." As Rosen concluded of the economy: "To sum up, the economic system of 'Izbet-Sartah is typical of a *sedentary* settlement based on agriculture and animal breeding" (1986: 151; emphasis mine). And one must add the paper by one of Finkelstein's own Field Supervisors, Zvi Lederman, entitled "Nomads They Never Were." Finkelstein never quotes any of the above information; I cannot help but think that he went to 'Izbet-Sartah with resedentarized nomads already in his field of vision, and there saw what he was conditioned to see. This is something that happens all too often in archaeology (although not, I presume, in reading texts!).

The third site that Finkelstein adduces to support his nomad theory is Tel Esdar, a site in the Negev twelve miles southeast of Beersheba. Kochavi excavated it in 1963-64. The plan of Stratum III does show part of what seems to be an oval-shaped settlement. But Esdar III is best dated to the late 11th or even the early 10th century B.C. Finkelstein considered it an Israelite site in 1988, describing it as being less than one acre in size, thus fitting his criterion of smallness (1988: 38). But Kochavi, the excavator, says that Tel Esdar was a five-acre site (1969: 2*).

Finkelstein's effort to see oval or circular plans at many Iron I sites ignores several critical points. (1) These early Iron Age villages are mostly hilltop sites. The easiest, most efficient, most sensible village plan would follow the natural contours of the hilltop — often bare bedrock. It would be a very strange geological formation indeed that would result in a rectangular hilltop. (2) Nearly all later Iron II sites, even large urban sites dating from the Monarchy, are also curvilinear — some, like Megiddo, almost perfectly circular in plan. Are these, too, sites that were established by nomads? The fact is that almost all tells or mounds in Palestine, regardless of period, have a circular or oval configuration. (3) The tendency to group dwellings together in a sort of ring, even at sites where there is no perimeter wall, is quite natural. Indeed, this plan may not reflect any perceived need for defense beyond the practical concern for keeping animal and human marauders out or animals in. Just as likely it indicates a universal psychological factor at work: the deeply felt human need to create a "liminal," or threshold, area in order to separate private, secure living space from the outside world. (4) Finally, ethnographers record that arranging tents in a circle was unusual even for Bedouin. It was a practice followed only in very hostile locales. What hostilities would our peaceful farmers in their mountain redoubts have had to fear? I have spent a good deal of time among the Bedouin of Israel and Jordan over the past forty years, and I have never seen a tent-circle. Bedouin line their tents up horizontally, facing east, with some space between each one.

Let me turn now to Finkelstein's second Iron I village-pastoral nomad connection: the typical pillar-courtyard house as a sort of domestic adaptation of a Bedouin tent (1988: 254-259). This idea was first developed in the 1970s by Volkmar Fritz, co-director of the Tel Masos excavations I mentioned above. Fritz took special note of the open central or side court-yard, flanked by a number of small rooms; he called these dwellings "broad-room" houses. It seemed to him that such a plan perpetuated the arrangement of Bedouin tents, the outdoor sitting area in front of Bedouin tents being the forerunner of the courtyards. His interpretation is prob-lematic, though, for these two living spaces have entirely different func-tions. The area directly outside a tent is usually a meeting place, where men congregate, talk, and offer hospitality (as I know from many a cup of bitter Bedouin coffee and endless small-talk). The house courtyard, on the other hand, serves mostly for food storage and preparation, feeding of animals, and other domestic chores usually carried out by women. A preferable model for the courtyard or broad-room house is really the Late Bronze Age Egyptian-style villa, examples of which are found in a number of resi-dencies of Egyptian high commissioners at various sites of the 14th-13th centuries B.C. A few others, including Aharon Kempinski, who was Fritz's co-director at Tel Masos, and Ze'ev Herzog, who excavated at Beersheba under Aharoni, share Fritz's preference for a tent prototype. Finkelstein differs from them only in seeing a more indirect lineage "from tent to house," positing an intervening early stage in which broad-room houses gradually grew by the addition of longrooms, and especially of the pillars that seem to develop by the 12th century B.C.

But few other scholars have been persuaded by the tent prototype. Stager's very detailed and sophisticated analysis puts it best:

> The pillared house takes its form not from some desert nostalgia monumentalized in stone and mudbrick, but from a living tradition. It was first and foremost a successful adaptation to farm life: the ground floor had space allocated for food processing, small craft production, stabling, and storage; the second floor (ʿaliyyah) was suitable for dining, sleeping, and other activities. . . . Its longevity attests to its continuing suitability not only to the environment, especially where timber was available, but also for the socioeconomic unit housed in it — for the most part, rural families who farmed and raised livestock. (1985: 17)

Robert Coote, a biblical scholar whose work I have mentioned above, notes that the "tent-to-house" theory, while once regarded as novel, is no longer widely held, and that there is no archaeological support for it. As he puts it:

There is no reason to wonder where the new settlers got their new housing ideas any more than their new building skills. Both lay quite within the capabilities of the lowland farming class, tribal and otherwise, of the thirteenth century and earlier. (1990: 133)

Once again the disinterested observer may get the impression that Finkelstein's overriding theory of the pastoral-nomadic origin of the earliest Israelites has influenced his interpretation of the archaeological evidence, as well as leading him into unwarranted speculation. I shall return to the larger issues of nomadism and tribalism in my own attempt at synthesis in the next chapter.

Reappearance of Cultural Traits

But first let me remark briefly on Finkelstein's final defense of resedentarized nomads in the hill country sites of Iron I: the supposed sudden reappearance of several cultural traits of the Middle Bronze Age five or six hundred years earlier, presumably after a long hibernation. His first comparison, of pillared houses, is too far-fetched for extended comment. An occasional Middle Bronze Age example of a house with some pillars or a courtyard adjoining some rooms does not provide a real connection. As for the lack of fortifications, the Middle Bronze Age is known precisely for its massive fortifications, even at small sites like Finkelstein's Shiloh. The assertion that these fortifications were constructed only at the end of the period (to support the notion of pastoral origins) is simply wrong. The most impressive Middle Bronze fortifications now known, at Ashkelon on the coast, where we have a huge multiple-entry city gate, belong to the very beginning of the period (as Finkelstein knows). The existence of open-air cult places in both periods (never mind that there is only one in Iron I) requires no explanation: they occur in all periods. Finally, Finkelstein's pottery "comparisons" are astounding, coming from a professional archaeologist. He states of the Middle Bronze Age pottery that its ceramic repertoire

was surprisingly limited, containing mainly storage jars and cooking pots. Pottery was apparently produced in local workshops. Mass production of vessels is evident only in subsequent periods (MB III). (1995: 359)

Bluntly put, none of this is true. All authorities stress the large and varied ceramic repertoire, the exquisite wheel production, and the mass-produced homogeneity of Middle Bronze pottery — with the very best of it beginning at the outset of the period.

There is only one conclusion that I can reach: an archaeologist who plays so loosely with well-known facts is too much in the grip of an *idée fixe*. As for Finkelstein's more recent argument that we cannot even identify these sedentarized nomads ethnically — as Israelites or anyone else — I shall address that presently.

CHAPTER 10

Yet Another Attempt at Synthesis: Early Israel as a Frontier Agrarian Reform Movement

By now the reader may have begun to think that biblical and archaeological scholarship are only so much mumbo-jumbo. But despite sharp differences over many details, it should be stressed that there has emerged over the past two decades or so a remarkable consensus on what I would argue are the main points regarding early Israel and its origins.

Toward a Consensus

1. The question of date has been resolved; the only horizon on which we can see Israel emerging in Canaan is that of the Late Bronze/Iron I transition, the late 13th–early 12th centuries B.C.

2. All older models are now obsolete overall, although some of their features may ultimately be retained.

3. Archaeology is and will continue to be the primary source of new data for rewriting Israel's early history. New readings of the biblical texts are welcome, however, and may be helpful in some cases — if there can be a constructive dialogue.

4. The recent archaeological evidence for indigenous origins of some sort is overwhelming. The only remaining question is *where* within Canaan. It is the continuities that are decisive.

5. Archaeology's best contribution will be to provide a context in which the settlement process can be better understood, but only an interdisciplinary inquiry will ultimately be productive.

The Late Bronze Age Context of Early Israel

First, it is evident to scholars and lay readers alike that early Israel did not arise in a historical and cultural vacuum, or without antecedents. Not even the most doctrinaire of the biblical writers thought that Israel dropped down from Heaven. Indeed, the biblical writers constantly portray Israel vis-à-vis its predecessors in the Land, the Canaanites. The prophet Ezekiel, for example, late in Israel's history, complains: "Your origin and your birth are of the Canaanites; your father was an Amorite, and your mother a Hittite" (16:3).

I will argue here that the historical memory of the Bible is accurate by and large. Throughout the foregoing discussion I have pointed out, as most scholars do today, the strong continuities between the Late Bronze Age Canaanite culture and that of the Iron I Israelites or "proto-Israelites." These continuities are most evident in some of the archaeological evidence, as we saw with the pottery of the two periods. But there are linguistic continuities as well; since the birth of modern linguistics it has been clear that biblical Hebrew is a Canaanite dialect. And many scholars have recently argued that even Israelite religion derives many of its supposedly unique features from Canaanite religion (which was what the prophets were complaining about).

"Con-textual" Evidence

Let me now be more specific about the Late Bronze Age context (that is, "con-text," *with* texts) by setting forth in simple terms what we know about Canaan in the 14th-13th centuries B.C. (or Late Bronze IIB). I shall use first the Amarna letters — letters written to the court of Pharaoh by native princes of Canaanite city-states, detailing local conditions. Then I shall juxtapose the contemporary archaeological evidence, some of it from these same city-states. Finally I shall compare some of the main tenets of the biblical traditions, although they are later (*ca.* 8th-7th centuries B.C.), to show how the biblical tradition grew out of earlier Canaanite culture while at the same time making a radical protest against its vestiges. Again, at the risk of oversimplifying, I shall do this in chart-form (see p. 169).

Two caveats are necessary before proceeding. (1) First, the biblical texts are, of course, later chronologically; they are not monolithic; and

Table 10.1. Comparative cultural features, Late Bronze to Iron Age

Late Bronze Age, 1400-1200 B.C.		Iron Age, 1200-600 B.C.
Amarna Letters (14th c.)	*Archaeological Data*	*Hebrew Bible*
1. City-states dominate	Declining urban culture at end	Ruralism, "nomadic ideal"
2. Canaanite overlords	Growing political disintegration	"No king but Yahweh"
3. Feudal society, economy	Evidence of local "elites," under Egyptian domination	Tribalism, "equality"
4. Social stratification; class conflict	Extremes of wealth and poverty in burials, and elsewhere	"Poor of the Land" idealized
5. Oppressive land-tenure systems	Overcentralization; declining agricultural production and trade	The Land as Yahweh's; "every man under his own fig tree"; "domestic mode of production"
6. Peasants disenfranchised; forced-labor (corvée)	Increasing poverty	Family inheritance "sacred"; "woe to those who add field to field"; opposition to corvée
7. Bureaucratic corruption; abuse of authority	"Palaces" of local rulers; conspicuous consumption	"Let justice roll down like waters"
8. Social unrest, ʿApiru and others	Gradual urban collapse; population displacement by end as refugees flee	Israelites a "displaced people"; Israel a "new creation"
9. Polymorphous religious expressions	Many temples, but all disappear by end	Religion as "social critique"; eventual development of monotheism

they often represent the religious ideal rather than the social reality. (2) Second, I am hardly the first to look to the Late Bronze context of early Israel, or to compare it with the biblical traditions. All I can claim is a novelty. Textual scholars have rarely added the archaeological evidence to the equation; and many archaeologists dismiss the biblical materials as irrelevant. Again, the better approach is interdisciplinary collaboration and dialogue between texts and artifacts.

It is one thing to argue that the early Israelites were in effect displaced Canaanites — displaced both geographically and culturally. That notion has been basic to the work of recent biblical scholars such as Gottwald, Chaney, Coote, Whitelam, and others. And archaeologists attracted to sociological thought have also pointed to Canaanite origins, among them Kempinski, Fritz, Bunimovitz, Stager, and even Finkelstein (despite his objections to this school generally). But what displaced these peoples who came to settle the highlands in the early Iron Age? And from where were they displaced? These questions — so fundamental to our inquiry — have to do with both the origins and the essential character of this movement.

Letters from Canaan

First, the general Late Bronze Age Canaanite background as outlined somewhat cryptically in Table 10.1 above requires further elaboration. A few quotations from some of the social commentary in the Amarna letters from Canaan may be illustrative. Even though these letters are prone to gossip, we can presume that they provide a candid and reasonably faithful portrait of the prevailing socio-economic conditions in the 14th and 13th centuries B.C. In particular, they illustrate the petty, back-biting rapacious behavior of the Egyptian puppets who ruled in Palestine — amusing in retrospect, but with tragic consequences for the masses living under them. Most of these letters are complaints and appeals to the infamous Akhenaten (Amenophis IV, ca. 1370-1353 B.C.), who appears to have been so busy with his beautiful Queen Nefertiti and his six beloved daughters that he never answered his mail. The letters were found in 1887 by a peasant woman among the ruins of Akhenaten's palace at el-Amarna, in Middle Egypt. (EA and RA in the following give the publication numbers; cf. Moran 1992.)

Here is part of an anonymous letter describing the general situation of chaos in Canaan; note the reference to the 'Apiru.

Let the king, my lord, learn that the chief of the 'Apiru has risen (in arms) against the lands which the god of the king, my lord, gave me; but I have smitten him. Also let the king, my lord, know that all my brethren have abandoned me, and (20) it is I and 'Abdu-Heba (who) fight against the chief of the 'Apiru. And Zurata, prince of Accho, and Indaruta, prince of Achshaph, it was they (who) hastened with fifty chariots — for I had been robbed (by the 'Apiru) — to my help but behold, they are fighting against me, so let it be agreeable to the king, my lord, and let him send Yanhamu, and let us make war in earnest, and let the lands of the king, my lord, be restored to their (former) limits! (RA XIX)

Here is an excerpt from the king of Acco, illustrating both the petty rivalry of the Canaanite kings and their ultimate dependence on Egypt.

Let the king, my lord, hear the word of his servant! [Zir] Damyashda has withdrawn from Biryawaza. [He was] with Shuta, the s[ervant] of the king in the city of [. . .] He did not say anything to him. The army of the king, my lord, has departed. He was with it in Megiddo. (20) I said nothing to him, but he deserted to me, and now Shuta has written to me: 'Give Zirlamyashda to Biryawaza!' But I did not consent to give him up. Behold. Accho is (as Egyptian) as Magdal in Egypt, but the king, my lord has not heard that [Shut]a has turned against me. Now let the king, my lord, send his commissioner and fetch him. (EA 234)

Here the king of Megiddo complains about his neighbor and rival at Shechem, Lab'ayu.

Let the king know that ever since the archers returned (to Egypt?), Lab'ayu has carried on hostilities against me, and we are not able to pluck the wool, and we are not able to go outside the gate in the presence of Lab'ayu, since he learned that thou hast not given archers; and now his face is set to take Megiddo, but let the king protect his city lest Lab'ayu seize it. Verily, the city is destroyed by death from pestilence and *disease.* Let the king give one hundred garrison troops to guard the city lest Lab'ayu seize it. Verily, there is no other purpose in Lab'ayu. He seeks to destroy Megiddo. (EA 244)

Even when one of the rascally rival kings died, like the notorious Lab'ayu of Shechem, there is no peace. Here, a complaint from the king of Hebron.

> Further, let the king, my lord, investigate; if I have taken a man or a single ox or an ass from him, then he is in the right!
> Further, Lab'ayu is dead, who seized our towns; but behold, 'Abdu-Heba is another Lab'ayu, and he (also) seizes our towns! So let the king take thought for his servant because of this deed! And I will not do anything until the king sends back a message to his servant. (EA 280)

There are constant conflicts over public and even private lands, which the local kings claim to hold for themselves, as seen in this letter from a king of Gezer. Note again the 'Apiru as a disruptive element.

> A servant of the king am I, and the dirt of thy two feet. Let the king my lord know that my youngest brother is estranged from me, and has entered Muhhazu, and has give his two hands to the chief of the 'Apiru. And now the [land of . . .] anna is hostile to me. Have concern for thy land! Let my lord write to his commissioner concerning this deed. (EA 298)

Each king tries to outdo the others, as well as impress Pharaoh, by forcing freemen into service on public works (the corvée system). Here, from the king of Megiddo.

> Let the king be informed concerning his servant and concerning his city. Behold, I am working in the town of Shunama, and I bring men of the corvée, but behold, the governors who are with me do not as I: they do not work in the town of Shunama, and they do not bring men for the corvée, but I alone bring men for the corvée from the town of Yapu. They come from Shu[nama], and likewise from the town of Nuribda. So let the king be informed concerning his city! (RA XIX)

Costly tributes were necessarily paid to the Egyptians to "buy them off," as we see in this letter from the Egyptian High Commissioner to the king of Gezer, Milkilu. The revenues, of course, are extracted from the populace at large.

> To Milkilu, prince of Gezer. Thus the king. Now I have sent thee this tablet to say to thee: Behold, I am sending to thee Hanya, the commissioner of the archers, together with goods, in order to procure fine concubines (i.e.) *weaving women*: silver, gold, (linen) garments, *turquoise*, all (sorts of) precious stones, chairs of *ebony*, as well as every good thing, totaling 160 deben. Total: 40 concubines: the price of each concubine is 40 (shekels) of silver. So send very fine concubines in whom there is no blemish. And let the king, thy lord, say to thee, 'This is good.' (RA XXXI)

If luxury goods and slaves aren't sufficient bribes, the kings can extend themselves a bit, as our friend Lab'ayu, king of Shechem, does in this letter.

> I have heard the words which the king wrote to me, and who am I that the king should lose his land because of me? Behold, I am a faithful servant of the king, and I have not rebelled and I have not sinned, and I do not withhold my tribute, and I do not refuse the requests of my commission. Now they wickedly slander me, but let the king my lord not impute rebellion to me!
>
> Further, my crime is namely that I entered Gezer and said publicly: 'Shall the king take my property, and not likewise the property of Milkilu?' I know the deeds which Milkilu has done against me.
>
> Further, the king wrote concerning my son. I did not know that my son associates with the 'Apiru, and I have verily delivered him into the hand of Adday. Further, if the king should write for my wife, how could I withhold her? If the king should write to me, 'Plunge a bronze dagger into thy heart and die!,' how could I refuse to carry out the command of the king? (EA 254)

Other local kings are threatened as well, as seen in this letter from Milkilu of Gezer, complaining about the king of Pella.

> Let the king, my lord, know the deed which Yanhamu did to me after I left the presence of the king, my lord. Now he seeks two thousand (shekels) of silver from my hand, saying to me: 'Give me thy wife and thy

children, or I will smite!' Let the king know this deed, and let my lord
send to me chariots and let him take me to himself lest I perish! (EA 270)

But in the end, all the intrigue fails, as 'Abdu-Heba the king of Jerusalem bemoans.

Twenty-one maidens (and) eighty captives, I delivered into the hand of
Shuta as a gift for the king, my lord. Let my king take thought for his
land! The land of the king is lost; in its entirety, it is taken from me: there
is war against me, as far as the lands of Seir (and) as far as Gath-carmel!
All the governors are at peace, but there is war against me. I have become
like an 'Apiru and do not see the two eyes of the king, my lord, for there
is war against me. I have become like a ship in the midst of the sea! (EA
288)

And the 'Apiru — often the scapegoats, blamed for the collapse of the system — were among the most despised victims, becoming social outcasts
and pariahs.

The Archaeological Context

There is not space to document here all the archaeological evidence that
we have for what I shall characterize as "collapse," but it is ample. Let us
look at some of it, referring to the categories enumerated in Table 10.1
(p. 169 above).

1. All the archaeological material culture data show a long, slow decline throughout the Late Bronze Age, from *ca.* 1500 B.C. onward, until the
lowest ebb is reached toward the end of the 13th century B.C. Canaan was
not isolated, however. Its collapse at that time marks, in fact, the well-
documented end of the 3,500-year-long Bronze Age in the entire eastern
Mediterranean world, from Greece to the Iranian plateau — the greatest
catastrophe that had befallen the region up to that time.

2. Following the disintegration of the Canaanite city-state system
and the disappearance of its local rulers, archaeological evidence such as
settlement type and distribution shows that Palestine regressed to political
anarchy that persisted for two centuries, until the rise of the Israelite Monarchy in Iron II.

3. The ruling elite minority is attested in the archaeological records by Egyptian-style "residencies" or palaces at several sites, among them the very ones from which the Amarna letters were written (such as Gezer).

4. Burials of the period show great extremes of wealth and poverty. Some tombs are filled with Egyptian, Cypriot, and Greek luxury items, while others are pitifully barren in grave goods.

5. The data show the concentration of impressive wealth and status symbols in the hands of a very few, while the culture as a whole was in decline.

6. Toward the end of the period, public building projects continue, but centrally managed maritime trade ceases completely, throwing the economy into a tailspin.

7. Here the evidence noted in nos. 3-6 above is compelling.

8. Demographic projections, based on archaeological data, show the gradual depopulation of the cities.

9. We have evidence of more than two dozen monumental temples — some sites have several — and elaborate cult paraphernalia. But all this disappears at the end of the period.

The End of the Bronze Age, and the Aftermath

Vibrant as the Late Bronze Age Canaanite culture may once have been, it was tottering toward collapse by the late 13th century b.c. Its end has fascinated ancient Near Eastern scholars almost as much as the fall of Rome has later historians — and it remains almost equally mysterious.

An earlier generation of scholars saw the end of the Bronze Age largely in terms of the catastrophic invasions of new peoples: "Sea Peoples" from the Mediterranean and, of course, our Israelites. In that scenario the end came quickly and dramatically, followed by a Dark Age lasting at least through the 12th century b.c. Later, some scholars invoked natural disasters, such as prolonged drought, as the cause (as Stiebing, above). More recently, technology has been seen as a factor, as in Robert Drews' *The End of the Bronze Age: Changes in Warfare and the Catastrophe ca. 1200 b.c.* (1993). But now almost all scholars recognize that such sweeping changes, which affected the entire Mediterranean world, cannot have been the result of any single cause, no matter how critical.

A recent Brown University symposium explored this problem with interesting results; the papers were published as *The Crisis Years: The 12th Century B.C. from Beyond the Danube to the Tigris* (1989). My contribution dealt with Palestine and events there in terms of systems collapse, using the approach outlined in Chapter 7. In this view, various cultural subsystems gradually deteriorated, until there occurred an inexorable downward spiral that fed on itself and eventually ended in the breakdown of the entire system. Some of the archaeological evidence has been presented above.

I would summarize matters by saying that (1) the economy of Palestine, always marginal, was adversely affected by the end of international trade, growing isolation, and perhaps declining agricultural production. (2) An outworn technology was not able to compensate, to "take up the slack." (3) A complex but delicately balanced social structure was upset by increasing conflict, made worse not only by local rebels, the ʿApiru, but also by intrusive people like Hurrians from Syria and the eventually invading "Sea Peoples." (4) An unwieldy, overly centralized, and corrupt bureaucracy either neglected matters or made them worse by meddling in systems that were never really understood (some things never change!). (5) The once-powerful integrating myths of religion — so eloquently attested in Canaanite texts from Syria — no longer seemed credible in the face of overwhelming challenges to the cultural system. At this point, even minor disturbances would have had a strong ripple effect throughout the system. The end finally came with the destruction or abandonment of many of the city-states, and then the disappearance of the Egyptian empire in Asia about 1160 B.C. Complete chaos ensued. A vacuum, which culture abhors as much as nature does, was created, and something would fill it.

Where within Canaan?

I hope that I have effectively made the case that Canaanite culture provides the general backdrop against which best to portray early Israelite culture. Assuming now that our highland colonists were dissidents and refugees of some sort within Canaan, where exactly was their point of departure? In the last chapter I gave many reasons why the most recent overarching theory, that of Israel Finkelstein, must be rejected on the basis of archaeological evidence. There is simply no way that the majority of those who settled in the hill country and came gradually to be known as Israelites could have been resedentarized local nomads, or even for that matter any sort of nomads from western Palestine, much less from Transjordan. The demographic data alone are decisive: there were not enough such nomads to account for the dramatic population growth we have in the 12th century B.C. hill country settlements.

There are other objections to Finkelstein's thesis. Nomads typically settle under duress, usually as a result of force from the outside world — as when governments try to bring them under state control. Emanuel Marx's detailed study *Bedouin of the Negev* (1967) documents how the sedentarization of the 15,000 or more Bedouin there began only in the 1870s under pressure from Ottoman Turkish rulers of Palestine. It was — and still is, under Israeli authorities — fiercely resisted. The Bedouin, who regard themselves as the only true Arabs, typically look down on the peasants as *fellahin,* or "settled farmers." This desert mystique goes back to some of our earliest Arabic sources, like the sociology of Ibn Khaldun, the 14th century A.D. historiographer. Marx has shown that the Bedouin lifestyle is rooted not so much in economic and political constraints, but in deeply held ideological beliefs and values. He relates how Bedouin who have been settled for two generations and are in fact peasant farmers, or even shopkeepers, still herd a few animals and think of themselves as pastoralists living a lifestyle of seasonal migrations.

I have seen this myself in Jordan, where the late King Hussein, himself of Bedouin lineage, tried unsuccessfully to settle the Bedouin in the south. I once saw a new, modern cinder-block village where the Bedouin had been confined; they were living in tents pitched in the yards, and had the sheep and goats stabled in the houses.

In the Late Bronze Age, the fact is that neither the Egyptian authorities, losing their grip on Canaan, nor the feuding local dynasties in Canaan had any effective control over the countryside — much less the steppes and the eastern frontiers. Both the Amarna letters dealing with the lawless 'Apiru and Egyptian texts describing the Shasu-Bedouin make that clear.

If one supposes rather that the local nomads had come up from the lowlands, or were already in the hill country, as Finkelstein argues, would they not, as refugees, have fled farther east, not west? The deserts of Transjordan would have been the safest refuge for anyone simply fleeing the breakdown of the urban centers and the chaos in the rural areas formerly under their control. Finkelstein proposes the large-scale and relatively sudden (re)sedentarization of pastoral nomads, but he offers no compelling rationale. Some such nomads probably did align themselves with the Iron I villagers, and even settled down permanently, as has always happened in the history of Palestine. But they were a minority.

Withdrawal?

Flight has often been invoked as the motive of peoples relocating in large numbers, which is the phenomenon that we must explain in Canaan in Iron I. Ethnographers sometimes picture this phenomenon of cyclical migration in terms not of sedentarization, but rather its exact opposite: retribalization. In extreme conditions, once-nomadic peoples who have long been settled have been known to revert to pastoral nomadism, throwing off government control for looser tribal affiliations. Sometimes this is called withdrawal; in fact, this is the very term used by Mendenhall and Gottwald. Like other urban dropouts, such as the 'Apiru, the early Israelites in this view were those who chose to withdraw from society, in this case migrating to the more remote and sparsely populated hill country.

I will argue that it is time to take up the notion of withdrawal again, but now with much more new supporting archaeological evidence, and with different ideas about its motives. It was not flight from intolerable conditions or necessarily a revolutionary Yahwistic fervor that propelled people toward the frontier, but rather simply a quest for a new society and a new lifestyle. They wanted to start over. And in the end, that *was* revolutionary.

In order to elaborate my thesis of withdrawal, however, I must first show that the Iron I hill country settlers had been sedentarized, and in the lowlands of Canaan at that, whether in the urban centers or in the countryside. My reasons for seeing these areas as the population pool (rather than the hinterland in the central hills or the eastern slopes) are the following:

(1) Anyone hoping to meet the challenges of colonizing the rural areas of the hill country frontier, and expecting to succeed as agriculturalists, must have had prior experience as subsistence farmers somewhere else in Canaan, as I have already suggested. It is inconceivable that nomads could have managed to do much more than to survive. Some probably did settle, as conditions allowed. But nomads alone cannot have created the extensive, highly integrated, successful agricultural society and economy that we have in the hill country in Iron I.

David Hopkins has recently analyzed these formidable difficulties in his *The Highlands of Canaan: Agricultural Life in the Early Iron Age* (1985). In particular, he enumerates the preconditions that had to be met. These include: (1) a close-knit social fabric; (2) the ability to mobilize labor on a large scale; (3) knowledge of environmental variations; (4) the technology necessary to clear forests, hew cisterns, and construct extensive terrace systems; (5) strategies for risk management and reduction; (6) the capacity to produce and store surpluses; and (7) provisions for long-term land tenure and conservation. Hopkins does not regard all these preconditions as necessarily preexisting among the hill country settlers (the art of terrace-building, for example, they would not have known beforehand). But he does show that they must have been conceivable, and that they developed successfully very soon. The earliest American colonists at Plymouth and Jamestown perished in large numbers, some the first year. The hill country settlers would have, too, had most of them not already been pre-adapted.

(2) Apart from agricultural experience and basic competence, there is, of course, the question of motive. Why would peasants, any more than pastoral nomads, want to uproot themselves, and in this case migrate to the inhospitable hill country frontier? The answer may be rather simple, if one accepts my picture above of the miserable conditions in the heartland of Canaan toward the end of the 13th century b.c. Canaan was on the verge of total collapse. Many villagers and peasant farmers, as well as the landless 'Apiru, were already impoverished and socially marginalized. They had little to lose. Withdrawing was prudent, if not necessary. It may even be that more than a century of rebellion and repression had given these various groups of dissidents some sense of social solidarity. There may have existed an ideology that made revolution seem possible, even inevitable. My theory is speculative, of course; and like Mendenhall's and Gottwald's peasants' revolt it has little direct archaeological evidence to support it. Nevertheless our current knowledge of the general archaeological context of Canaan toward the end of the Late Bronze Age makes this scenario quite realistic. In the words of the distinguished sociologists Lenski and Lenski, frontiers

> provide a unique opportunity for departures from the sociocultural patterns so deeply entrenched in agrarian societies. Those who respond to the challenge of the frontier, to its dangers and its opportunities, are primarily men with little to lose, with little at stake in the established order. Thus they are likely to possess a willingness to take great physical risks

and a proclivity for independence and innovation. As a result, new ways of life commonly develop in frontier areas, innovations are readily accepted, and older rigidities give way. (1978: 229)

This sounds to me like an apt description of the early Israelites.

The Highland Frontier

Before going further, let me examine the basic notion here, that of the "frontier." I do not mean, of course, a national frontier or border in the modern sense. The whole of what is today Israel, the West Bank, Jordan, and southern Lebanon and Syria was at the time all part of greater Canaan, which the Egyptians usually designated "the Land of the Hurru," that is, of the Hurrians. The real borders within this larger entity were ecological, and they were constantly shifting with changing environmental conditions. These were marginal lands, not only geographically but perceptually as well. Even in good times they were considered remote and hostile areas even though they were not that distant physically.

Michael Rowton has characterized the landscape of these regions of the Middle East as "dimorphic," or characterized as having two basic configurations. What is unique is that here, in contrast to the Great Desert of Arabia, arid and semi-arid zones are interspersed with arable lands in a sort of jigsaw pattern. Thus pastoralists roaming the steppes were frequently in contact with townspeople, as they still are today. In fact, Bedouin cannot prosper or even survive without trading their surplus animals and animal products to more sedentary peoples. (Finkelstein's theory of supposedly isolated nomads in the hill country in the Late Bronze Age ignores this well-known phenomenon.) Thus both the geographical and the psychological boundaries are always in flux. What all of the foregoing implies is that tribal peoples could settle from time to time, and settlers could easily become retribalized. Urban folk could gravitate to small villages in the hinterland; villagers could flock to the big city.

By the end of the 13th century B.C., however, with disaster looming on the horizon, the traffic was becoming more one-way. The frontier was open and attractive. Even earlier in the Late Bronze Age there were only a few large Canaanite city-states in the hill country, as we know from the Amarna letters. In the entire central hill country from the Jezreel Valley to

Beersheba, the only large cities mentioned are Megiddo, Taʿanach, Shechem, Jerusalem, and perhaps Hebron. These urban centers were on the average between twenty and twenty-five miles apart. The sphere of influence of each cannot have extended very far. And even though they were in contact with others, the competition and hostility suggests that none of these centers effectively controlled the countryside.

The Israeli surveys show that Late Bronze II satellite settlements are few in number, small, and relatively dispersed. That is precisely why the ʿApiru could operate so freely, well beyond the law. Finkelstein has objected to my 1992 argument that the intervening frontier zones in the central hills were sparsely occupied before Iron I, although my "sparsely" was relatively speaking. He counts some 150 Middle Bronze sites in this region (1992: 66). But he neglects to tell the reader that his own figures (1991: 27) yield only some six very large sites (10-20 acres) and six large sites (3-4 acres). The rest are small towns, villages, hamlets, and isolated cemeteries. The total Middle Bronze hill country population is unknown, but in my judgment it would have been well below what we call the carrying capacity of the region. Estimates of Broshi and Gophna in 1986 yielded a total of 138 Middle Bronze sites in the hill country, with about 4,100 acres of built-up occupied area. That would work out to a maximum population of some 40,000. But the significant fact here is that by Finkelstein's own estimate, the population had dwindled to not more than 12,000 by the end of the Late Bronze Age. So for all practical purposes, the frontier on the eve of the 13th/12th century transition was underpopulated, especially in the rural areas.

A Motley Crew?

I have already stressed the heterogeneous nature of the people of Late Bronze Age Canaan, their longtime adaptation to the shifting frontier, and their growing restiveness by the end of the period. It should therefore be no surprise that I will now advocate explicitly a model for the Iron I hill country colonists — my "proto-Israelites" — that accounts for a variety of groups, all of them dissidents of one sort or another. Among them I would include the following: (1) Urban dropouts — people seeking to escape from economic exploitation, bureaucratic inefficiency and corruption, taxation, and conscription. (2) ʿApiru and other "social bandits" (Hobsbawm's term), rebels already in the countryside, some of them highwaymen, brigands, former soldiers and mercenaries, or entrepreneurs of various sorts — freebooters, in other words. (3) Refugees of many kinds, including those fleeing Egyptian "justice," displaced villagers, impoverished farmers, and perhaps those simply hoping to escape the disaster that they saw coming as their society fell into decline. (4) Local pastoral nomads, including some from the eastern steppes or Transjordan (Shasu), and even perhaps an "Exodus group" that had been in Egypt among Asiatic slaves in the Delta. All of these peoples were dissidents, disgruntled opportunists ready for a change. For all these groups the highland frontier would have held great attractions, despite the obstacles to be overcome. A new beginning!

The idea of early Israel as a motley crew is not all that revolutionary. The biblical tradition, although much later, remembers such diverse origins. It speaks not only of Amorites and Canaanites in close contact with Israelites, but also "Jebusites, Perrizites, Hivites" (the latter probably neo-Hittites), and others. All could have been part of the Israelite confederation at times. The Gibeonites and Shechemites, for instance, are said to have been taken into the Israelite confederation by treaty. Some were born Israelites; others became Israelites by choice. The confederation's solidarity, so essential, was ideological, rather than biological. As for Israelite ethnicity — what made them all Israelites — I shall deal with that presently. Needless to say, I do not share Finkelstein's skepticism about their identity. They knew who they were; and it is up to us to find out if possible.

Revolting Peasants?

The biblical tradition adheres strongly to the notion of tribal origins and tribal organization in the formative phase in Canaan. As I have noted above, however, the much-discussed nomadic ideal of the Hebrew Bible may be just that: a nostalgic notion of some later writers, rather than the reality of any given period. Truly tribal origins would require that all, or nearly all, of those who constituted early Israel had in fact descended from Jacob and were kin-affiliated or blood related. Most modern Arab tribes in the Middle East today do claim to be what anthropologists call agnatic, or related through male descent. But even the members of these tribes often recognize that their traditions are vastly exaggerated, even in some cases simply origin myths. The fact is that there are many other factors beside kinship, real or imagined, that may bind groups of individuals into a close-knit social unit called a tribe or clan. A common desert origin is not one of those factors, since villagers and even urban inhabitants may claim to be tribally organized. There are many social, economic, and political factors that go into creating and sustaining tribes and tribal ideologies.

The sense of social solidarity that is implicit here often has more to do with property rights and laws of inheritance — that is, with maintaining the status of both family networks and the larger unit. And in the ancient Near East, as is the case in many places today, property means land, because in nearly all preindustrial societies tilling the land was the basic means of food production. Thus social class and ethnic conflict — "who *we* are" — was usually not a contest between local peoples and invaders who usurped authority. It was rather a contest between competing groups within the society over who owned land, managed it, and reaped its reward, both social and economic. It was this contest that often pitted the urban authorities against rural elements.

Now I return to Mendenhall's and Gottwald's peasants. By "peasant" we mean essentially an individual who lives off the land, a farmer (the word itself comes from the French *pays,* "country"), someone in the rural areas, by implication a rustic. And rural folk are not only much more closely bonded to the land, they are more likely than urbanites to be kin-related, bonded to each other. Thus the sense of tribe, despite some fictive aspects, creates a sort of social contract, expressing common allegiances, obligations, and rights. And when tribal affiliations are traced back many generations through genealogies, as they are in the biblical tradition, then this contract is regarded as binding. It is rooted in history, in what is right because it is traditional; it may even be regarded as ordained by the gods.

Now all of this may seem speculative, may even sound like a bit of populist propaganda. But we do have actual evidence for land tenure systems in the century or two preceding Israel's emergence in Canaan, as discussed above. It is noteworthy that several of the Amarna letters quoted above deal explicitly with land rights. Local kings acknowledge that Pharaoh, the Sovereign, owns all the land; but they claim that the management has been entrusted to them personally. That is, the land becomes a fief, as it was in medieval European feudal systems, or heritable land held in return for service.

Many of the protests to the Pharaoh in the Amarna letters have to do with claims to these lands, and even its usurpation by rival kings or by rebellious elements like the 'Apiru. Local kings organize and even compel labor (the corvée), and they claim all the land's benefits. It is clear from the socioeconomic system that the Amarna texts presume that most of those who worked the land were either what we would call in a feudal model peasants, serfs, or slaves. The latter had no rights at all; serfs would have rented the land from the crown or landed gentry in exchange for a large share of their produce and services. But as serfs they were bound to the land, even though they did not own it, and they could be transferred with the land like attached property. Only peasants would actually have owned small plots of land. They were, in effect, freeholders, or citizens with certain theoretical rights, including title to heritable land. But even these property-holders were subject to constant harassment, sometimes including confiscation of their land, by both local rulers and Egyptian overlords.

Both Mendenhall and Gottwald appealed to the Amarna letters in support of their peasant revolt theory. Oddly enough, neither made much reference to the pioneering studies of the anthropologist Eric Wolf in the 1960s, such as *Peasants* (1966) and *Peasant Wars of the Twentieth Century* (1969). Gottwald only cites Wolf once, saying that "most, if not all, of the conditions contributory to a cohesive and revolutionary peasantry cited by Wolf appear to have been present in thirteenth to eleventh-century B.C. Canaan" (1979: 586). Mendenhall (1973) does not cite Wolf at all. Coote and Whitelam (1987) cite Wolf twice, but only in passing. Stager (1985), even though he is generally very widely read in anthropology, does not mention Wolf's works.

The only scholar in our fields to make any extended use of Wolf's studies of modern peasants in class-structured societies is Marvin Chaney, whose 1983 publication I have mentioned above in presenting various models for early Israel. Chaney observed this of Wolf's work, even before the current archaeological evidence became available:

> While such comparative studies cannot prove that ancient Israel emerged from a Palestinian peasant's revolt, they can allow us to determine whether there existed in Late Bronze and early Iron I Palestine a concatenation of conditions which in other agrarian societies have proved conducive to broader peasants' revolts. (1983: 61)

Chaney goes on to summarize Wolf's argument that among the requisite conditions for revolt are (1) a "tactically mobile" segment of the population, mobile both physically and ideologically. (2) A group that is thus "able to rely on some external power to challenge the power that challenges them," without which revolutions are never successful. (3) The areas where dissident elements have their effectiveness strengthened still further will be those that "contain defensible mountain redoubts." Finally (4) the possibilities for success will be enhanced if there are "reinforcing cleavages," or painful sources of social conflict, such as national, ethnic, or religious divisions.

Chaney correctly notes that Wolf's conditions for social revolt are amply reflected in the Amarna letters. He is one of the very few scholars (and no archaeologists) to have made such a connection, although it seems obvious. Consider:

1. The Late Bronze/early Iron I population of Canaan was certainly mobile, as made clear both by texts describing the elusive 'Apiru already dispersed in the countryside, and by archaeological evidence documenting a major population shift to the hill country.

2. As for leadership, or external sources of power, it is noteworthy that the Amarna letters mention "chiefs of the 'Apiru." The Hebrew Bible, of course, attributes the role of leadership first to Joshua and then to his successors, the judges. These early folk-heroes were essentially successive charismatic military leaders who are portrayed in Judges precisely as men (and a woman) of unusual talents who were able to rally the tribes against the Canaanites. Direct archaeological evidence for any of these specific persons is lacking, of course, since the archaeological record without texts is anonymous (although not mute). But the Iron I hill country villages do exhibit a remarkable homogeneity of material culture and evidence for family and clan social solidarity. Such cohesiveness — a fact on the ground — had to have come from somewhere. And as Lenski and Lenski have observed (above), the challenges and hardships of the frontier would have tended to strengthen whatever sense of solidarity already existed.

3. As for defensible mountain redoubts where the rebels could take refugee from the urban authorities, the central hill country of Palestine, now extensively colonized, fits the description perfectly: the (relatively) distant frontier.

4. The highly polarized society of Late Bronze Age Canaan, clearly evident in both the textual and the archaeological records, is an excellent example of Wolf's cleavages that often serve as the catalyst for social revolutions.

As I noted above, however, many scholars have objected to the peasants' revolt model on the grounds that (1) the notion of "peasants' wars" itself is a modern construct, projected arbitrarily back upon ancient Canaan and Israel; (2) the biblical tradition has no memory of such conflicts and presents instead a military invasion from outside; and (3) there is no physical or archaeological evidence of such peasant wars. Yet we can easily refute such arguments.

1. Unless one assumes that ancient societies measured up to an egalitarian ideal in which there were no class conflicts, it is evident there were always peasants' revolts. But most were unsuccessful; and since history is written by winners, as the saying goes, the losers have had no voice. The anthropologist Clifford Geertz has called such folk "the people without a history" — that is, without a written history, told from their perspective, that has survived.

2. It is simply not true that the biblical tradition has no knowledge of early Israel as a peasants' war of liberation. Chaney asserts that the persistent rhetoric against the Canaanites in the Hebrew Bible, early and late, is less a rejection of their gods (who were sometimes adapted) as it is a radical critique and rejection of Canaanite "agrarian monarchy and its concomitants" (1983: 71). I would say it is particularly a protest against a corrupt landed aristocracy that disenfranchised the peasant class. This is evident in early stories of the killing of Canaanite kings, the seizure of their property, and the devotion (*herem,* above) of it to Yahweh, its rightful Lord. It is also seen in the prophet Samuel's unwillingness to appoint a king over Israel, warning precisely that a king would conscript citizens for his own service, stripping them not only of their freedom but of their rightful wealth as well. Above all, a king would create a classed society, dominated by elites (1 Sam. 8).

That was what happened, of course, in time. Yet in the 8th century B.C., the prophet Isaiah could still condemn those "who join house to house, and add field to field, until there is no more room" (5:8). Micah complained about the comfortable urban upper class and their ill-gotten gains, who "covet fields, and seize them; and houses, and take them away" (2:2). Throughout the Hebrew Bible, the democratic social ideal is that conveyed by the frequent phrase "the poor of the Land" (Heb. *'am ha-'arets*), who are Yahweh's own. I would contend that almost everywhere in the biblical tradition the demand for social justice revolves around the land and its uses — entrusted to Israel as Yahweh's steward, governed by divine law, inalienable, and an inheritance forever. In the well-known story of King Ahab's seizure of the vineyard of Naboth, a poor peasant, not even the king escaped the prophet's condemnation and Yahweh's wrath. And in the end, the vision of Israel's restoration as the true kingdom of God embraces the picture of "every man sitting under his vine and under his fig tree, and none shall make them afraid" (Micah 4:9). Here again, the emphasis is on land; private ownership of property; freedom from oppression; Yahweh as sole Sovereign. The biblical social and ethical values are those that protect and empower the proletariat (to borrow Marx's term, although not necessarily his sense of it) — the working class.

Some would dismiss the biblical tradition as fiction: late, unhistorical, and romantic — the product of nostalgia for a past that never was, hope for a future that never would be. But insofar as this tradition is both ancient and unique among the other literature of the time, some explanation is required. I suggest simply that the biblical notion of what we would now call "agrarian land reform" is deeply rooted in historical memory, specifically in a long oral tradition that reaches back to the social and economic realities of Canaan of the end of the Bronze Age. There is a reason why in the Hebrew Bible the Canaanites are always the bad guys.

One apparent vestige of early egalitarianism, or at least of nomadic and pre-state ideals, is the report of Jeremiah concerning a group of extreme reformists of his day. As an object lesson, Jeremiah invites members of the family of one Rechab to the Temple and offers them wine. They refuse, claiming that their ancestor Yonadab, the son of Rechab, had commanded them, "You shall never drink wine, neither you nor your children; nor shall you ever build a house, or sow seed; nor shall you plant a vineyard, or even own one; but you shall live in tents all your days, that you may live many days in the land where you reside" (35:6-7). Yet the Rechabites admit that by now they have come to live in Jerusalem, surely in houses. Thus the Rechabite tradition was more ideal than reality. Yet I would argue that this reactionary social movement, if it was that, surely had some basis in earlier Israelite history, culture, and social structure (not to mention religion).

3. The third objection to the idea of a peasant revolt — that it has no archaeological support — is the easiest to overrule. This opinion was voiced largely before the current archaeological data surveyed here became available, and it is simply obsolete today. The evidence surveyed here of social upheaval, mass migration to the hill country, and the relatively sudden emergence of a distinctive rural lifestyle, is all best explained by positing a

social revolution of some kind. And if land and landholding were the bones of contention, then most of those involved were by definition peasants, seeking land reform perhaps more than anything else.

Agrarianism and Land Reform

At this point I want to introduce the other element in my agrarian frontier reform model — the term "agrarian." It refers essentially to land and landholding, originating with the agrarian laws (Latin *agrarius*, from *ager*, "field, open country") of ancient Rome, which were intended to distribute conquered and other public lands equally among all citizens. In practice, however, most agrarian reforms either were never really instituted, or else the reform movements failed. As we have seen, ancient Canaan did not acknowledge even the theoretical principle of agrarianism. All public lands belonged to the Sovereign — the Pharaoh or his surrogates, local Canaanite kinglets who were even more rapacious.

The new mode of production saw the sovereign displaced, and the family unit substituted for the state apparatus. Perhaps the anthropologist Marshall Sahlins put it best in his *Stone Age Economics*, when he described this family-based community as "the tribal community in miniature . . . politically underwrit[ing] the condition of society — society without a Sovereign" (1972: 95). Sahlins was not writing about the Israelites, but I cannot think of a more apt description of our early Israel, or of its anti-statist protest. The biblical writers downplay the sociology of Israel's beginnings, but it is evident nevertheless in the theology they have preserved. And while some may see their work simply as a later rationalization, I prefer to regard it more realistically as part of an authentic folk memory.

Despite its apparent explanatory power in the case of early Israel, the notion of agrarianism has seldom been employed among biblical scholars, and never by archaeologists. Neither Gottwald nor Hopkins mentions agrarianism. Yet to my mind, land reform must have been the driving force behind, and the ultimate goal of, the early Israelite movement. No other scenario really makes sense of what we now know from all sources. Chaney ends his very provocative 1983 study with these prescient words:

> While it remains a working hypothesis, a model of peasant and frontier revolt has been found to accommodate and illuminate the data provided

by the Amarna archive, Syro-Palestinian archaeology, and the biblical tradition, and to do . . . so within parameters defined by the comparative study of agrarian societies by social scientists. . . . The writer will consider this paper a success if it serves to enlist new results in that ongoing process. (1983: 72)

It is a shame that so few scholars have enlisted themselves in this process.

If early Israel indeed constituted an agrarian movement with strong reformist tendencies driven by a new social ideal, it would not be unique. Agrarianism is about more than land; it is Utopian. There have been countless such rural revolutionary movements in history, many of them as small, isolated, and insignificant as that of early Israel seemed to be. One needs look no further than an American history textbook: the Oneida Community of the 1800s in New York was founded as a perfectionist society on biblical principles of absolute equality. Unfortunately their Utopian views on marriage and family life went too far, and the movement was bitterly criticized. Another experiment in rural communal living was carried out in the early 1800s at New Harmony in southwestern Indiana, founded by strict religionists of German extraction. Better known, of course, is the 18th-century Shaker movement. It was characterized by a deep religious spirit, commitment to absolute equality, temperance, and simplicity in all things. Unfortunately, the Shakers also practiced chastity and celibacy, and so eventually became extinct. The Amish in Pennsylvania constitute a far more successful rural communitarian movement — an excellent example of the phenomenon of withdrawal, and of course based on religious notions. All these and many other reformist movements in history are essentially agrarian — that is, based on principles of land reform and shared agricultural production.

CHAPTER 11

Who Were the Early Israelites?
Ethnicity and the Archaeological Record

Thus far I have characterized the Iron I hill country pioneers as agrarian reformers with a new social vision, and I have gone so far as to identify these peoples as early Israelites. But what evidence is there for such an ethnic label? Is that not simply reading the later biblical Israel back into earlier history, into an archaeological epoch that is anonymous? Some would say so. If Israel Finkelstein is a skeptic about any historical "early Israel," as we have seen, then the biblical revisionists are nihilists. When these "historians" are finished deconstructing history and archaeology, there is no Israel, early or late. The most radical of them, Thomas Thompson, has gone so far as to have stated recently that

> Ethnicity is hardly a common aspect of human existence at this very early period. Whatever we might assert to be "markers" of an unknown ethnicity, such factors as Dever has pointed to, are distinguishable material aspects of human experience . . . that tend to coalesce on the basis of their functional — not their ideological — relevance. (1977: 175)

Elsewhere Thompson has described these ethnic markers as "accidental, even arbitrary." Thus it appears that he thinks (1) that ancient people did not know who they were, had no sense of "peoplehood" (Greek *ethnos*, "people"); (2) that in any case what makes peoples different from one another is not their ideas, but only their technology; and (3) that even these differences are not a part of cultural patterning, but are only accidental. Such statements are too absurd to require further comment. They call to mind Thompson's colleague Niels Peter Lemche's comment that "the Canaanites of the ancient Near East did not know that they were themselves Canaanites" (1991: 152). But *Lemche* knows that they were not!

Other biblical scholars have also weighed in recently concerning "ethnicity in the archaeological record." Diana Edelman, now with Philip Davies at Sheffield, begins her chapter in the volume *Ethnicity in the Bible* on "Ethnicity and Early Israel" with the statement that "given the present state of textual and artifactual evidence, nothing definitive can be said about the ethnicity of premonarchic Israel" (1996: 25). Well, that settles that! Edelman does acknowledge that "it is possible to draw up a list of ways in which (ethnicity) is manifested in some form or another" (1996: 39), so she deals briefly but inconclusively with such markers as site layout, domestic house-form, social organization, pottery, burial customs, cultic items, and foodways. This is what archaeologists call an "ethnic trait-list," and as a specialist in material culture, I have dealt with all this and other evidence above. Again Edelman, like Finkelstein, assumes that without contemporary texts (the Hebrew Bible came later, of course) we are only wishing upon a star. She does mention the Merneptah Stele and its reference to "Israel." But she decides that this text "yields almost no firm data," and that maybe it really read "Jezreel" (that is, the northern valley) instead of "Israel" (1996: 35). As for the data the Merneptah text yields, I shall return to that issue; but the notion that the reading "Israel" is questionable is astounding. No competent Egyptologist has ever read it otherwise. "Israel" means Israel — some Israel in history. At issue here is (1) what is "ethnicity"? and (2) can it be recognized and identified in material remains?

Defining "Ethnicity"

Like many other scholars, I have utilized the definition of the well-known ethnographer Fredrik Barth in *Ethnic Groups and Boundaries: The Social Organization of Culture Difference* (1969). Barth defines an ethnic group as a population or people who

1. are biologically self-perpetuating;
2. share a fundamental, recognizable, relatively uniform set of cultural values, including language;
3. constitute a partly independent "interaction sphere";

4. have a membership that defines itself, as well as being defined by others, as a category distinct from other categories of the same order;
5. perpetuate their self-identity both by developing rules for maintaining ethnic boundaries as well as for participating in inter-ethnic social encounters.

I have translated Barth's trait-list into categories of archaeological data that may be supposed to yield information on ethnicity. Let me summarize these, with emphasis on continuity and discontinuity on the Late Bronze Age–Iron I horizon. There is general agreement that this is often our best clue to cultural change, which is the phenomenon we are seeking to understand here. In short, how different was the Iron I hill country culture? And is that difference attributable to its being ethnically Israelite? Again, I shall use a simple General Systems Theory outline.

Table 11.1. Comparison of traits and their implications for ethnicity on the Late Bronze Age–Iron I horizon

Trait	LB-Iron I Continuity	If New, Indicates What?
1. Settlement type and distribution	Discontinuous	Rural dispersion
2. Demography	Discontinuous	Population explosion in the hill country(?)
3. Technology (pottery, etc.)	Continuous	Local origins, but now "degenerate"; few new elements indicate agriculture
4. House-form	Discontinuous	Extended family, clan
5. Economy	Discontinuous	Agrarian; "domestic mode of production"
6. Social structure	Discontinuous	Communitarian
7. Political organization	Discontinuous	Tribal; pre-state
8. Art; ideology; religion; language	Continuous	Reflex of Canaanite culture

Proto-Israelites?

Nearly all commentators consider that the archaeological evidence just summarized indicates that the Iron I hill country culture, while continuous in general with that of Late Bronze Age Canaan, exhibits enough changes to mark it as something new. Apart from the question of where the innovations came from, discussed in detail above, the only remaining issue today is what to call this new culture. In Finkelstein's latest treatment he avoids all ethnic labels; other scholars, including most archaeologists, are less skeptical but stress that the Iron I population was heterogeneous, as I have also noted above. For that reason not all groups should be labeled Israelite, nor should the early hill country colonists simply be equated directly with the Israel of the Hebrew Bible. That particular Israel comes into existence only with the Divided Monarchy in the 10th century B.C., and it is the Israel attested first in 9th century B.C. Neo-Assyrian and Tel Dan texts and then in the biblical texts, mostly 8th century B.C. and later.

Thus the peoples of the highlands were not yet citizens of a State of Israel with fixed boundaries, a unified sense of ethnic identity, and passports saying "Israelite." But I will argue that these were the *ancestors* — the authentic and direct progenitors — of those who later became the biblical Israelites. This is why a decade ago I proposed the provisional term "proto-Israelite." Several other scholars had in fact used this term on occasion, Gottwald among them. But they did not do so in a specific sense, or with any reference to the Iron I archaeological data. In 1992 Finkelstein, who was beginning to abandon the more explicit term "Israelite," thought my suggestion "excellent" (1992: 64). Later he sometimes used the term himself (1997: 230, for example). In his most recent work, however, he seems to ignore it, or mention it without comment (1998: 9), despite the fact that the term has come into wide usage.

I have advanced one common-sense argument and two scholarly arguments in defense of the term "proto-Israelite." The common-sense argument is that no cultural development occurs overnight; all have a rather long formative stage. Archaeologists and ancient historians recognize this fact when they coin and use such common terms as "proto-literate" for late 3rd millennium B.C. Mesopotamia; "pre-Dynastic" for Egypt in the same period; and "proto-urban" for contemporary Palestine. Despite the objection of some biblicists, "proto-" terminology is standard practice in archaeology.

194

The more significant arguments for the term "proto-Israelite" are (1) continuities in material culture from Iron I into Iron II, or the period of the Israelite Monarchy; and (2) the reference to "Israel" on the Merneptah Stele. Let us consider each of these in turn.

1. In the same way that I summarized the continuities from the Late Bronze Age into Iron I in chart-form in Table 11.1 above, I will present the continuities (and discontinuities) from Iron I, the putative period of the "proto-Israelites" (12th-11th centuries B.C.), into Iron II, the well-documented era of the Israelite Monarchy (10th-7th centuries B.C.).

While the main lines of development are clear — showing that biblical Israel is the direct outgrowth of my "proto-Israel" — some trait-by-trait commentary is necessary. (1) No one disputes that the general trend

---

Table 11.2. Development of major archaeological diagnostic traits from proto-Israel into the Israelite Monarchy

Trait	Iron I	Iron II
1. Settlement type and distribution	Rural, dispersed; principally in hill country	Urban, centralized; spreading beyond hill country
2. Demography	Population *ca.* 55,000	Population to *ca.* 150,000
3. Technology: terraces, cisterns, iron, pottery	Systems built. Many in domestic areas. Sporadic iron tools. Continuation of LB; limited repertoire	Systems expanded. Also municipal waterworks. Iron more common. Direct continuity of many forms; more homogeneity
4. House-form	Pillar-courtyard houses	The standard house
5. Economy	Primarily agro-pastoral; little industry, trade	Agriculture intensifies; more industry, trade
6. Social structure	Communitarian	More stratified
7. Political organization	Tribal; pre-state	National states of Israel, Judah
8. Art; ideology; religion; language	Little art; religion non-Establishment; proto-Canaanite	Considerable art; established priestly cult, temples; Hebrew fully developed

by the 10th century B.C. is toward centralization and urbanization, although it is difficult to quantify this. On the one hand many of the Iron I hill country sites, including all of those excavated thus far, seem to have been abandoned by the 10th century B.C., as new, larger, more centralized towns were established elsewhere. But on the other hand they are not abandoned en masse. I have emphasized this gradual shift from ruralism to urbanism more than most. Finkelstein points out that according to his calculations some 76 out of 115 Iron I sites surveyed in the Samaria hill country continued into Iron II. Very well; but what kind of sites were they? To judge from the published data, the vast majority of these sites in the Monarchy were still small villages, only a few having developed into urban centers. Thus the strong trend toward urbanization argued here is not called into question.

At least a dozen of the Iron I sites that do continue provide especially significant evidence for Israel as the descendant of proto-Israel. In the north Dan, Hazor, Beth-shan, Megiddo, and Ta'anach had all grown into large fortified cities by the 10th century B.C., now clearly Israelite. In the central hills Tell el-Far'ah (Tirzah), Shechem, and Beth-shemesh had the same thing happen. In the south Tell Beit Mirsim and Beersheba continued into Iron II and became fortified cities. And of course many other sites beside these evolved into major urban centers, like Lachish in Judah and Israel's new capital of Samaria.

The point is simply that the formative phase of proto-Israelite/ proto-urban in Iron I developed directly and even predictably into an urbanized state in Iron II. It also expanded now from the original heartland into Galilee and parts of the coastal plain, although the former area retained some of its Aramaean character, and the latter its Phoenician and Philistine character. Nevertheless the borders of the new Israelite state represent its expansion to its natural and cultural limits — the crystallization of the multi-ethnic mix already present in Iron I. This is not an intrusive state, but the outgrowth and maturation of an indigenous polity (some would say a chiefdom).

2. The trebling of the hill country populations from some 55,000 to 150,000 for the entire area by the 7th century B.C. is again to be expected, the natural result of the evolution of the state, now relatively stable and prosperous. Note that there are no more sudden population explosions such as those that accompanied the pioneer colonization, but only the steady growth of a long-resident population.

3. In technology the continuity is also what we would expect. Terraces and cisterns continue, the former probably expanding to keep pace with the need for increased agricultural production. But larger cities gradually required highly engineered public water systems, and such sites as Hazor, Megiddo, Gibeon, Jerusalem, and probably Gezer exhibit them. Iron comes into more widespread use. The pottery of Iron II develops out of Iron I, and the forms of such items as cooking pots, bowls, and juglets show continuous evolution. The occasional hand burnish (or polish) of Iron I became much more common, and by the 9th century B.C. it was usually done on the potter's wheel. The most conspicuous ceramic changes in the Monarchy were the expansion of the repertoire, a natural tendency toward mass-production and standardization, and the proliferation of imported wares. All these are, of course, the expected consequences of state-level expansion.

4. The most striking continuity between Iron I and Iron II is seen in the extensive use of the pillar-courtyard house until the end of the Monarchy, not only in rural areas but also in built-up urban areas. It becomes, in fact, the standard Israelite house; this is an extremely important clue to ethnicity. As anthropologists and ethnographers have long recognized, house-form is a fundamental cultural and ethnic trait, perhaps revealing more about social organization, lifestyle, and shared values than any other single indicator. And if the pillar-courtyard house is ethnically Israelite in Iron II, its predecessors were certainly to be found in Iron I. The continuity alone should be conclusive. Nor do recent examples of such houses found in Iron I in Transjordan really change the picture. The form is authentically Israelite, even if not exclusively so. Several younger Israeli archaeologists formerly skeptical about the positivist views of their teachers have recently argued that the characteristic, preferred Israelite house, from the beginning of the nation's history to its end, gives us unique insights into "Israelite" mentality, especially its celebration of the family as the basic unit of society. That is certainly an inheritance from our Iron I proto-Israelite culture.

5. The development of small family-owned farms into a sort of agribusiness is predictable — although the Hebrew Bible holds on to the original ideal. As the rural sector declines, the state increasingly takes over production, and it expands the economy by fostering industry, local exchange, and international trade.

6-7. The emergence of the Israelite state represents the natural, almost universally attested process by which tribes and chiefdoms evolve into states. In retrospect, such social and political evolution in ancient Israel was perhaps inevitable, even though it was resisted by some parties who still cherished the early communitarian ideal. In any case there is a direct line of development, whether a progressive one or not. The early Israelite democratic society becomes inevitably a petty Oriental state with all the usual trappings: dynastic succession, often disputed; overweening bureaucracy; highly stratified society; centralized economy; international ambitions. But here, too, the biblical writers enter a vigorous critique, undoubtedly rooted in the pre-Monarchic tradition. Ironically but not surprisingly, history repeats itself: Monarchic Israel becomes precisely the kind of oppressive, elitist state that early Israel came into being to protest, complete with Canaanite-style overlords who usurp the land. None of the prophets were more eloquent in their disgust than Amos:

> Alas for those who lie on beds of ivory,
>   and lounge on their couches,
> and eat lambs from the flock,
>   and calves from the stall;
> who sing idle songs to the sound of the harp,
>   and like David improvise on
>   instruments of music;
> who drink wine from bowls,
>   and anoint themselves with the
>   finest oils,
>   but are not grieved over the ruin
>   of Joseph!
> Therefore they shall now be the
>   first to go into exile,
>   and the revelry of the loungers
>   shall pass away. (6:4-7)

8. In the areas of ideology and aesthetics, including religion, archaeology provides less direct evidence, as I have pointed out above. Nevertheless, it is clear that the scant primitive art of Iron I is eclipsed in the Monarchy, as expected, by much more sophisticated art forms, often Phoenician-inspired (as the Bible correctly notes). Carved and inlaid ivory panels for decorating furniture are well attested, as for instance at Samaria, the capital. Again, the

prophets observe the conspicuous consumption of the upper classes with contempt. In the passage already quoted, Amos condemns those "who lie on beds of ivory"; and elsewhere predicts that "the houses of ivory shall perish" (3:15). I would argue that the 8th-century prophetic protest against social injustice was not a new reform movement, but was deeply rooted in the egalitarian traditions of early Israel and its ideal of agrarian reform.

Religious beliefs can only be inferred from material culture remains, but cultic practices are often clear. I have mentioned above the only indisputable early Israelite cult installation that we know, Mazar's "Bull Site" in the tribal territory of Manasseh, the bronze bull obviously an El icon. Beginning with the Monarchy, however, we have relatively numerous private and public shrines, sanctuaries, and even local temples (not to mention the Jerusalem Temple, for which there is ample indirect evidence from archaeology). Today we also have a whole range of cultic paraphernalia attested by archaeology — altars, offering stands, and vessels, model temples, female (Asherah) fertility figurines, texts with blessing formulae, and so on — as well as evidence for an established priestly class. Yet despite the development of religion, and no doubt about the existence of a state cult, there are very strong continuities going back to Iron I and even to the Canaanite era.

The old male gods El and Baʿal, along with Asherah the Mother Goddess, live on in Monarchical Israel, attested not only as shadowy figures in biblical texts, but also as vibrant deities witnessed in abundant archaeological remains. The name "El" and several El-epithets occur significantly in some of the oldest textual traditions in the Hebrew Bible, as scholars have long known.

The fertility themes so prevalent in Canaanite religion, and no doubt typical of early Israelite religion, continue throughout as the fundamental aspect of Israelite religion. Note that here again the focus of religion is on the land: insuring its fruitfulness, enhancing its capacity to nourish and sustain humans and animals, holding it in sacred trust in perpetuity. Today it is politically incorrect in some circles to emphasize the central role of sex and reproduction in Canaanite and Israelite religion. But this "new prudery" overlooks the fact that religion is essentially concerned with ultimate reality. And nothing was as ultimate as the continued fertility of fields, beasts, and humans in an agricultural society and economy; it was literally a matter of life and death.

The more we learn about official religion and especially about popu-

199

lar or folk religion in the entire biblical period, the more we see that it is an outgrowth of Canaanite religion, no matter how much Yahwism eventually transformed it later in the Monarchy. The Israelite sacrificial system goes back to Canaanite culture. Even the liturgical calendar has a Canaanite and agricultural basis. The old Canaanite Fall harvest and New Year's festivals celebrated the bounty of Nature and the onset of the annual life-giving rains. They became theologized in Israel as Succoth, when the harvesters lived temporarily in booths in the fields; Rosh ha-Shanah, the celebration of the New Year; and Yom Kippur, or the day of repentance. The common Semitic early spring festival, originally a pastoral feast celebrating the birth of new lambs, became connected in Israelite traditions with the blood of lambs on the doorposts in Egypt that heralded Israelite deliverance. Thus historicized it became Passover, or the Festival of Unleavened Bread. The later spring harvest of firstfruits, principally grains, became Shavuot ("seven weeks"), still basically a harvest festival.

Under rubric no. 8 I have also included language, which all commentators recognize as one of the most essential and illuminating ethnic markers. Here there is no debate. Linguists and philologists have known for two hundred years that the Hebrew of both the Bible and our growing corpus of archaeologically-recovered inscriptions is a dialect of Canaanite. So are its other West Semitic cousins: Aramaic, Phoenician, Ammonite, Moabite, and Edomite (all these other ethnic groups remaining Israel's neighbors in the Iron II period). From Iron I we have only the handful of Hebrew inscriptions noted above, still written in the Old Canaanite script of the Late Bronze Age. But the hundreds of later Iron II Hebrew inscriptions that we now have — on pottery, stone, plastered walls, seals, and personal items — are all written in a script directly descended from that of early Israel and Late Bronze Age Canaan. Finally, many biblical scholars have argued that some of the oldest literature in the Bible, written in an archaic Hebrew — mainly poems in the Pentateuch and some of the Psalms — is very close to Canaanite poetry and mythology known to us from hundreds of 14th-13th century B.C. texts found at Ugarit, on the coast of Syria. Here there is a striking cultural continuity even in the basic literary forms of the Hebrew Bible.

Where Is Merneptah's "Israel"?

Apart from the considerable archaeological evidence for Monarchical Israel being the continuation of my proto-Israel, there is an even more compelling — I would say conclusive — piece of evidence justifying the term. That is the reference to Israel on the "Victory" Stele of Ramses II's successor, Merneptah. This inscription was discovered in the late 19th century in the ruins of Merneptah's mortuary temple at Thebes and is now in the Cairo Museum. It is a royal inscription celebrating the Pharaoh's victory over the Libyans, but it also commemorates his victories in Asia — whether real or imaginary at this point is irrelevant.

The Merneptah or "Victory"
Stele, ca. 1210 B.C.
Jürgen Liepe

The portion of this long poem that interests us here runs as follows:

The princes are prostrate, saying "Mercy!"
    Not one raises his head among the Nine Bows.
Desolation is for Tehenu; Hatti is pacified;
    Plundered is the Canaan with every evil;
Carried off is Ashkelon; seized upon is Gezer;
    Yanoam is made as that which does not exist;
Israel is laid waste; his seed is not;
    Hurru is become a widow for Egypt!
All lands together, they are pacified.

This is the earliest reference to Israel outside the Hebrew Bible — indeed the earliest anywhere. It pre-dates biblical texts mentioning Israel by at least two hundred years, if not more. Let us see what reliable historical information we can glean from this unique, priceless inscription. (1) First, we may be able to locate Merneptah's Israel in Canaan by identifying and locating the other peoples listed. "Tehenu" refers to Libya, whose conquest is the main theme of the poem. "Hatti" denotes Hittites, who inhabited large parts of northern Syria. The meaning of "Canaan" is obvious: southern Syria and Palestine. "Yanoam" is usually identified as an important town in northern Canaan, perhaps *el-'Abeidiyeh* in the Jordan Valley. "Ashkelon" and "Gezer" are the well-known cities by those names along the coastal road, both of which do show some archaeological evidence for destruction at this time. "Hurru" is the Egyptian equivalent of "Hurrians," the bulk of the population of Syria in the Late Bronze Age, and the name often given by the Egyptians to Greater Canaan in New Kingdom times. That leaves only "Israel" unidentified. Or does it? Skeptics like the revisionists would say yes; but we shall see.

All Egyptologists are agreed that the names of Ashkelon, Gezer, and Yanoam refer to city-states in Canaan, as shown by the fact that the Egyptian scribe has attached to these what is called a "determinative sign," that is, a sign that specifies what the place is. In these three instances, the sign is that for "three hills," signifying lands outside the Nile Valley and the Delta. But the name Israel is followed by a different sign: "man + woman + three strokes," which refers to peoples in contrast to nation-states or their capitals — in other words, to an ethnic group. In fact, as the distinguished Egyptologist Kenneth Kitchen points out, this sign cannot be read as referring to a place, as some biblicists contend (as we will see below). The determinative sign in the Egyptian text is a gentilic, that is, one designating a specific people, and it is in the plural. So any objective scholar must read the Stele thus: "The Israelite peoples are laid waste; their seed [land or progeny] is not." But let us see how the biblical revisionists and even some archaeologists interpret this text.

All the principal biblical revisionists have commented in some way or another on the Merneptah reference to Israel, not surprisingly to discredit it, since in their view there cannot have been an early Israel. Davies (no Egyptologist he) simply declares that "the determinative is not unambiguous," so Merneptah's Israel could be simply a place in Canaan (1992: 61-63).

Whitelam, whose Israel is invented by the biblical writers, is equally predictable. He, too, makes the judgment (paraphrasing Davies?) that the Merneptah inscription "offers very little unambiguous evidence about the nature and location of ancient Israel." He thinks that while some Israel may be referred to, "the Stele represents a particular perception of the past embodying important ideological and political claims on behalf of the Egyptian Pharaoh" (1996: 209, 210). How does Whitelam know that this is only a perception? He does not explain.

Lemche, as usual the least extreme (and a far better scholar), acknowledges that the Merneptah inscription does testify in the late 13th century B.C. to "some sort of ethnic unity, which was identifiable as far as it had its own name, Israel." He even allows that this Israel can be located in northern Canaan or the central hill country, and this may "indicate some sort of political or ethnic relationship between this Israel and the later Kingdom of this name in the Iron Age" (1998: 37, 38). Yet the remainder of his book, *The Israelites in History and Tradition*, argues that we can say little about this Israel. On the next to last page he writes,

> The Israel of the Iron Age proved to be most elusive, in historical documents as well as in material remains, where hardly anything carries an ethnic tag that helps the modern investigator to decide what is Israelite and what is not. (1998: 160)

Apparently Lemche's problem is that Merneptah's Israel is not the same as the biblical Israel. But why should we expect it to be?

The other scholars often placed in the revisionist camp are the late

Gösta Ahlström and his protégé Diana Edelman. Ahlström's argument that Merneptah's Israel is a place rather than a people is effectively disposed of by Kitchen.

Thomas Thompson deserves separate treatment simply because his interpretation is so drastic. He declares categorically that Merneptah's Israel "does not correspond with the highland Israel or any biblical Israel" (1999: 79). He thinks that the terms "Canaan" and "Israel" on the Stele are both "metaphorical parents of three towns destroyed by the Egyptian army" (i.e., Ashkelon, Gezer, and Yanoam; 1991: 81). At an international symposium in Copenhagen in 2000, where he and I squared off against each other, he even went so far as to suggest that the Egyptian scribe came up with the name "Israel" more or less by chance, so the use of this reference as a datum is improper. What can one say in response to this? There is no basis on which to even have a discussion.

Finally there is Finkelstein, who these days flirts with revisionism, though not of the extreme variety. He knows the Iron I highland complex firsthand better than anyone else in the field. Nevertheless, in his major 1996 treatment of ethnicity he never mentions the Merneptah evidence except in citing my views. This was not always the case. In 1988 he thought the inscription relevant to his then-Israelites (1988: 28). But his 1995 survey mentions the Stele only once, dismissing its reference to Israel as "vague" (1995: 351). And that remains the case in his recent popular book (with Neil Silberman; 2001: 101), *The Bible Unearthed*. Does Finkelstein's progressive downplaying of the Merneptah data have anything to do with its being inconvenient for his theory of anonymous hill country settlers?

It seems that Merneptah knew something none of the revisionists knows: that there *was* an early Israel. He also knew where it was in Canaan, something we can know, too, by the process of elimination. Consider: (1) Merneptah's Israel cannot have been along the coast or in the Jezreel Valley, that is, the lowlands, because these areas were not those of "peoples" but of city-states, and furthermore they were under at least nominal Egyptian rule. (2) Merneptah's Israel was not in Galilee, since that was the northern part of Egyptian-controlled Hurru, or Canaan. (3) Finally, Merneptah's Israel cannot have been in the Negev or southern Transjordan, for other New Kingdom Egyptian texts make it abundantly clear that those marginal areas were inhabited by the nomadic Shasu, who although "peoples," like the Israelites, could not be ad did not need to be subdued.

A simple glance at the map here of Merneptah's Canaan on page 205

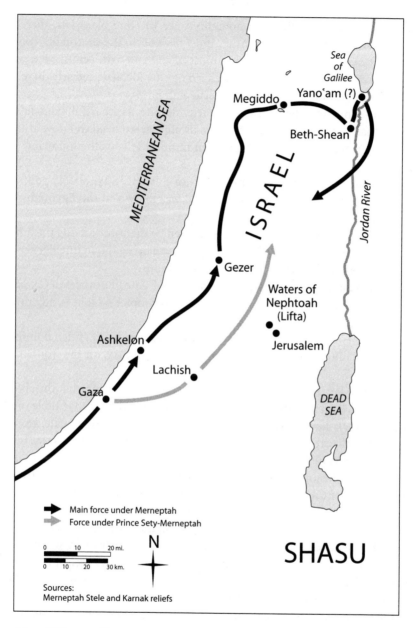

Map of Merneptah's campaign to Canaan, showing in the central area a lacuna
where the "Israelite peoples" would have been located
Adapted from *BAS*

will show anyone with an unprejudiced eye the one place left, the one where Israel in the late 13th century must have been: the central hill country. Is it merely a coincidence that most of the 13th-12th century B.C. villages recently brought to light by archaeology are located precisely there? It seems we can indeed know what Merneptah knew.

In summary, the Merneptah Stele, despite its boastful (and false) claim that "Israel was laid waste," tells us all that we need to know at this point — if we come to it with an open mind. It tells us the following:

1. There existed in Canaan by 1210 B.C. a cultural and probably political entity that called itself "Israel" and was known to the Egyptians by that name.
2. This Israel was well enough established by that time among the other peoples of Canaan to have been perceived by Egyptian intelligence as a possible challenge to Egyptian hegemony.
3. This Israel did not comprise an organized state like others in Canaan, but consisted rather of loosely affiliated peoples — that is, an ethnic group.
4. This Israel was not located in the lowlands, under Egyptian domination, but in the more remote central hill country, on the frontier.

The Merneptah Stele is, in fact, a goldmine of information about early Israel. And it is just what skeptics, mistrusting the Hebrew Bible (and archaeology), have always insisted upon as corroborative evidence: an extrabiblical text, securely dated, and free of biblical or pro-Israel bias. What more would it take to convince the naysayers?

In conclusion, then, my argument for proto-Israelites in the Iron I hill country of Canaan would be confirmed by the Merneptah reference to Israel alone. In fact, some of my colleagues (Amihai Mazar for one) chide me for being so cautious: Why not simply call them Israelites? I admit that I am tempted, but I hesitate for two reasons. (1) I prefer to err on the side of caution, since defining ethnicity in the archaeological record is admittedly difficult (although not impossible: we know exactly who the Philistines were); and (2) my proto-Israelites were not, at least not yet, Israelites in the full sense of being part of the later state of Israel (that is, biblical Israelites). Yet they were their authentic progenitors.

Recently several scholars have gone beyond the textual reference to Israel on the Merneptah Stele and have argued that this Pharaoh has even

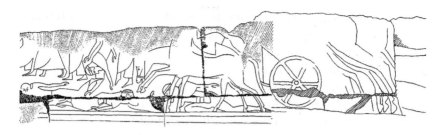

Yurco's "Israelites" on the Karnak reliefs
Biblical Archaeology Society

Rainey's "Israelites" on the Karnak reliefs
Biblical Archaeology Society

left us an eyewitness pictorial representation. In 1990 Frank Yurco argued that the famous battle scenes on the walls of the Temple of Karnak, bearing cartouches of Amenmose (1202-1199 B.C.) and Seti I (1199-1193 B.C.), were really executed by their immediate predecessor Merneptah (1212-1202 B.C.). He even showed convincingly how these pretenders had partly erased and recarved Merneptah's name, replacing it with their own and thus usurping the victories he claimed in Palestine. In this light the Karnak reliefs would have to be read in conjunction with the famous Victory Stele. Yurco then argued that one scene actually portrays our proto-Israelites being trampled under the hooves of Pharaoh's horses and chariots. Elsewhere on the reliefs, it seems to be the well-known Shasu nomads who are depicted; and the Israeli scholar Anson Rainey prefers to see these peoples, also being trampled, as Israelites. In any case, with or without the scenes at Karnak, the detailed and accurate knowledge of Egyptian intelligence is significant — Merneptah's boastful claims aside.

Were All the Hill Country Settlers Proto-Israelites?

Thus far I have tried to be consistent in focusing mainly on the Iron I settlers of the central hill country, identifying them tentatively as proto-Israelites. But what of the other hill country sites, as for instance upper and lower Galilee?

Upper Galilee

I have already discussed the Israeli surveys that have provided the source of much of our recent information on the Iron I period generally. Yohanan Aharoni's surveys of upper Galilee in the 1950s were followed up by the more systematic surveys of Raphael Frankel in the late 1970s, reported in English in 1994. There are some twelve Late Bronze Age archaeological sites, most known also from Egyptian texts such as those of Thutmosis III or the Amarna letters, and most located in the lowlands. Two have been excavated, Dan and Hazor, and both are strategically located on low ridges overlooking the upper Jordan and Huleh Valleys. Both were major Canaanite city-states (see above on Hazor) destroyed in the mid-13th century B.C. or so, then sparsely reoccupied sometime later (Dan VI and Hazor XII), perhaps after a gap in occupation.

Frankel documented a major shift in settlement patterns in the 12th century B.C., with some forty Iron I sites now in evidence. He thinks that these sites did not overlap with the few Late Bronze Age Canaanite urban settlements, but were founded somewhat later. Thus the evidence from upper Galilee could accommodate any of the three older models. But Frankel

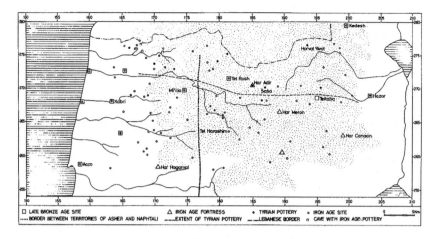

Late Bronze and Iron I sites in Upper Galilee
Israel Finkelstein and Nadav Na'aman, *From Nomadism to Monarchy*

prefers to see the local population as continuous from Late Bronze II into early Iron I. These indigenous folk, both pastoral nomads and villagers, may later have become part of the biblical tribes of Asher and Naphtali. Frankel concludes as follows:

> The transition from the Late Bronze Age to the Iron Age in the country in general, and in Upper Galilee in particular, combined change and continuity. Change is manifested in the destruction of the large cities in the lowlands, and in the emergence of a new settlement pattern of small sites in the mountains. Continuity is expressed in the ceramic assemblages and in the geopolitical division of the country. In the main, the changes are part of a momentous process that occurred in the whole of the Eastern Mediterranean. (1994: 34)

The biblical traditions in Judges 1 and 13–18 imply that the tribe of Dan was initially supposed to settle in upper Galilee, but it was unable to prevail over the Amorites there. Only later was Laish (or Tel Dan) destroyed, its name changed to Dan. According to Judges, the tribe of Asher was to have pressed westward to Acco on the coast, but it was unable to do so. Naphtali suffered the same lack of success, but it is said to have "dwelt among the Canaanites" (1:33).

In all this, the memory (or the sources) of the biblical writers seems to have been generally correct. The excavation of Dan and Hazor may be interpreted as corroborating the biblical story. Hazor was destroyed and then resettled by squatters after a hiatus of perhaps a hundred years. At Dan the pre-Israelite name Laish is confirmed by Egyptian texts. The 13th century B.C. destruction claimed by Avraham Biran, the excavator, is not yet well published. But subsequently Dan does have collar-rim storejars and other pottery similar to that of the central hill country Iron I settlements. Nevertheless, Frankel's conclusion that "there is little evidence for an early 'Israelite' penetration into upper Galilee" seems sound. The area probably remained Phoenician for some time.

Lower Galilee

Lower Galilee, also examined by Aharoni, was extensively surveyed in the 1970s by Zvi Gal, who published his results fully in 1992. Here there are very few Late Bronze Age sites known either from textual or archaeological data. Hannathon, northwest of Nazareth (unexcavated), is the only site mentioned in the Amarna letters. For the 12th century B.C., however, Gal found some 30 sites, most newly-founded settlements in the intermontane valleys such as the Beth-netofah north of the Nazareth hills. Much of the hill country here was apparently forested at the time, and that would have been a barrier to settlement. Gal connects the several dozen Iron I settlements, some of which have collar-rim jars, with the biblical tribes of Zebulun and Naphtali to the west and Issachar to the east. I have noted the biblical account of Naphtali above. Zebulun is said in Judges 1:30 to have persisted in a Canaanite enclave. Issachar is not mentioned in Judges 1, but elsewhere biblical tradition identifies it with Zebulun (as in Deuteronomy 33:18-19).

Any direct identification of the Iron I sites in lower Galilee with the biblical tribes seems questionable. Both Finkelstein and Kochavi are of the opinion that these sites (and those of upper Galilee) are more Phoenician in character, with Galilean storejars that seem to point northward to Tyre on the coast of modern-day Lebanon. The Canaanite-Phoenician cultural influence may have persisted in the north as late as the 10th century B.C., according to Finkelstein's latest reconstructions — a sort of Neo-Canaanite reincarnation in Iron I.

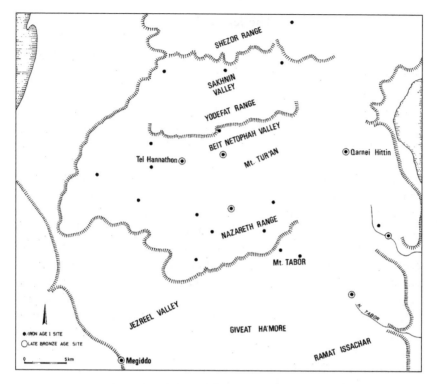

Late Bronze and Iron I sites in Lower Galilee
Israel Finkelstein and Nadav Na'aman, *From Nomadism to Monarchy*

One of the lower Galilean sites surveyed by Gal, Tel Vavit (Tell el-Wawiyat), has now been excavated by students of mine. It is in the Beth-netofah valley just north of Nazareth. It seems to have been a sort of rural manor house in the 13th century B.C., with substantial building remains and imported luxury items. Its Canaanite occupation continued throughout the 12th century B.C., until the site was abandoned *ca.* 1100 B.C. (An 11th-century squatter occupation reusing some of the ruined structures may have been Israelite, but that is speculative.)

Another site in lower Galilee excavated by Arizona students is Tell 'Ein-Zippori, some five miles south of Wawiyat. There another small Late Bronze Age Canaanite village, with some monumental architecture, continued into the Iron I period and was destroyed by unknown agents in the mid-10th century B.C.

The Jezreel Valley

Moving south, we come to the broad, fertile Jezreel Valley, stretching all the way from the Mediterranean coast eastward to the Jordan Valley. However, since the valley was marshy until modern times, there are almost no ancient sites in its floor. Around the hill borders and near the passes giving access to the valley, there are a number of large Late Bronze Age city-states, so we may look at this area along with the hill country proper.

Large Late Bronze Age sites in the valley include Tell Keisan on the bay of Acco; Megiddo and Taʿanach along the southern reaches; and Beth-shan guarding the eastern end of the valley. All four (if we count Acco) are mentioned in the Amarna letters. There are also smaller Late Bronze Age settlements, like those recently excavated at Jokneam and Tel Qiri. It is noteworthy that all of these sites show strong continuity from the 13th century B.C. into the 12th, and even into the 11th century B.C. Israelite occupation here may not have begun before the 10th century, under the aegis of the United Monarchy (Finkelstein would say the 9th century B.C.). Beth-shan clearly remained an Egyptian garrison until the time of Ramses VI (1141-1133 B.C.). And Megiddo, which I have discussed above, is still strongly in the local Canaanite tradition until the massive destruction of Stratum VIA (which I would date *ca.* 1000 B.C., but which Finkelstein dates to *ca.* 930 B.C.). Thus the biblical battle of Deborah and Barak against Sisera and his "nine hundred chariots of iron" (Judges 4) has no archaeological context. In fact, the biblical text itself admits that after the battle, Yabin, the king of Hazor, still dominated the area (despite the Israelite destruction claimed there earlier; compare Josh. 11:1-15 and Judg. 4:23, 24).

The Judean Hills

Most of the hill country that I have discussed thus far lies north of Jerusalem. The hill country to the south, as well as Jerusalem and its environs, has a somewhat different settlement history in Late Bronze-Iron I.

Israeli surveys in the Judean hills were carried out in the 1980s by Avi Ofer, published in 1994. Ofer found only six Late Bronze Age sites, including remains at Hebron, known from the Amarna letters as the main, probably the only, city-state in the region. Kh. Rabûd, possibly biblical "Debir"

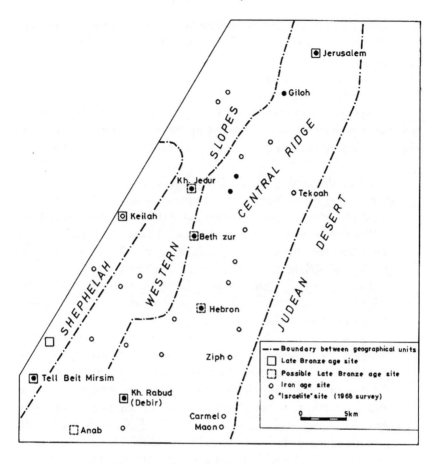

Late Bronze and Iron I sites in the Judean hillcountry
Israel Finkelstein, *Archaeology of the Israelite Settlement*

(above), was the only other important site, and it extended over only about two acres.

In Iron I, however, the number of Judean settlement sites grew to 17-18, with a total built-up area of some 30-45 acres, which would yield a population of 3,000-4,500 by the usual demographic criteria. These are all, however, small villages, subsisting mostly on dry farming and animal husbandry. Ofer disagrees with Finkelstein, who argues that the Judean hill country was settled only in the 11th century B.C. by people migrating southward from the hill country north of Jerusalem. He regards the set-

213

tlers in the south as descendants of the local Canaanite population who gradually became more sedentary, a settlement pattern that did not peak until the 9th century B.C. By that time there are a few larger urban sites, such as Lachish (above), and the area becomes part of the Judean Kingdom. Ofer stresses, however, that the archaeological record does not indicate any newcomers in Iron I. And he declines to make any connections with the biblical tribes, apart from noting the traditions about Caleb and Judah. He concludes thus:

> Groups of diverse origins settled in the Judean Hills, having diverse relations among themselves and with families throughout the entire south and center of the country, on both sides of the Jordan. In some cases the settling families had closer ties with the inhabitants of regions outside of the Judean Hills than with their neighbors. In all the early sources regarding the establishment of the Davidic monarchy, there is no concrete evidence of an organization, beyond family ties bearing the name 'Judah'. This indicates that 'Judah' is the name of the region in which these different families settled.
>
> The settlement of these groups in nearby regions intensified their common characteristics and created economic and social ties. The impetus for their unification in an all-encompassing framework was provided by the appearance of common enemies. The settling population shifted directly from a family and subtribal system to a national state structure. But in this process the extended family, especially the separate paternal houses within it, continued to retain their former importance. The concept of a 'tribe' for Judah lacks any concrete content, and seems to be a late, artificial application to the history of the families which settled in the land of Judah. (1994: 117)

The Beersheba Valley

I have already discussed the major Iron I sites known south of the Judean hills, near the limits of settled occupation in the Beersheba Valley, on the border of the Negev Desert. Among these sites are Tel Masos, Tel Esdar, Arad, and Beersheba itself. The surveys of Ze'ev Herzog, who was a senior staff member of the excavations at Arad and Beersheba, did not locate any more than a handful of other 12th century B.C. settlements, all very

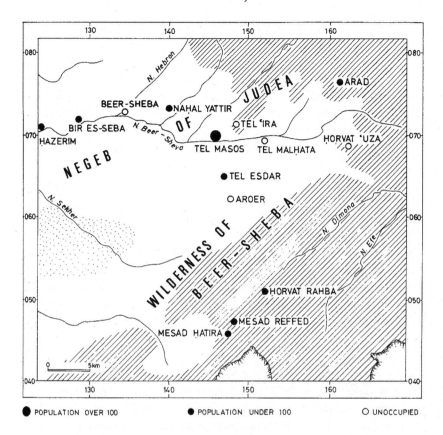

Beersheba valley sites at the end of the 11th century B.C.
Israel Finkelstein and Nadav Na'aman, *From Nomadism to Monarchy*

small. Settlement of the areas was gradual, and by the late 11th century B.C. it was not estimated to total more than about 1,500 people. Tel Masos, at some seven to eight acres, was apparently the nucleus of regional settlement. Because of its sophistication and ceramic connections with the coast, Masos may have served as a center for trade and distribution. I have suggested that Tel Masos might be among my proto-Israelite sites, although it is not in the hill country proper. Finkelstein strongly denies this, and the question may perhaps best be left open. Herzog's conclusion is as follows:

> The 'Israelite Settlement' was a complex process of socioeconomic change that took place in most of the regions of Canaan. In a long pro-

cess that started at the end of the thirteenth century BCE, most of the cultivable regions of the country were settled by small groups of heterogeneous ethnic and social origins. The consolidation of the Israelite national and ethnic identity reached its climax with the emergence of the United Monarchy. But the pan-Israelite ethnic identity existed for only about one hundred years, from the late eleventh to the late tenth century BCE, and broke down with the division of the United Monarchy. It was mostly in the ideological sphere of the Old Testament that the Israelite identity obtained its eternal survival. (1994: 149)

Jerusalem: A Special Case?

According to biblical tradition, Jerusalem, in the heart of the central hills, remained in the hands of the "Jebusites" until David seized it by a ruse in the early 10th century B.C. (2 Sam. 5:6-10; compare Josh. 15:63). We do not know who the Jebusites were and can only suppose that Jebus was the name of a local Canaanite clan (as in Gen. 10:16). Jerusalem has never been extensively excavated inside the Old City walls. But Dame Kathleen Kenyon dug part of the spur of the Ophel to the south — the "City of David" — in the 1960s, and the late Yigal Shiloh excavated extensively there between 1978 and 1985. Very little of the Iron I city has been reached, however, or for that matter much of the 10th century B.C. Many of the revisionists noted above deny that there was even an important town there, much less a state capital, before the 8th century B.C. But that is an argument from silence, easily dismissed.

The environs of Jerusalem, although part of the hill country of Judah, may be treated separately. The most comprehensive survey is that of Amihai Mazar, who directed the excavation of one of the most important proto-Israelite sites, Giloh, on the southwestern outskirts of modern Jerusalem. Several Israeli surveys beginning in 1968 have brought to light some thrity small Iron I settlements, mostly to the north and west of Jerusalem — that is, in biblical Benjamin. Elsewhere Finkelstein has stressed the relative lack of Iron I sites around Jerusalem, estimating that the total population of the area was about 2,200. Mazar's conclusion, however, is as follows:

> An approach denying the value of archaeology as a source for studying the Israelite culture during the period of settlement and the Judges must

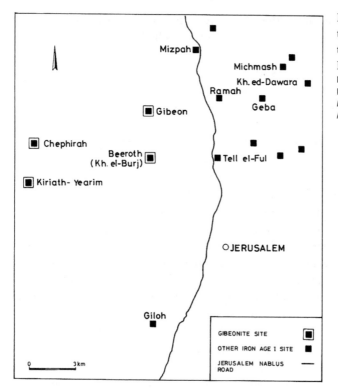

Iron I sites in the tribal territory of Benjamin

Israel Finkelstein and Nadav Na'aman, *From Nomadism to Monarchy*

be rejected. The emergence of Israel constituted complex processes, which involved other ethnic groups as well. The settlers in the region, whatever their origin, might not have identified themselves as part of an Israelite nation in this early stage; but they are certainly part of the population groups that provided the nucleus for the rise of the Israelite state, and thus they can be defined as Israelites, in the broadest meaning of the term. (1994: 91)

Proto-Israelites — and Others?

The foregoing survey of regions other than the central hill country, especially north of Jerusalem, suggests that my proto-Israelites are to be located for the most part precisely where a map of Merneptah's late 13th century B.C. Stele would place them. Elsewhere in Canaan, both surveys and excavations have shown that there are significant regional differences in the material culture in the Iron I settlements, which I have surveyed here in some detail. These differences imply that we should not attempt to force all the various Iron I peoples into one ethnic group, at least in the present state of our knowledge. Nevertheless, there are some generalizations that seem reasonable, summarizing the extensive data presented in several chapters above.

1. All the various Iron I regional assemblages develop out of general continuity with the last stages of the Late Bronze Age Canaanite culture, which we might also call the post-Amarna period. The continuity is best seen perhaps in the local pottery. Thus despite new technology, shifts in settlement patterns, and socio-economic changes, the overall population probably remained Canaanite well into the early Iron Age.

2. The changes that do take place, which are most readily observable through archaeology, are complex, gradual, and do not necessarily proceed at the same pace in all regions. The eventual emergence of new Iron Age ethnic identities by the 10th century B.C., at latest, crystallizes into regional settlement patterns and regional socio-political entities or petty states that persist until the Neo-Assyrian and Neo-Babylonian destructions in the late 8th–early 6th centuries B.C. These entities within former Canaan — each with related but distinguishable cultural characteristics — include (1) the Aramaeans in Syria and northern Canaan; (2) Phoenicians along the northern coast; (3) Philistines and other "Sea Peoples" along the central and southern coast; (4) the evolution of the proto-Israelites into the small state of Israel (soon divided into northern and southern kingdoms); (5) the tribal states of Ammon, Moab, and Edom in Transjordan. All these new Iron Age ethnic entities and socio-political configurations come to fill the vacuum left in the wake of the gradual collapse of the long Bronze Age Canaanite civilization. Merneptah's "Israelite peoples" are a small but significant part of the resultant heterogeneous ethno-cultural mix.

3. Despite the lack of conclusive proof (rarely available in any reconstruction of the past), the Iron I colonists in the central hill country of Canaan may be tentatively identified as proto-Israelites, that is, as the initial settlers in the area whose culture evolved by the 10th century B.C. into the Israel of the Monarchy, if not the ideal Israel of the Hebrew Bible. There is extrabiblical textual support for this identification, not available this early for any of the other ethnic groups, namely the Victory Stele of Merneptah.

4. The written sources in the Hebrew Bible, commencing probably in

the 8th century B.C., give us an official version of "all Israel" that supposedly dominated almost the entire region of former Canaan from the beginning. Yet the overall tradition, probably based on both older oral and written sources, correctly remembers the *diverse* cultural origins and the multi-ethnic makeup of Canaan in what we now know as the Iron I period.

It may be helpful at this point to summarize what we know of these other Iron Age ethnic groups.

1. Canaanites. I have used this term throughout for the indigenous population of Bronze Age (and early Iron Age) Canaan, a standard usage. A generic term, it denotes the West Semitic peoples of what is now southern Syria, the Lebanon coast, Israel, the West Bank, and Jordan. The name is first clearly attested in texts from about 1500 B.C., but there are a few possible earlier occurrences. "Canaanite" is by far the most common ethnic term in the Hebrew Bible. The pattern of polemics suggests that most Israelites knew that they had a shared common remote ancestry and once-common culture.

2. Amorites. The etymology of the name means "West Semites," and it often denotes a people of pastoral-nomadic origins. The Amorites are widely attested in texts from Mesopotamia and Syria from the late 3rd millennium B.C. onward. For all practical purposes (certainly in the biblical texts) they can be equated with the Canaanites, perhaps as the earlier, more nomadic element of the native population of the region.

3. Hittites. The Hittites were non-Semitic peoples who ruled a great empire in Anatolia (modern Turkey) and north Syria from the 2nd millennium B.C. until its collapse at the end of the Bronze Age *ca.* 1200 B.C. They never penetrated into southern Canaan, however, and the references in the Hebrew Bible are to the surviving Neo-Hittites in Syria, now related to the emergent Aramaeans. The biblical usage therefore refers to an ethnic group farther north in Canaan, with whom Israel had only distant connection.

4. Perizzites. The Hebrew etymology may mean either "dwellers in open country" or "those who live in unwalled villages." The term occurs 23 times in the Hebrew Bible and is often associated with hill country sites like Shechem and Bethel.

5. Hivites. The term "Hivite" is of unknown origin, and most authorities regard it as the result of the biblical writer's confusion with "Horite" (below; very similar in Hebrew), or possibly "Hittite." The parallel lists of the table of nations in Genesis 10 and Genesis 15:18-21 suggest that "Hivite" and "Hittite" could be used interchangeably.

Before listing other ethnic groups, we should note that in both the passages just cited, all four (or five) of the groups discussed thus far are mentioned together. The biblical tradition thus regards these as the oldest and principal ethnic groups in pre-Israelite Canaan (although some others are listed less consistently).

6. Horites. The apparent etymology of this rare term derives from Hebrew *hôr*, meaning "cave," thus presumably the primitive "cave-dwellers" of Canaan. But we now know that the proper spelling and etymology is "Hurrians." The Hurrians were non-Semitic peoples of northern Syria and Mesopotamia, archrivals of the 2nd millenium B.C. Hittites. They had migrated to southern Canaan after 1500 B.C. in such large numbers that the Egyptians typically called the area "the Land of the Hurru" in the Late Bronze Age (as in the Merneptah Stele). Many kings of the Canaanite city-states in the Amarna period have Hurrian names.

7. Jebusites. I have discussed the Jebusites above in connection with Jerusalem, but we know little about them except their association with the central hill country. The etymology of the name is unknown. Texts such as Judges 9:1 list them along with the Canaanites, Amorites, Hivites, and Perizzites.

8. Amalekites. The Amalekites are pictured as the nomadic descendants of Esau, Jacob's disinherited brother, and are usually associated with Edom in southern Transjordan. It is worth noting that even the inimical references in the Hebrew Bible tacitly acknowledge that the Israelites and Amalekites shared a remote common ancestry.

9. Philistines. The Philistines, known from biblical and Egyptian texts, and now extremely well-documented archaeologically, were one group of the "Sea Peoples" checked by Ramses III about 1180 B.C. The Philistines then invaded and settled the southern coast of Canaan. They are correctly omitted from the tables of nations in Genesis, but then they appear in Joshua and Judges as contemporaries and rivals of the early Israelites — another correct description. Many Philistine sites have now been excavated, among them Ashkelon, Ashdod, Ekron, and Gath, four of the five cities of the biblical pentapolis. But both the textual and the archaeological record show that the Philistines remained confined largely to the coast and foothills and thus did not often encounter the early Israelites directly (despite the biblical stories). For instance, there is scarcely a sherd of painted Philistine pottery in any of the hill country proto-Israelite sites.

To sum up, the later writers of the Hebrew Bible clearly know something about the diverse population of Canaan in the early Iron I period, and even before that in the Bronze Age. But it is clear that all these groups are used mostly as foils for their story of Israelite conquest and annihilation, which as we have seen scarcely describes the actual ethnic situation in Canaan. It would be tempting to push the historical memory of the Hebrew Bible back into the 12th-11th centuries and thus identify the peoples and nations of the text with the various regional archaeological assemblages that we have distinguished. And some scholars have attempted to do just that, as we have seen — even going so far as to connect the biblical twelve tribes (however artificial they may be) with specific regions. But in my opinion, that is going well beyond the evidence that is currently available. If I am right (and not too bold) in identifying mainly the central hill country sites as the area inhabited by proto-Israelites, that might suggest a connection of this region with the tribes of Manasseh, Ephraim, and Benjamin, who are situated there. I will explore that possibility in the next chapter.

CHAPTER 12

Salvaging the Biblical Tradition: History or Myth?

The foregoing has been a critical analysis of both the archaeological and the biblical data that we have on the origins of Israel. Throughout I have tried to show that the newer and sometimes revolutionary archaeological evidence must now become our primary source for writing (or rewriting) any history of early Israel.

Yet the problem raised by such a categorical assertion about the primacy of archaeology is that it relegates the biblical text with its grand tradition to a secondary place as a historical source. Indeed, it can be interpreted as discrediting the Bible altogether. This in turn makes it easy to dismiss the biblical stories of Israel's origins and early history as much later theocratic propaganda — entertaining perhaps, even edifying, but entirely fictional. And it opens the door for biblical revisionists to seize upon the skepticism of archaeologists in justifying their own nihilistic agenda. Hence the crisis I described in the introduction to this book.

Simply put, the issues are these: If the Hebrew Bible is not historically true, then how can it be true at all? If the biblical stories are not historically accurate, how did they come to be written in the first place? And why were they preserved and handed down as the core of the tradition, considered valid even to this day? Is the Bible, after all, a monstrous literary hoax?

Archaeologists and Other Troublemakers

Few (if any) of us archaeologists, who helped to start the fuss in the first place, rarely trained as we are in literary criticism, theology, or even history, seem sensitive to these issues or even aware of them. To their credit, Finkelstein and Silberman's *The Bible Unearthed* is the first attempt from archaeologists to come to grips with the larger intellectual issues (albeit somewhat superficially). Many others either make sensationalistic statements to the media or ignore altogether the crisis that they helped to provoke. To me that seems irresponsible scholarship. Scholars have an obligation to enlighten the public that subsidizes them, not merely to titillate or confuse. (And journalists have the same obligation.)

Many biblical scholars, theologians, seminary professors, and clergy are also culpable in what amounts to deceiving the public. "New" histories of ancient Israel continue to be published that are no more than rational paraphrases of the Hebrew Bible, as the revisionists rightly charge. Scholars and religious leaders in the academy and in church and synagogue proceed by ignoring skeptical voices (and possibly even their own doubts) in the interest of doing "business as usual." Would that more followed the refreshing example of Rabbi David Wolpe of Sinai Temple in Westwood, in Los Angeles, whose Passover sermon informed his congregation of two thousand that

> The truth is that virtually every archaeologist who has investigated the story of the Exodus, with very few exceptions, agrees that the way the Bible describes the Exodus is not the way it happened, if it happened at all.

Lecturing a few weeks later to a standing-room-only audience at the Wilshire Boulevard Temple in Los Angeles, I was besieged by earnest questioners who were deeply disturbed and wanted to know the answer to the questions posed by this book's title: *Who were the early Israelites, and where did they come from?* And these were not fundamentalists. Most were enlightened and sophisticated readers of the Bible: some were Jews, some were Christians, and others were secularists who nevertheless found the Hebrew Bible morally edifying and a vital part of the Western cultural tradition.

Both Rabbi Wolpe's sermon and my lecture made the front page of the religion section of the *Los Angeles Times*. And recent books by Finkelstein and Silberman *(The Bible Unearthed)* and by me *(What Did the Biblical Writers Know, and When Did They Know It?)* received a great deal of media attention over the spring and summer of 2001. It is this public outcry that prompted me to sit down and write this book in the fall of 2001.

What in God's Name(!) Did the Biblical Writers Think They Were Doing?

Let me begin to formulate an answer to some of the questions raised above by giving the Hebrew Bible the benefit of the doubt. I shall assume that those who wrote, collected, and edited the Bible's stories were not charlatans, deliberately perpetrating what they knew to be a hoax. But in what sense were they — or did they think that they were — historians, by ancient or modern standards?

Baruch Halpern in his provocative book *The First Historians: The Hebrew Bible and History* (1988) suggests that one criterion for distinguishing real historians from myth-makers is *intentionality*. That is, apart from adequate sources and competent methods, which we might assume, what did ancient writers, whether those who produced the Hebrew Bible or Greek writers like Herodotus and Thucydides, want to accomplish? To put it another way: Did they think that they were telling the truth?

Using these criteria let me suggest three alternatives for assessing the writers, compilers, and editors of the Hebrew Bible as historians:

Scenario 1

They were in possession of adequate sources, oral and written, earlier and contemporary. And they told the story as it really happened, as best they could, with only the expected literary flair and editorial biases. In that regard, they were like other competent ancient historians. They did not intend to deceive, and indeed they believed that they were telling the truth. This is the conventional or conservative view of the biblical writers, focusing on what we might call "narrative history."

Scenario 2

The biblical writers and editors had some genuine sources, but they did not hesitate to manipulate them. They did this not only with exaggerations and embellishments, but also with additions and even outright inventions, in order to make the stories serve their own ideological agenda. In this regard, they were like most ancient historians. Nevertheless, they still need not be regarded as charlatans, even though their view of history was naïve. They, too, thought that they were telling the operative truth — that is, they were simply writing well-intentioned propaganda. This may be called "historicized myth," and that is how much of modern, liberal, critical scholarship regards the Hebrew Bible. Nevertheless, even propaganda and myth, like caricature, must necessarily contain some objective truths, lest they be completely unbelievable and thus ineffective.

Scenario 3

Those who produced the Hebrew Bible and its story of ancient Israel had few if any real sources at all. They simply made it up. They deliberately invented a story, with no regard whatsoever for facts (provided that they even knew any), and passed it off as historical truth. They were charlatans. This we may call "history as hoax," or at best ancient revisionist history. This is the view modern revisionists take of the Hebrew Bible, an extreme one that I have repudiated at length elsewhere (especially in *What Did the Biblical Writers Know?*).

My position here, after a lifetime of struggling with the historical difficulties in both the textual and the archaeological evidence that we have, is aligned with the middle-of-the-road option in Scenario 2 above. That is, the basic traditions about ancient Israel now enshrined in the books of Exodus-Numbers and Joshua through Kings cannot be read uncritically as a satisfactory history, but neither can they be discarded as lacking any credible historical information. The challenge for both critical scholars and the enlightened public is to sort out fact from fiction; and it is only modern archaeology, as an independent witness to the events of the past, that may enable us to do that. That task is what this book has undertaken.

Convergences

In terms of methodology I would suggest that the dialogue between text and artifact that I envision will proceed most effectively by searching for what may be called "convergences." These convergences are points at which the two lines of evidence, when pursued independently and as objectively as possible, appear to point in the same direction and can be projected eventually to meet. At these points we may be reasonably sure that we have facts upon which an adequate history of ancient Israel can be based. But it is archaeology that provides the control — the corrective — because of the context that it supplies. For without some historical and cultural context, the biblical stories seem to float in an unreal, fantastic, unverifiable world. Archaeology can often make the stories more tangible, more credible, by situating them in a real time and place and thus giving us a context in which to relate them to us in our world. That does not mean, however, that archaeology can "prove the Bible to be true" — either in terms of what really happened in the past, or of what the biblical writers thought that these supposed events meant. In the end, with all our best efforts, we moderns may come up with a sort of minimal "core history." But each of us will have to decide for ourselves what we think the ethical, moral, and religious significance of that history was and is.

When we look for convergences, how do the various books of the Hebrew Bible fare as a history? A story on this very topic appeared in *The New York Times* on July 19, 2000, entitled "The Bible, as History, Flunks New Archaeological Tests." But does it? Perhaps the books of Exodus and Numbers do, because as we have seen their accounts of escape from Egypt, of wandering in the wilderness, and of massive conquests in Transjordan are overwhelmingly contradicted by the archaeological evidence. That may make many uncomfortable, but it is a fact, one from which no open-minded person can escape. There is little real history in these books, although there may be some vague memories of actual events, as I shall argue presently. For example, we may suppose that a historical figure like the biblical Moses did exist and was recognized as a leader among a group of Semitic slaves in Egypt, someone who indeed seemed to be a miracle-worker, and perhaps the mediator of knowledge about the new deity Yahweh (see further below).

But what about the conquest and settlement of Canaan as depicted in the books of Joshua and Judges? As we have seen, there is little that we can salvage from Joshua's stories of the rapid, wholesale destruction of Canaanite cities and the annihilation of the local population. It simply did not happen; the archaeological evidence is indisputable. It is conceivable that there was a military chieftain and folk hero named Joshua, who won a few skirmishes here and there. But there simply was no Israelite conquest of most of Canaan. Mendenhall was right about that forty years ago, as were Continental biblical scholars even earlier. Most of those who came to call themselves Israelites, and were so designated by the contemporary Egyptians, were or had been indigenous Canaanites. There was no wholesale conquest, no need for it.

Here is where a reevaluation of the book of Judges is both necessary and helpful. Of the two accounts of the emergence of Israel in Canaan now placed back-to-back in the Hebrew Bible, Judges far more than Joshua has the ring of truth about it. Its stories of a two-century sociological and religious struggle against the prevailing local Canaanite culture fits astonishingly well with the current archaeological facts on the ground. Thus there is good reason to think that Judges, so realistic about the humble origins of early Israel, rests on much older and more authentic traditions than Joshua, both oral and written. We can only be grateful that the final editors of the Hebrew Bible chose to include it despite its obvious contradictions with the conquest recounted in Joshua. Perhaps these editors were both more honest and more sophisticated than we give them credit for being.

What Gave Rise to the Dominant Biblical Tradition?

But however much we may admire the historically more accurate but politically incorrect version of Israel's origins in Judges, the fact is that it is a minority opinion. It cannot be denied that the main thrust of the biblical tradition overall is that Israel came into existence as the Chosen People of God by a unique, miraculous intervention of its god Yahweh in history. Its conquest of the Land and eclipse of Canaanite religion and culture was foreordained, not simply another stage of socio-cultural evolution. The promise to the Patriarchs; the liberation from Egyptian bondage; the crossing of the "great and terrible wilderness" guided by God's own hand; the conquest of Canaan; the gift of the Land; the heritage of the people of Israel forever — these are the events upon which Israel's faith and destiny were predicated throughout the Hebrew Bible. As my revered teacher

G. Ernest Wright once wrote, "In Biblical faith everything depends upon whether the central events actually occurred"; and the events he meant were the Exodus and Conquest. But what if they didn't occur? Where would that leave us?

The "House of Joseph" — an Exodus Group?

Let me take this dilemma seriously but suggest a possible way out, in particular a way to explain how the Exodus-Sinai tradition might have come into being in the first place. There are several stages in the argument.

1. Biblical scholars have long noted that two of the central tribes — Ephraim and Manasseh — are sometimes linked together and designated the "House of Joseph" — that is, those who were thought to be direct descendants of the Patriarch Joseph (Hebrew *benei-yosef*, "sons of Joseph"; cf. Joshua 16:1; 17-18; Judges 1:22, 35). Sometimes it is implied that the territory of the small tribe of Benjamin in the Jerusalem hills was also reckoned with the House of Joseph (the boundaries of their territories also overlap somewhat). Several things are significant here, all possibly indicating a historical basis of sorts for the central place of the Exodus-Sinai tradition in the Hebrew Bible as we have it.

2. A disproportionate amount of space in Genesis, the primary document, is taken up with the so-called Joseph Cycle, which sets the stage for the overarching saga of descent into Egypt, enslavement, and liberation from bondage (Genesis 37–50, nearly one-third of the book). Many scholars believe that this dramatic story — a sort of self-contained historical romance — may have originated and once circulated independently from the other Patriarchal narratives. The locale was perhaps in the regions of Shechem and Dothan, where the story begins with Joseph as a lad. This area later becomes part of the tribal territory of Ephraim, who according to tradition was Joseph's son and Manasseh's younger brother.

3. Many aspects of the Joseph Cycle make it unique among the biblical literature. While its carefully structured plot and narrative themes are found elsewhere in popular sagas of the ancient Near East, there are elements of the story that are distinctly Egyptian. The richly textured story of Joseph and Potiphar's wife, in particular, has a distinctly Egyptian flavor (it has often been compared with the well-known 13th century b.c. Egyptian "Tale of Two Brothers"). In addition, much of the Cycle takes place in

Egypt; thus it contains numerous Egyptian personal- and place-names. Many authorities find the most likely context for these Egyptian elements not in the 15th-13th centuries B.C., when the biblical stories are supposedly set, but rather in the Iron Age or even the Persian (Saite) period, when the narrative as we have it is likely to have been edited. My point here is simply that this most Egyptian of all the biblical story cycles may preserve some historical memories. It may even reflect the actual experience in Ramesside Egypt of small groups of Semitic peoples who a bit later found themselves part of Merneptah's coalition of Israelites in Canaan. Thus while the Joseph Cycle as it now stands may be largely fiction (but for all that a great story) it can be read as providing an actual Egyptian background for some elements in early Israel, however small. These elements could later have been associated with central-southern tribes bearing the names of Joseph's two sons Ephraim and Manasseh and known collectively as the House of Joseph — Joseph, who had been in Egypt.

4. By the time of the Monarchy, the term "House of Joseph" is sometimes extended to apply also to the ten northern tribes — that is, to designate all Israel (as in Ezekiel 37:16 and Psalm 80:1), just as the name of Joseph's father Jacob had done. This reflects the dominant role that Ephraim, Manasseh, and probably Benjamin — central and southern tribes — played in Israel's national life from earliest times. That pivotal role is underlined if we note that in two of the most archaic poems in the Hebrew Bible, the Blessing of Jacob (Genesis 49) and the Blessing of Moses (Deuteronomy 33), Joseph is praised all out of proportion to the other tribes.

5. It has long been known that southern groups, largely Judean, shaped the literary traditions that we now have in the Hebrew Bible. This is seen in the editorial work of the so-called "J" (or "J/Yahweh") school that flourished in Judah in the 8th-6th centuries B.C., and which produced the first version of (or collection of materials that formed) the Pentateuch. A northern school, "E" (after the other divine name preferred, "Elohim"), partly contemporary, also had a hand in shaping these books. But in its final form the Pentateuch is the product of another southern school, the "P" ("Priestly") school of the exilic or post-exilic period. Needless to say, the Exodus-Sinai tradition is contained entirely in the Pentateuch. As for the other relevant biblical traditions that we have sought to assess — the materials in the 7th-6th century B.C. "Deuteronomistic" work that extends from the book of Deuteronomy through Kings — this, too, was compiled in the south, clearly reflecting the typical Judean bias against the Northern King-

dom. Finally, as though to underscore the southern provenience of the Hebrew Bible as it has come down to us, scholars have long known that its language largely reflects the southern or Judahite dialect of classical Hebrew.

The point of the foregoing is that among the principal architects who shaped the biblical overall tradition we assume that there were elements of the House of Joseph. Although a minority, they told their story as the story of all Israel. That would explain how the Exodus/Sinai tradition came into being. Some of these groups probably had come out of Egypt to Canaan, and in a way that upon reflection seemed miraculous to them. Later they assumed (or dictated?) that other of the heterogeneous groups that had made up early Israel had had the same experience. So they reworked the Exodus (and Conquest) stories and included them as part of the great national epic when this took final shape in writing toward the end of the Monarchy. This version of events, however skewed, was soon to become Scripture and thus prevailed, as it still does in many circles today. It is not the whole story of Israelite origins, to be sure; but I would suggest that it may rest on some historical foundations, however minimal. To the theological ramifications, which are more important in my judgment, I shall return presently.

6. Thus far I have focused on only one possible set of historical circumstances that could explain how the literary traditions originated and why they were preserved. But this is admittedly quite speculative (although in line with much of mainstream biblical scholarship). Is there any tangible, archaeological evidence — that is, a historical context — for such a scenario as I have sketched? It happens that there now is. It will be recalled that all along I have pointed out that the vast majority of the Iron I hill country settlements now known, including nearly all those extensively excavated, are located precisely in the tribal territories that the biblical tradition assigns to the central and southern tribes that constituted the House of Joseph: Manasseh, Ephraim, and to a lesser degree Benjamin. This is the central hill country extending from Jerusalem northward to the Jezreel Valley. And here is where virtually all of the sites with what I have called proto-Israelite material culture attributes are located.

I suggest that this region was the heartland of nascent Israel. It was where the earliest and most characteristic highland settlements were located. This was also where the stories of the Exodus from Egypt, the Sinai Covenant, the crossing of the Great Desert, and the entry into Canaan from the east probably first circulated and gained a tenacious foothold. If the House of Joseph really did have a disproportionate influence upon the formation of the later literary tradition in the Hebrew Bible, then it is really no surprise that its stories eclipsed those of other proto-Israelite groups. These peoples remain anonymous because they do not happen to have left us their "Bibles." Yet archaeology attests to their presence.

The Exodus Myth: A Metaphor for Liberation

The miraculous, larger-than-life story of the Exodus as it now stands in the Bible cannot be corroborated as factual history. Nor do we even need to presume such a series of events in a far off foreign land, given archaeology's recent documentation of the rise of early Israel within Canaan. To put it simply, there is no longer a place or a need for the Exodus as a *historical* explanation for the origins of Israel. The story, however dramatic, however central to the self-identification of later biblical Israel — or even our own identity in the West — is best regarded as a myth. In this case, it is just the sort of origin myth that has characterized many other peoples past and present.

Yet the very word "myth," commonly used by scholars, alarms many lay folk who fervently want the Bible to be true. It may be helpful, therefore, to define the word and the way I will use it here. According to Webster's dictionary, a myth is

> A traditional story of unknown authorship, ostensibly with a historical basis, but serving usually to explain some phenomenon of nature, the origin of man, or the customs, religious rites, etc. of a people; myths usually involve the exploits of gods and heroes.

This definition fits the Exodus story precisely, in the sense that I suggest we understand it.

Before going any further, we should note that calling something a myth does not mean that it is without any historical basis whatsoever, much less false or untrue. A myth is rather supra-historical, true on a higher and more profound level. Thus the dilemma so keenly felt by many sincere readers of the Bible at this point is, I suggest, a false one. It is the result of a superficial and literalistic notion of what truth is, especially truth in the religious sense. How the Bible can be morally and ethically true when it is not historically true in all details is a non-question once we understand the nature of religious (dare I say *spiritual?*) truth.

Rather than attempt to defend the factual historicity of the Exodus traditions, I suggest that we must understand the Exodus story precisely as a myth, specifically as a "metaphor for liberation." Instead of demanding to know "what really happened" that might have given rise to the story (beyond speculating as I have above), we need to ask what the story meant in ancient times, and what it can mean today.

Only a general answer can be given to the first inquiry, because it is obvious that, like all great and immortal literature, the biblical story meant different things to different interpreters over the centuries. Simple folk in ancient Israel probably understood the long oral tradition and read early written versions of it as factual history, as many readers of the Bible still do. But I suspect that the later compilers and editors of the Hebrew Bible, and certainly the sages of later Judaism, were more sophisticated than we often give them credit for being. Thus they grasped the larger dimensions of the saga of slaves miraculously liberated from bondage in Egypt. It was a story about the victory of the oppressed and powerless over all the might of the world's greatest empire. The Exodus story was not only a reaffirmation of justice, but it was a promise of a life of full self-realization — a story about the ultimate triumph of the human spirit. Who can fail to resonate with such a story? True? Yes, and profoundly so!

I do not think this is simply romanticizing a biblical tale. There is ample evidence that the Exodus story was read metaphorically already in ancient times, certainly so by the early rabbis and by later rabbinical commentaries. It continues in Jewish tradition to this day: a vital part of the Passover feast that remembers and celebrates the Exodus story is the recitation of the *Haggadah*. This is a traditional, centuries-old compilation of stories and various commentaries about the deliverance from Egypt. It is partly historical, partly fanciful, even humorous — a retelling of the Exodus story for each new generation. Thus in the prayers and blessings that are interspersed around the Passover table in the *Haggadah* that forms the libretto to the dramatic reenactment of the Exodus, Jews say: "It is as though we had been in Egypt, and have been delivered by the Almighty to this very day."

But literally speaking, "we" were never in Egypt. Most of us came to our Promised Land from the ghettoes of Eastern Europe, as slaves from Africa, as refugees from Asia. My ancestors, for instance, came over from Ireland during the potato famine in the 1840s. Yet we can all resonate with the Exodus story because we instinctively recognize that it is a metaphor for liberation, one of universal and timeless appeal. Originally told thousands of years ago by and about a small and obscure immigrant group within the society of early Israelite peoples, and based in all likelihood on some actual historical experience of some of them in Egypt (perhaps the House of Joseph characterized above) the Exodus story eventually came to be told as though it had been true for all Israel. And this accounts for its enduring place in the literary traditions that found their final expression in the Hebrew Bible.

There is a parallel in more recent history for a feast that celebrates a metaphor of liberation: that most American of holidays, Thanksgiving. On Thanksgiving Day we all gather around the table not just to stuff ourselves with turkey, but also to remember with gratitude the founders of our country, often with great nostalgia. On this day, despite the diversity of origins I sketched above, all we Americans *metaphorically* came over on the *Mayflower*. We know, factually speaking, that most of our ancestors did not come to America then and there, and that the first Thanksgiving in all likelihood was not on a Thursday in late November. But in a burst of patriotism, on this holiday spiritually (yes!) we are all Pilgrims, newcomers to our own Promised Land. That is what makes us Americans. An origin myth? To be sure — an extraordinarily powerful one, constitutive of a great nation. And, of course, derived from the original biblical myth of the Exodus.

What Ever Happened to Moses?

But however "sensible" it may seem, the reconstruction of Israelite origins that I have suggested here will be unpersuasive to many readers for obvious reasons. Primary among these is that it contradicts the fundamental theological themes of the literary traditions of the Hebrew Bible in the form in which we have them. The recurrent motifs are (1) miraculous deliverance of the Israelite tribes from Egypt under Moses' leadership; (2) the sojourn in the wilderness and the revelation of the divine law, or Ten Commandments, at Mount Sinai; (3) the covenant of Yahweh with his chosen people and the gift of the Promised Land; and (4) the unified and complete conquest of Canaan and its apportionment among the twelve tribes as their inheritance forever. These incidents, and the themes that accompany them, are the very foundations of the epic story of Israel in the Hebrew Bible, in the New Testament, and in both the later Jewish and Christian communities, and indeed in much of the Western cultural tradition until recently. That leaves us where we began: with the crucial question of whether the Bible's stories are history or myth, fact or fiction.

I may have rationalized the biblical accounts of the Exodus and conquest, but have Moses and the Sinai covenant not disappeared in the process of providing "secular explanations"? Archaeologists whose discoveries have provoked much of the controversy too often blithely sidestep the religious issues here. For current theories of "indigenous origins" for early Israel have no place for Moses, nor any *need* of him. It would be easy to conclude, along with Freud's classic study *Moses and Monotheism,* that Moses was simply invented out of deep subconscious human desires. But here I wish at least to make an attempt to be theologically sensitive and responsible — that is, to reconcile, if possible, the probably-mythical Moses of the texts with a possible Moses-like figure who may have been historical. The issue for critical scholarship is how to account for the "Mosaic traditions," even if found mostly in later literature, if they did not have *some* historical foundations. Where and when could such an original tradition have come from? And how did it come to be preserved and handed down as credible for some five or six centuries before it was codified in writing? The revisionists simply dispose of this issue: in their estimation, Moses and the Law are simply part of second-century-B.C. origin myths and have no historical basis.

On the negative side, we must confront several theoretical objections. (1) There is absolutely no external — that is, extrabiblical — witness to Moses, either textual or archaeological. (2) The portrait of a "miraculous Moses" who performs stupendous feats and contends face-to-face with God strains modern readers' credulity. (3) The notion of a revolutionary new religion that emerged complete overnight and never required or underwent revolutionary development is similarly unconvincing. And the ideal in fact is contradicted by the reality of later Israelite belief and practice, which many of the texts of the Hebrew Bible candidly acknowledge. In short, taken at face value, much of the Moses-Sinai-Covenant story is hard for modern readers to swallow.

Then there are several well-established facts. (1) As biblical scholars have long noted, in the oldest reference to the Exodus, Miriam's "Song of the Sea" (Exod. 15), Moses is not even named. (2) Furthermore, Israel's most ancient creedal recital, the *Magnalia Dei* (Deut. 26:5-10), makes no mention of Moses in connection with the deliverance from Egypt. (3) Finally, outside of Exodus-Numbers, scant attention is paid to Moses. Even in the pre-Exilic prophetic literature, only Jeremiah (15:1) and Micah (6:4) mention him by name. It is *only* in the book of Deuteronomy and the sweeping historical epic of Joshua through Kings, shaped by the "Deuteronomistic school" of the era of Josiah in the late seventh century B.C. — at the very end of the Monarchy — that Moses looms large. There, as the focus of the "Yahweh-alone" reform movement, Moses appears as lawgiver and the founder of Israelite religion. But scholars have long regarded these materials as largely nationalist and orthodox propaganda. The basis for the attempted Josianic reform — a scroll containing a long-lost sermon by Moses himself, and supposedly rediscovered in the archives of the Jerusalem Temple (2 Kings 22:8-13; 23:13) — is suspected by scholars to have been our present book of Deuteronomy (or "Second Law"), written and planted by some other reformist parties. In this view, the "larger-than-life" biblical Moses would be mostly a later literary invention — although invented for theological purposes that some might deem legitimate. After all, for an attempted reformation to have authority, it must call believers back to *some* original, "pure" version of religion.

As for the Ten Commandments, attributed by later tradition to Moses, many biblical scholars point out that both the versions in Exodus 34 and Deuteronomy 5 appear to have no direct connection with major strands of the Pentateuch. Versions of the Ten Commandments probably circulated for a long time in independent circles. And while the oral traditions of the Decalogue (and many of the dozens of other "laws") may go back quite early, virtually no authority today would date the present form before the eighth or seventh century B.C., much less attribute it to a thirteenth-century-B.C. Moses.

Nevertheless, the commonsense arguments requiring some "founder" of Israelite religion in whatever form, and taking the literary tradition seriously, however late and tendentious, should not be brushed aside for lack of demonstrable "proof." There is also at very least a context, as pointed out above, for Asiatics escaping servitude in Egypt, and even for the knowledge in Egyptian texts of the Late Bronze Age of a deity called "Yhw" in connection with the Shasu nomads of southern Transjordan. After all, it was there, in the "land of Midian," according to the Bible, that Moses learned of the existence of this deity in one view from his father-in-law. And numerous later biblical passages depict Yahweh, the God of Israel, "coming forth from Seir" (that is, southern Edom; see Judg. 5:4 and Deut. 33:2) .

For these reasons, even some rather radical scholars would take seriously the notion that some of these "Shasu of Yhw" were among the tribal peoples who became early Israel, and that they may indeed have been guided through the desert by a charismatic, sheikh-like leader with the Egyptian name of "Moses." In folk religion these pre-Israelite traditions, partly mythological, may have survived well into the late Monarchy. They could then have been incorporated into the national epic that crystallized as the old agrarian ideal was giving way to urbanization, national security, and religious conformity. As Baruch Halpern has eloquently put it, this reform "successfully defined traditional as un-Israelite, as pagan, as inferior, a position that Western literary religions have continued to maintain ever since" (1991: 91).

Conclusion

I began this book by sketching the current controversy about the origins of ancient Israel. I justified yet another review of the issues by suggesting that much of the heat, if not the light, generated by this controversy is due to the fact that for many in the West this is not simply another antiquarian pursuit. It is very much a question of our own self-identity, for in some ways we see ourselves as the New Israel. But we in Europe and the New World no longer are the only ones who perceive the issues this way.

Palestinians as the New Canaanites?

There is now a stream of popular literature on Israelite origins that drags our topic into the current political situation in the Middle East. Some of it equates modern Israelis with ancient Israelite conquerors, modern Palestinians with the beleaguered ancient Canaanites. And archaeology is now being used in some circles to justify each group's exclusive right to the Land: "We were here first!" Or a more strident claim: "Your people didn't really exist here at all; your religious myths have invented them!" Thus revisionist rhetoric from biblical and archaeological scholarship is being subverted to serve nationalist agendas, whether extreme forms of Zionism or those of Muslim Fundamentalists. In the Middle East, this is akin to shouting "Fire!" in a crowded theater.

One of the earliest examples appeared in the *Jerusalem Post International* in October 1997. There Michael Arnold documented the fact that the Palestinian Authority in the West Bank, through its Internet sites, television programs, national celebrations, and school textbooks, is offering the world a new (read: "revisionist") reading of the region's history, which in essence writes ancient Israel out of that history. This amounts to taking a page from early Zionism's book, which similarly tried to deny the existence of the other party. But this time the appeal is to archaeology.

Other Palestinian archaeologists are excavating Early Bronze Age sites in the region (3rd millennium B.C.) and claiming that these are sites occupied by Canaanites, the Palestinians' direct ancestors. This has led to renewed interest in these ancestors and their practices. According to Michael Arnold, in the summer of 1996 the Palestinian Authority staged an elaborate ceremony reenacting the worship of the Canaanite god Ba'al, dancing around an elated Palestinian Minister of Culture, Yasser Adb-Rabbo. The Palestinian media has picked up on the revisionists' claims as well. The Authority's official television station aired a program that placed the entire biblical story of Israel in Yemen, based on a notorious book by Kamal Salibi, a Lebanese writer (thoroughly discredited, of course, by critics on all sides). Of course some Palestinian spokespersons downplay all this propaganda, protesting that only extremists or a poorly-informed public would buy it. Yet Hamdan Taha, the director of the Palestinian Authority's Ministry of Tourism and Antiquities, is inclined to defend his colleagues' tactics as fair turnabout. And in any case, why should Israelis care about what Palestinian revisionism claims?

But there are also some Israeli archaeological revisionists who fuel the fire. The first sign of their existence was a story in the Israeli newspaper *Ha'aretz* of October 29, 1999, in which Tel Aviv University archaeologist Ze'ev Herzog went public for the first time with the indigenous origins theory of the emergence of Israel that he and his colleagues had been espousing quietly for a decade (as I do here). Secular intellectuals and post-Zionist historians were for the most part unfazed by his claims, but they provoked cries of outrage from the religious right, especially the settlers in the "territories," whose claim to the land was that God has given it to them (sound familiar?).

The international media picked up Herzog's story and the reaction to it immediately. They were also the subjects of an extended story in the *Chronicle of Higher Education* of January 21, 2000. The *Chronicle* also covered a conference in December, 1999, of the Herzog Teacher Training College, an institution located in an Israeli West Bank settlement and associated with the country's religious Zionist movement. There Herzog, a "post-Zionist," argued that

> The Jews in Israel no longer need the Bible to justify their presence in the Middle East. We're here because we're here. We no longer need excuses — we're natives.

Many Israeli archaeologists, much more moderate, rejected the post-Zionist argument as aligned with the minimalist or revisionist schools of biblical scholarship at Copenhagen and Sheffield, which I have characterized above as essentially nihilist — those for whom there was no early Israel, and no need for one.

Erasing Ancient Israel from History?

The growing controversy was aired in an excellent series of articles by Michael Balter in an issue of *Science* magazine on January 7, 2000, entitled "Archaeology in the Holy Land." In Israel, Balter interviewed Herzog; his senior colleague at Tel Aviv, Israel Finkelstein; and many other Israeli and American archaeologists, including me. He carefully documents the way in which various religious and political ideologies are now appealing to archaeology for support, however misguided. I told him

> We fought so hard to make archaeology a respectable discipline and to free it from these kinds of emotional issues. . . . And now we are back in the middle of it again.

Balter rightly picks up on the link between the original biblical and the new archaeological revisionism. He recounts how Hamid Salim, a young Palestinian archaeologist from Birzeit University (who did his M.A. with me at Arizona), is delighted to be excavating at last in his own land. And he cites Khaled Nashef, director of the Institute of Archaeology at

Birzeit University. European-educated, extraordinarily urbane and articulate (as I know from personal acquaintance), Nashef is an outspoken and often very effective proponent of the involvement of local archaeology in the Palestinian cause. He argues that the history of Palestine for too long has been written by Christian and Israeli "biblical archaeologists." Now, he says, Palestinians themselves must rewrite that history, beginning with the archaeological recovery of ancient Palestine.

But where does this recent insistence on a Palestinian archaeology and history written by real Palestinians come from? I recall that even before the biblical revisionist Keith W. Whitelam published his book *The Invention of Ancient Israel: The Silencing of Palestinian History* in 1996 I predicted that it would become the "Bible" of the Palestinian revisionists. Indeed, it soon appeared in Arabic translation in East Jerusalem bookshops, and Nashef and many other Palestinian political activists have obviously read it. Yet as several reviewers, including myself, have pointed out, Whitelam's charge that Israelis and Jewish-inspired Christians have invented ancient Israel and have thus deliberately robbed Palestinians of their history is extremely inflammatory; indeed, it comes dangerously close to anti-Semitism. And the storm shows no signs of abating: Thomas L. Thompson's even more rabid book *The Mythic Past: Biblical Archaeology and the Myth of Israel* (1999) has also now appeared in Arabic.

That Nashef and other Palestinians are being profoundly influenced by the revisionists' rhetoric is clear. Nashef is the editor of a new journal of Birzeit University, the *Journal of Palestinian Archaeology*. For the first issue, published in July of 2000, Nashef wrote an editorial entitled "The Debate on 'Ancient Israel': A Palestinian Perspective." (It was partly an attack on my views, despite my attempts to be resolutely non-political — and in fact sometimes rather critical of Israeli archaeology.) Most of his comments were supportive of the biblical revisionists, explicitly naming all the principals: Philip Davies, Niels Peter Lemche, Thomas L. Thompson, and Keith W. Whitelam. Nashef declares that

> The fact of the matter is, the Palestinians have something completely different to offer in the debate on "ancient Israel," which seems to threaten the ideological basis of *BAR* (the American popular magazine, the *Biblical Archaeology Review*, which turned down this piece — WGD): they simply exist, and they have always existed on the soil of Palestine. . . . There is indeed a crisis of history in the study of the origins of

Jewish people. . . . But in reality, the crisis was always there, and always will be, as long as Palestinians are silenced and deprived of their history and their land.

These final words come almost verbatim from Whitelam. Yet even some of his fellow revisionists have pointed out what Nashef surely knows and what archaeology tells us: The fact of the matter is that there were no Palestinians in the Bronze and Iron Ages, but rather the various peoples of the land the Romans later called Palestine, including the ancestors of both the Israelis and the Palestinians.

Still the controversy rages on. Along with Finkelstein and Silberman, I am often described as holding the middle ground in what Stuart Schoffman, a reporter for the *Jerusalem Report,* recently described as a "controversy for the sake of heaven." This appellation, drawn from the Mishnah, is not necessarily apt, since all the authors under review here are secularists. But it is a controversy that is engaged in all moral earnestness with issues that are of life-and-death importance. And for my own passion in the engagement I make no apologies.

As the anthropologist and social philosopher Eric Hobsbawm once remarked, there are facts; facts matter; and some facts matter a great deal. The reality of ancient Israel is just such a fact. The ancient Israelites were a real people, in a real time and place. And their historical experience, however tantalizingly incomplete its portrait may be in the Hebrew Bible, still has much to teach us — in America, in Europe, and in the Middle East.

Some Basic Sources
(Usually in Chronological Order)

General Reference Works

1. Geography and Topography

Aharoni, Y. *The Land of the Bible: A Historical Geography.* Philadelphia: Westminster, 1979.

2. Archaeological Sites

Stern, E., editor. *The New Encyclopedia of Archaeological Excavations in the Holy Land.* New York: Simon & Schuster, 1993.

3. Archaeological Handbooks

Mazar, A. *Archaeology of the Land of the Bible 10,000-586 B.C.E.* New York: Doubleday, 1990.

Ben-Tor, A., editor. *The Archaeology of Ancient Israel.* New Haven: Yale University Press, 1992.

Levy, T. E., editor. *The Archaeology of Society in the Holy Land.* New York: Facts on File, 1995.

4. "Biblical" and Syro-Palestinian Archaeology

Dever, W. G. "Syro-Palestinian and Biblical Archaeology." 31-79 in *The Hebrew Bible and Its Modern Interpreters.* Edited by D. A. Knight and G. M. Tucker. Philadelphia: Fortress, 1985.

Drinkard, J. E., G. L. Mattingly, and J. M. Miller, editors. *Benchmarks in Time and Culture: An Introduction to Palestinian Archaeology.* Atlanta: Scholars Press, 1988.

Moorey, P. R. S. *A Century of Biblical Archaeology.* Louisville: Westminster/John Knox, 1991.

Dever, W. G. "Palestine, Archaeology of Bronze and Iron Ages." III:545-58 in *The Anchor Bible Dictionary.* Edited by D. N. Freedman. New York: Doubleday, 1992.

Fritz, V. *An Introduction to Biblical Archaeology.* Sheffield: JSOT Press, 1994.

5. Handbooks on Method in Biblical Scholarship, Particularly on Historiography

Knight, D. A., and G. M. Tucker, editors. *The Hebrew Bible and Its Modern Interpreters.* Chico, Calif.: Scholars Press, 1977.

Barton, J. *Reading the Old Testament: Method in Biblical Study.* Philadelphia: Westminster, 1984.

Halpern, B. *The First Historians: The Hebrew Bible and History.* San Francisco: Harper & Row, 1988.

McKenzie, S. L., and S. R. Haynes, editors. *To Each Its Own Meaning: An Introduction to Biblical Criticisms and Their Application.* Louisville: Westminster/John Knox, 1993.

Millard, A. R., J. K. Hoffmeier, and D. W. Baker, editors. *Faith, Tradition, and History: Old Testament Historiography in Its Near Eastern Context.* Winona Lake, Ind.: Eisenbrauns, 1994.

Brettler, M. Z. *The Creation of History in Ancient Israel.* London: Routledge, 1995.

Dever, W. G. "Philology, Theology, and Archaeology: What Kind of History Do We Want, and What Is Possible?" 290-310 in *The Archaeology of Israel: Constructing the Past, Interpreting the Present.* Edited by N. A. Silberman and D. Small. Sheffield: Sheffield Academic Press, 1997.

Baker, D. W., and B. T. Arnold, editors. *The Face of Old Testament Studies: A Study of Contemporary Approaches.* Grand Rapids: Baker, 1999.

Long, V. P., editor. *Israel's Past in Present Research.* Winona Lake, Ind.: Eisenbrauns, 1999.

Barr, J. *History and Ideology in the Old Testament: Biblical Studies of the End of a Millennium.* Oxford: Oxford University Press, 2000.

6. On the Pentateuch

Friedman, R. E. *Who Wrote the Bible?* Englewood Cliffs, N.J.: Prentice, 1987.

Blenkinsopp, J. *The Pentateuch: An Introduction to the First Five Books of the Bible.* New York: Doubleday, 1992.

7. On the Deuteronomistic School Specifically

Coogan, M., and H. Tadmor. *II Kings.* Garden City, N.Y.: Doubleday, 1983.

McKenzie, S. L. *The Trouble with Kings: The Composition of the Book of Kings in the Deuteronomistic History.* Leiden: Brill, 1991.

Provan, I. W. *1 & 2 Kings.* Peabody, Mass.: Hendrickson, 1997.

Knoppers, G. N., and J. G. McConville, editors. *Reconsidering Israel and Judah: Recent Studies on the Deuteronomistic History.* Winona Lake, Ind.: Eisenbrauns, 2000.

8. Handbooks and Histories of Ancient Israel

Noth, M. *The History of Israel.* London: A. & C. Black, 1958. Revised 1965.

Hayes, J. H., and J. M. Miller, editors. *Israelite and Judean History.* Philadelphia: Westminster, 1977.

Bright, J. *A History of Israel.* Philadelphia: Westminster, 1959. Revised 1981.

Rendtorff, R. *The Old Testament: An Introduction.* Philadelphia: Westminster, 1983.

Soggin, J. A. *A History of Ancient Israel from the Beginnings to the Bar Kochba Revolt,* A.D. *135.* Philadelphia: Westminster, 1985.

Miller, J. M., and J. H. Hayes. *A History of Ancient Israel and Judah.* Philadelphia: Westminster, 1986.

Coogan, M. D., editor. *The Oxford History of the Biblical World.* New York: Oxford University Press, 1995.

Shanks, H., editor. *Ancient Israel from Abraham to the Roman Destruction of the Temple.* Washington: Biblical Archaeology Society, 1999.

McNutt, P. *Reconstructing the Society of Ancient Israel.* Louisville: Westminster/ John Knox, 1999.

For a list of revisionist histories, see Chapter 1.

9. Society; Family and Daily Life; Folklore

Kirkpatrick, P. G. *The Old Testament and Folklore Study.* Sheffield: Sheffield Academic Press, 1988.

Matthews, V. H. *Manners and Customs in the Bible: An Illustrated Guide to Daily Life in Bible Times.* Peabody, Mass.: Hendrickson, 1991.

Matthews, V. H., and D. C. Benjamin. *Social World of Ancient Israel, 1250-587* BCE. Peabody, Mass.: Hendrickson, 1993.

Perdue, L. G., J. Blenkinsopp, J. J. Collins, and C. Meyers. *Families in Ancient Israel.* Louisville: Westminster/John Knox, 1997.

McNutt, P. M. *Reconstructing the Society of Ancient Israel.* Louisville: Westminster/ John Knox, 1999.

King, P. J., and Stager, L. E. *Daily Life in Ancient Israel.* Louisville: Westminster/ John Knox, 2001.

Chapter 1. The Current Crisis in Understanding the Origins of Early Israel

1. Revisionist Works and Critiques

Davies, P. R. *In Search of "Ancient Israel."* Sheffield: JSOT Press, 1992.

Thompson, T. L. *Early History of the Israelite People from the Written and Archaeological Sources.* Leiden: Brill, 1992.

Halpern, B. "Erasing History: The Minimalist Assault on Ancient Israel." *Bible Review* 11/6, 1995. 26-35, 47.

Dever, W. G. "Will the Real Israel Please Stand Up? Archaeology and Israelite Historiography: Part I." *Bulletin of the American Schools of Oriental Research* 197, 1995. 37-58.

Whitelam, K. W. *The Invention of Ancient Israel: The Silencing of Palestinian History.* New York: Routledge, 1996.

Grabbe, L. L., editor. *Can a "History of Israel" Be Written?* Sheffield: Sheffield Academic Press, 1997.

Lemche, N. P. *The Israelites in History and Tradition.* Louisville: Westminster/John Knox, 1998.

Japhet, S. "In Search of Ancient Israel: Revisionism at All Costs." 212-233 in *The Jewish Past Revisited: Reflections by Modern Jewish Historians.* Edited by D. N. Meyers and D. R. Ruderman. New Haven: Yale University Press, 1998.

Thompson, T. L. *The Mythic Past: Biblical Archaeology and the Myth of Israel.* New York: Basic, 1999.

Finkelstein, I., and N. A. Silberman. *The Bible Unearthed: Archaeology's New Vision of Ancient Israel and the Origin of Its Sacred Texts.* New York: Free Press, 2000.

Dever, W. G. *What Did the Biblical Writers Know and When Did They Know It? What Archaeology Can Tell Us about the Reality of Ancient Israel.* Grand Rapids: Eerdmans, 2001.

Chapter 2. The Exodus — History or Myth?

1. Commentaries on Exodus

Propp, W. *Exodus.* New York: Doubleday, 1999.

2. General Works

Finegan, J. *Let My People Go: A Journey through Exodus.* New York: Harper & Row, 1963.

Hermann, S. *Israel in Egypt.* Naperville, Ill.: Allenson, 1973.

Sarna, N. M. *Exploring Exodus: The Heritage of Biblical Israel.* New York: Schocken, 1986.

Halpern, B. "The Exodus from Egypt: Myth or Reality?" 86-113 in *The Rise of Ancient Israel*. Edited by H. Shanks. Washington: Biblical Archaeology Society, 1992.

Frerichs, E. S., and L. H. Lesko, editors. *Exodus: The Egyptian Evidence*. Washington: Biblical Archaeology Society, 1993. Essays by W. G. Dever, A. Malamat, D. B. Redford, W. A. Ward, J. M. Weinstein, and F. J. Yurco.

3. Conservative Reactions

Bimson, J. *Redating the Exodus and Conquest*. Sheffield: University of Sheffield Press, 1981.

Krahmalkov, C. R. "Exodus Itinerary Confirmed by Egyptian Evidence." *Biblical Archaeology Review* 20/5, 1994. 55-62, 79.

Hoffmeier, J. K. *Israel in Egypt: The Evidence for the Authenticity of the Exodus Tradition*. New York: Oxford University Press, 1996.

Currid, J. D. *Ancient Egypt and the Old Testament*. Grand Rapids: Baker, 1997.

Kitchen, K. A. "Egyptians and Hebrews, from Ra'amses to Jericho." 65-131 in *The Origin of Early Israel — Current Debate: Biblical, Historical and Archaeological Perspectives*. Edited by S. Ahituv and E. D. Oren. Beersheba: Ben-Guryon University of the Negev Press, 1998.

Millard, A. "How Reliable Is Exodus?" *Biblical Archaeology Review* 26/4, 2000. 50-57.

Chapter 3. The Conquest of Transjordan

1. Older Works

See works cited above for Chapter 2, especially those of Khramalkov, Hoffmeier, and Kitchen, all very traditional.

2. More Recent Treatments

See the general articles by J. A. Dearman, G. L. Mattingly, and J. M. Miller in *Biblical Archaeologist* 60/4, 1997. The whole issue is devoted to Moab.

3. Edom and Moab

Bienkowski, P., editor. *Early Edom and Moab: The Beginning of the Iron Age in Southern Transjordan*. Sheffield: JSOT Press, 1992.

4. Ammon

MacDonald, B., and R. W. Younker, editors. *Ancient Ammon*. Leiden: Brill, 1999.

Chapter 4. The Conquest of the Land
West of the Jordan: Theories and Facts

1. Ancient Near Eastern Conquest Accounts

Younger, K. L., Jr. *Ancient Conquest Accounts: A Study in Ancient Near Eastern and Biblical History Writing.* Sheffield: JSOT Press, 1990.

2. The Book of Joshua Specifically

Soggin, J. A. *Joshua: A Commentary.* Philadelphia: Westminster, 1972.

Boling, R., and G. E. Wright. *Joshua: A New Translation with Notes and Commentary.* Garden City, N.Y.: Doubleday, 1984.

Na'aman, N. "The 'Conquest of Canaan' in the Book of Joshua and in History." 218-81 in *From Nomadism to Monarchy: Archaeological and Historical Aspects of Early Israel.* Edited by I. Finkelstein and N. Na'aman. Washington: Biblical Archaeology Society, 1994.

Nelson, R. D. *Joshua: A Commentary.* Louisville: Westminster/John Knox, 1997.

3. The Book of Judges

Boling, R. G. *Judges.* Garden City, N.Y.: Doubleday, 1975.

4. On the Conquest Model

Albright, W. F. "The Israelite Conquest of Canaan in the Light of Archaeology." *Bulletin of the American Schools of Oriental Research* 74, 1939. 11-23.

Wright, G. E. "Epic of Conquest." *Biblical Archaeologist* 3, 1940. 25-40.

Lapp, P. W. "The Conquest of Palestine in the Light of Archaeology." *Concordia Theological Monthly* 38, 1967. 495-548.

Yadin, Y. "Is the Biblical Conquest of Canaan Historically Reliable?" *Biblical Archaeology Review* 8, 1982. 16-23.

Malamat, A. "How Inferior Israelite Forces Conquered Fortified Canaanite Cities." *Biblical Archaeology Review* 8, 1982. 24-35.

See also works cited under Chapter 2.

5. On the Peaceful Infiltration/Immigration Model

Alt, A. *Essays on Old Testament History and Religion.* Oxford: Oxford University Press, 1966.

Noth, M. *The Deuteronomistic History.* Sheffield: JSOT Press, 1981.

Weippert, M. *The Settlement of the Israelite Tribes in Palestine: A Critical Survey of Recent Scholarly Debate.* Naperville, Ill.: Allenson, 1971.

6. On the Peasant Revolt Model

Mendenhall, G. E. "The Hebrew Conquest of Palestine." *Biblical Archaeologist* 25, 1962. 66-87.

Mendenhall, G. E. *The Tenth Generation: The Origins of the Biblical Tradition.* Baltimore: Johns Hopkins University Press, 1973.

Gottwald, N. K. *The Tribes of Yahweh: A Sociology of the Religion of Liberated Israel, 1250-1050 B.C.E.* Maryknoll, N.Y.: Orbis, 1979.

Gottwald, N. K. "Method and Hypothesis in Reconstructing the Social History of Early Israel." *Eretz-Israel* 24, 1993. 70-82.

7. On Pastoral Nomadism, with Reference to Both the Patriarchal and Conquest Models

Johnson, D. L. *The Nature of Nomadism: A Comparative Study of Pastoral Migrations in Southwestern Asia and Northern Africa.* Chicago: University of Chicago Press, 1969.

Dever, W. G. "The Patriarchal Traditions. Palestine in the Second Millennium BCE: The Archaeological Picture." 70-120 in *Israelite and Judean History.* Edited by J. H. Hayes and J. M. Miller. London: SCM, 1977.

Saltzman, D. C., editor. *When Nomads Settle.* New York: Praeger, 1980.

Cribb, R. *Nomads in Archaeology.* Cambridge: Cambridge University Press, 1991.

Bar-Yosef, O., and A. Khazanov, editors. *Pastoralism in the Levant: Archaeological Materials in Anthropological Perspective.* Madison, Wis.: Prehistory Press, 1992.

Hopkins, D. C. "Pastoralists in Late Bronze Age Palestine: Which Way Did They Go?" *Biblical Archaeologist* 56/4, 1993. 200-211.

8. On the 13th Century B.C. Destruction at Hazor

Ben-Tor, A. "Excavating Hazor, Part II: Did the Israelites Destroy the Canaanite City?" *Biblical Archaeology Review* 25/3, 1999. 22-39.

Chapter 5. Facts on the Ground: The Archaeological Rediscovery of the Real Israel

1. Major Excavated Sites

Tel Esdar

Kochavi, M. "Excavations at Tel Esdar." *'Atiqot* 5, 1969. 14-48. In Hebrew.

Kh. Raddana

Callaway, J. A., and R. E. Cooley. "A Salvage Excavation at Raddana, in Bireh." *Bulletin of the American Schools of Oriental Research* 201, 1971. 9-19.

Giloh

Mazar, A. "Giloh: An Early Israelite Site Near Jerusalem." *Israel Exploration Journal* 13, 1981. 1-36.

Tel Masos

Fritz, V. "The Israelite 'Conquest' in the Light of Recent Excavations at Khirbet el-Meshash." *Bulletin of the American Schools of Oriental Research* 241, 1981. 61-73.

'Izbet Sartah

Finkelstein, I. *'Izbet Sartah: An Early Iron Age Site near Rosh Ha'ayin, Israel.* Oxford: Oxford University Press, 1986.

Shiloh

Finkelstein, I., editor. *Shiloh: The Archaeology of a Biblical Site.* Tel Aviv: Tel Aviv University, 1993.

2. Minor Sites

See individual entries in Stern, *The New Encyclopedia of Archaeological Excavations in the Holy Land,* under General Reference Works, above.

Chapter 6. More Facts on the Ground:
Recent Archaeological Surveys

1. Israeli Surveys in the West Bank

Finkelstein, I. *The Archaeology of the Israelite Settlement.* Jerusalem: Israel Exploration Society, 1988.

Gal, Z. *Lower Galilee During the Iron Age.* Winona Lake, Ind.: Eisenbrauns, 1992.

Finkelstein, I., and N. Na'aman. *From Nomadism to Monarchy: Archaeological and Historical Aspects of Early Israel.* Washington: Biblical Archaeology Society, 1994.

Finkelstein, I., and Z. Lederman, editors. *Highlands of Many Cultures. The Southern Samaria Survey: The Sites.* Tel Aviv: Tel Aviv University, 1997.

2. Interpretation of Results

Dever, W. G. Review of Finkelstein and Lederman 1997. *Bulletin of the American Schools of Oriental Research* 313, 1999. 87, 88.

3. On Late Bronze–Iron Age Demography

Shiloh, Y. "The Population of Iron Age Palestine in the Light of a Sample Analysis of Urban Plans, Areas, and Population Density." *Bulletin of the American Schools of Oriental Research* 239, 1980. 25-35.

Gonen, R. "Urban Canaan in the Late Bronze Period." *Bulletin of the American Schools of Oriental Research* 253, 1984. 61-73.

Chapter 7. A Summary of the
Material Culture of the Iron I Assemblage

1. Relevant Works of W. G. Dever

Recent Archaeological Discoveries and Biblical Research. Seattle: University of Washington Press, 1990.

"Archaeology and Israelite Origins: A Review Article." *Bulletin of the American Schools of Oriental Research* 179, 1990. 89-95.

"Archaeological Data on the Israelite Settlement: A Review of Two Recent Works." *Bulletin of the American Schools of Oriental Research* 284, 1991. 77-90.

"Unresolved Issues in the Early History of Israel: Toward a Synthesis of Archaeological and Textual Reconstructions." 195-208 in *The Bible and the Politics of Exegesis: Essays in Honor of Norman K. Gottwald on His Sixty-Fifth Birthday.* Edited by D. Jobling, P. L. Day, and G. T. Sheppard. Cleveland: Pilgrim, 1992.

"How to Tell an Israelite from a Canaanite." 27-56 in *The Rise of Ancient Israel.* Edited by H. Shanks. Washington: Biblical Archaeology Society, 1992.

"The Late Bronze-Early Iron I Horizon in Syria-Palestine: Egyptians, Canaanites, 'Sea Peoples,' and 'Proto-Israelites.'" 99-110 in *The Crisis Years: The 12th Century B.C. From Beyond the Danube to the Tigris.* Edited by W. A. Ward and M. S. Joukowsky. Dubuque, Iowa: Kendall/Hunt, 1992.

"Ceramics, Ethnicity, and the Question of Israel's Origins." *Biblical Archaeologist* 58/4, 1995. 200-213.

"The Identity of Early Israel: A Rejoinder to Keith W. Whitelam." *Journal for the Study of the Old Testament* 72, 1996. 3-24.

"Revisionist Israel Revisited: A Rejoinder to Niels Peter Lemche." *Currents in Research: Biblical Studies* 4, 1996. 3-24.

"Archaeology and the Emergence of Early Israel." 20-50 in *Archaeology and Biblical Interpretation.* Edited by J. R. Bartlett. New York: Routledge, 1997.

"Is There Any Archaeological Evidence for the Exodus?" 67-83 in *Exodus: The Egyptian Evidence.* Edited by E. S. Frerichs and L. H. Lesko. Winona Lake, Ind.: Eisenbrauns, 1997.

"Archaeology, Ideology, and the Quest for an 'Ancient' or 'Biblical' Israel." *Near Eastern Archaeology* 6/1, 1998. 39-52.

"Israelite Origins and the 'Nomadic Ideal': Can Archaeology Separate Fact from Fiction?" 197-237 in *Mediterranean Peoples in Transition, Thirteenth to Early*

Tenth Centuries BCE. Edited by S. Gitin, A. Mazar, and E. Stern. Jerusalem: Israel Exploration Society, 1998.

2. Relevant Works of Israel Finkelstein

'Izbet Sartah: An Early Iron Age Site near Rosh Ha'ayin, Israel. Oxford: Oxford University Press, 1986.

The Archaeology of the Israelite Settlement. Jerusalem: Israel Exploration Society, 1988.

"The Emergence of Israel in Canaan: Consensus, Mainstream and Dispute." Scandinavian Journal of the Old Testament 2, 1991. 47-59.

"Response." 63-69 in The Rise of Israel. Edited by H. Shanks. Washington: Biblical Archaeology Society, 1993.

Finkelstein, I., S. Bunimovitz, and Z. Lederman, editors. Shiloh: The Archaeology of a Biblical Site. Tel Aviv: Tel Aviv University, 1993.

Finkelstein, I., and N. Na'aman, editors. From Nomadism to Monarchy: Archaeological and Historical Aspects of Early Israel. Washington: Biblical Archaeology Society, 1994.

"The Great Transformation: The 'Conquest' of the Highlands Frontier and the Rise of the Territorial States." 349-65 in The Archaeology of Society in the Holy Land. Edited by T. E. Levy. New York: Facts on File, 1995.

"Ethnicity and Origin of the Iron I Settlers in the Highlands of Canaan: Can the Real Israel Stand Up?" Biblical Archaeologist 59, 1996. 198-212.

"Pots and Peoples Revisited: Ethnic Boundaries in the Iron Age." 216-37 in The Archaeology of Israel: Constructing the Past, Interpreting the Present. Edited by N. A. Silberman and D. Small. Sheffield: Sheffield Academic Press, 1997.

Finkelstein, I., and Z. Lederman, editors. Highlands of Many Cultures. The Southern Samaria Survey: The Sites. Tel Aviv: Tel Aviv University, 1997.

Finkelstein, I., and N. A. Silberman. The Bible Unearthed: Archaeology's New Vision of Ancient Israel and the Origin of Its Sacred Texts. New York: Free Press, 2000.

3. On Early Iron I Agriculture

Hopkins, D. C. The Highlands of Canaan: Agricultural Life in the Early Iron Age. Sheffield: Almond, 1985.

Borowski, O. Agriculture in Iron Age Israel. Winona Lake, Ind.: Eisenbrauns, 1987.

4. On Technology

McNutt, P. M. The Forging of Iron: Technology, Symbolism, and Tradition in Ancient Society. Sheffield: Sheffield Academic Press, 1990.

Stager, L. E. "The Archaeology of the Family in Early Israel." Bulletin of the American Schools of Oriental Research 260, 1985. 1-35.

5. On the Significance of Pig Bones

Hesse, B., and P. Wapnish. "Can Pig Bones Be Used for Ethnic Diagnosis in the Ancient Near East?" 238-70 in *The Archaeology of Israel: Constructing the Past, Interpreting the Present*. Edited by N. A. Silberman and D. Small. Sheffield: Sheffield Academic Press, 1997.

6. On Tribal Structure

Khoury, P. S., and J. Kostiner, editors. *Tribes and State Formation in the Middle East*. Los Angeles: Tauris, 1990.
See also Gottwald, as cited in Chapter 4.6 and also works on pastoral nomadism cited in Chapter 4.7.

7. On Ceramic Analysis

London, G. "A Comparison of Two Contemporaneous Lifestyles in the Late Second Millennium B.C." *Bulletin of the American Schools of Oriental Research* 273, 1989. 37-55.
Wood, B. G. *The Sociology of Pottery in Ancient Palestine: The Ceramic Industry and the Diffusion of Ceramic Style in the Bronze and Iron Ages*. Sheffield: Sheffield Academic Press, 1990.

8. On Burial Practices

Bloch-Smith, E. *Judahite Burial Practices and Beliefs about the Dead*. Sheffield: JSOT Press, 1992.

9. On Religion and Cult, Especially Popular

Dever, W. G. "The Contribution of Archaeology to the Study of Canaanite and Early Israelite Religion." 209-47 in *Ancient Israelite Religion: Essays in Honor of Frank Moore Cross*. Edited by P. D. Miller Jr., D. D. Hanson, and S. D. McBride. Philadelphia: Westminster, 1987.
van der Toorn, K. *From Her Cradle to Her Grave: The Role of Religion in the Life of the Israelite and Babylonian Woman*. Sheffield: Sheffield Academic Press, 1994.
Berlinerblau, J. *The Vow and the "Popular Religious Groups" of Ancient Israel: A Philological and Sociological Inquiry*. Sheffield: Sheffield Academic Press, 1996.
van der Toorn, K., editor. *The Image and the Book: Iconic Cults, Aniconism, and the Rise of Book Religion in Israel and the Ancient Near East*. Louvain: Peeters, 1997.
Halpern, B. "Jerusalem and the Lineages in the Seventh Century B.C.E.: Kinship and the Rise of Individual Moral Liability." 11-107 in *Law and Ideology in

Monarchic Israel. Edited by B. Halpern and D. W. Hobson. Sheffield: Sheffield Academic Press, 1991.

Miller, P. D. *The Religion of Ancient Israel.* Louisville: Westminster/John Knox, 2000.

10. On Iron I Cult Places

Mazar, A. "The 'Bull Site': An Iron Age I Open Cult Place." *Bulletin of the American Schools of Oriental Research* 247, 1982. 27-42.

Zertal, A. "Has Joshua's Altar Been Found on Mt. Ebal?" *Biblical Archaeology Review* 11/1, 1985. 26-43.

Chapter 8. Previous Attempts at a Synthesis of Textual and Artifactual Data on Early Israel

Albright, W. F. *From the Stone Age to Christianity: Monotheism and the Historical Process.* Garden City, N.Y.: Doubleday, 1940.

Kaufmann, Y. *The Biblical Account of the Conquest of Palestine.* Jerusalem: Magnes Press, 1953.

Kaufmann, Y. *The Religion of Israel.* Chicago: University of Chicago Press, 1960.

Weippert, M. *The Settlement of the Israelite Tribes in Palestine.* Naperville, Ill.: Allenson, 1971.

Aharoni, Y. "Nothing Early and Nothing Late: Re-Writing Israel's Conquest." *Biblical Archaeologist* 3, 1976. 55-76.

Aharoni, Y. *The Land of the Bible: A Historical Geography.* Philadelphia: Westminster, 1979.

Fritz, V. "The Israelite 'Conquest' in Light of Recent Excavations at Khirbet el-Meshash." *Bulletin of the American Schools of Oriental Research* 241, 1981. 61-73.

Mazar, A. "Giloh: An Early Israelite Site Near Jerusalem." *Israel Exploration Journal* 31, 1981. 1-36.

Freedman, D. N., and D. F. Graf, editors. *Palestine in Transition: The Emergence of Ancient Israel.* Sheffield: Almond, 1983.

Halpern, B. *The Emergence of Israel in Canaan.* Chico, Calif.: Scholars Press, 1983.

Callaway, J. A. "A New Perspective on the Hill Country Settlement of Canaan in Iron Age I." 31-49 in *Palestine in the Bronze and Iron Ages: Papers in Honour of Olga Tufnell.* Edited by J. N. Tubb. London: Institute of Archaeology, 1985.

Kochavi, M. "The Israelite Settlement in Canaan in the Light of Archaeological Surveys." 54-60 in *Biblical Archaeology Today: Proceedings of the International Congress on Biblical Archaeology, Jerusalem, April 1984.* Edited by J. Amitai. Jerusalem: Israel Exploration Society, 1985.

Mazar A., "The Israelite Settlement in Canaan in Light of Archaeological Excavations." 61-71 in *Biblical Archaeology Today: Proceedings of the International Congress on Biblical Archaeology, Jerusalem, April 1984*. Edited by J. Amitai. Jerusalem: Israel Exploration Society, 1985.

Stager, L. E. "The Archaeology of the Family in Early Israel." *Bulletin of the American Schools of Oriental Research* 200, 1985. 1-35.

Ahlström, G. W. *Who Were the Israelites?* Winona Lake, Ind.: Eisenbrauns, 1986.

Coote, R. B., and K. W. Whitelam. *The Emergence of Early Israel in Historical Perspective*. Sheffield: Almond, 1987.

Stiebing, W. H. Jr. *Out of the Desert? Archaeology and the Exodus/Conquest Narratives*. Buffalo, N.Y.: Prometheus, 1989.

Redford, D. B. *Egypt, Canaan, and Israel in Ancient Times*. Princeton: Princeton University Press, 1992.

Fritz, V. "Conquest or Settlement? The Early Iron Age in Palestine." *Biblical Archaeologist* 50/2, 1987. 84-100.

Coote, R. B. *Early Israel: A New Horizon*. Minneapolis: Fortress, 1990.

Halpern, B. "The Exodus from Egypt: Myth or Reality?" 87-113 in *The Rise of Ancient Israel*. Edited by H. Shanks. Washington: Biblical Archaeology Society, 1992.

Bunimovitz, S. "Socio-Political Transformations in the Central Hill Country in the Late Bronze-Iron I Transition." 179-202 in *From Nomadism to Monarchy: Archaeological and Historical Aspects of Early Israel*. Edited by I. Finkelstein and N. Na'aman. Jerusalem: Israel Exploration Society, 1994.

Stager, L. E. "Forging an Identity: The Emergence of Ancient Israel." 123-75 in *The Oxford History of the Biblical World*. Edited by M. D. Coogan. New York: Oxford University Press, 1998.

Rainey, A. F. "Israel in Merneptah's Inscription and Reliefs." *Israel Exploration Journal* 51, 2001. 57-75.

In addition, see the works of Hermann, Miller and Hayes, Shanks, and Soggin cited for the Introduction; of Davies, Grabbe, Lemche, and Thompson for Chapter 1.1; Yadin for Chapter 4.4; and Alt and Noth for Chapter 4.5.

Chapter 9. Toward Another Synthesis on the Origins and Nature of Early Israel

See the works of Finkelstein and Dever cited for Chapter 7.1, 2.
See also works on pastoral nomadism cited for Chapter 4.7.

Chapter 10. Yet Another Attempt at Synthesis:
Early Israel as a Frontier Agrarian Reform Movement

1. On Canaan in the Late Bronze Age

Leonard, A. "The Late Bronze Age." *Biblical Archaeologist* 52/1, 1989. 4-38.

Gonen, R. "The Late Bronze Age." 211-57 in *The Archaeology of Ancient Israel.* Edited by A. Ben-Tor. New Haven: Yale University Press, 1992.

Singer, I. "Egyptians, Canaanites and Philistines in the Period of the Emergence of Israel." 282-338 in *From Nomadism to Monarchy: Archaeological and Historical Aspects of Early Israel.* Edited by I. Finkelstein and N. Na'aman. Jerusalem: Israel Exploration Society, 1994.

Bunimovitz, S. "On the Edge of Empires — Late Bronze Age 1500-1200 BCE. " 320-31 in *The Archaeology of Society in the Holy Land.* Edited by T. E. Levy. New York: Facts on File, 1995.

2. On the Amarna Age

Chaney, M. L. "Ancient Palestinian Peasant Movements and the Formation of Premonarchic Israel." 39-90 in *The Emergence of Ancient Israel.* Edited by D. N. Freedman and D. F. Graf. Sheffield: Sheffield Academic Press, 1983.

Moran, W. L. *The Amarna Letters.* Baltimore: Johns Hopkins University Press, 1992.

Finkelstein, I. "The Territorio-Political System of Canaan in the Late Bronze Age." *Ugarit-Forschungen* 28, 1996. 221-55.

Na'aman, N. "The Network of Late Bronze Kingdoms and the City of Ashdod." *Ugarit-Forschungen* 29, 1997. 599-626.

3. On the End of the Late Bronze Age

Dever, W. G. "The Late Bronze–Early Iron I Horizon: Egyptians, Canaanites, 'Sea Peoples,' and Proto-Israelites." 99-110 in *The Crisis Years: The 12th Century B.C. From Beyond the Danube to the Tigris.* Edited by W. A. Ward and M. S. Joukowsky. Dubuque, Iowa: Kendall/Hunt, 1992.

Gitin, S., A. Mazar, and E. Stern, editors. *Mediterranean Peoples in Transition: Thirteenth to Early Tenth Centuries BCE.* Jerusalem: Israel Exploration Society, 1998.

4. On Peasants, Peasant Agriculture,
and the Domestic Mode of Production

Hobsbawm, E. J. *Primitive Rebels: Studies in Archaic Forms of Social Movements in the 19th and 20th Centuries.* New York: Praeger, 1965.

Wolf, E. R. *Peasants.* Englewood Cliffs, N.J.: Prentice Hall, 1966.

Wolf, E. R. *Peasant Wars of the Twentieth Century.* New York: Harper & Row, 1969.

Sahlins, M. P. *Stone Age Economics*. Chicago: University of Chicago Press, 1972.

Hobsbawm, E. J. "Social Banditry." 142-157 in *Rural Protest: Peasant Movements and Social Change*. Edited by H. A. Landsberger. New York: Macmillan, 1973.

Lenski, G., and J. Lenski. *Human Societies: An Introduction to Macrosociology*. New York: McGraw-Hill, 1978.

Gottwald, N. K. *The Tribes of Yahweh: A Sociology of the Religion of Liberated Israel, 1250-1050 B.C.E.* Maryknoll, N.Y.: Orbis, 1979.

Hopkins, D. C. *The Highlands of Canaan: Agricultural Life in the Early Iron Age*. Sheffield: Sheffield Academic Press, 1985.

Gottwald, N. K. "Method and Hypothesis in Reconstructing the Social History of Early Israel." *Eretz-Israel* 24, 1993. 77-82.

5. On Ethnicity in the Archaeological Record

Edelman, D. V. "Ethnicity and Early Israel." 25-55 in *Ethnicity and the Bible*. Edited by M. G. Brett. New York: Brill, 1996.

See also the works of Lemche and Thompson as cited for Chapter 1.1; and of Dever and Finkelstein, as cited for Chapter 7.1, 2.

6. On Urbanization Following the Iron I Period

Fritz, V. *The City in Ancient Israel*. Sheffield: Sheffield Academic Press, 1995.

Herzog, Z. *Archaeology of the City. Urban Planning in Ancient Israel and Its Social Implications*. Tel Aviv: Tel Aviv University, 1997.

7. On the Merneptah Stele

Hasel, M. G. "'Israel' in the Merneptah Stele." *Bulletin of the American Schools of Oriental Research* 196, 1994. 45-61.

Yurco, F. J. "Merneptah's Canaanite Campaign and Israel's Origins." 27-55 in *Exodus: The Egyptian Evidence*. Edited by E. S. Frerichs and L. H. Lesko. Winona Lake, Ind.: Eisenbrauns, 1997.

Kitchen, K. "Egyptians and Hebrews, From Ra'amses to Jericho." 65-131 in *The Origin of Early Israel — Current Debate: Biblical, Historical and Archaeological Perspectives*. Edited by S. Ahituv and E. D. Oren. Beersheba: Ben Guryon University, 1998.

See also the works of Davies, Lemche, and Thompson as cited for Chapter 1.1; and the works of Ahlström, Rainey, and Stager as cited for Chapter 8.

8. On Pastoral Nomadism

See the works cited for Chapter 4.7.

9. On Various Ethnic Groups in Bronze and Iron Age Canaan

Wiseman, D. J., editor. *Peoples of Old Testament Times*. Oxford: Clarendon, 1973.

Chapter 12. Salvaging the Biblical Tradition: History or Myth?

1. Revisionist Works, to the Left

Davies, P. R. *Whose Bible Is It Anyway?* Sheffield: Sheffield Academic Press, 1995.
See also Davies, Lemche, Thompson, and Whitelam as cited for Chapter 1.1.

2. Conservative Works, to the Right

Millard, A. R., J. K. Hoffmeier, and D. W. Baker, editors. *Faith, Tradition, and History: Old Testament Historiography in Its Near Eastern Context.* Winona Lake, Ind.: Eisenbrauns, 1994.

Harrisville, R. A., and W. Sundberg. *The Bible in Modern Culture: Theology and Historical-Critical Method from Spinoza to Käsemann.* Grand Rapids: Eerdmans, 1995.

Baker, D. W., and B. T. Arnold, editors. *The Face of Old Testament Studies: A Survey of Contemporary Approaches.* Grand Rapids: Baker, 1999.

3. Mainstream or Centrist Works

Barr, J. *The Bible in the Modern World.* New York: Harper & Row, 1973.

Barr, J. *Fundamentalism.* Philadelphia: Westminster, 1977.

Spong, J. S. *Rescuing the Bible from Fundamentalism: A Bishop Rethinks the Meaning of Scripture.* San Francisco: HarperSanFrancisco, 1991.

Barton, J. *What Is the Bible?* London: SPCK, 1991.

Barton, J. *Reading the Old Testament: Method in Biblical Study.* Louisville: Westminster/John Knox, 1996.

See also Dever, W. G. *What Did the Biblical Writers Know and When Did They Know It? What Archaeology Can Tell Us about the Reality of Ancient Israel.* Grand Rapids: Eerdmans, 2001.

Index of Authors

Index of Subjects

Aaron, 23, 24
Abel, 28
Acco, 171, 212
Achshaf, 68
Adullam, 68
agrarianism, 188, 189. *See also* reform
   movements; ruralism
agriculture, 105-8, 113-18, 147, 164, 178-80,
   185. *See also* economy; family; peas-
   ants; social structure; technology
ʿAi, 37, 38, 46-48, 88, 106
ʿAin Qudeis, 19, 20
Amalek, 27, 28, 220
Amarna letters, 73, 74, 168-74, 183, 184
Amman (Rabbath-Ammon), 31, 35
Ammonites, 70, 218
Amphictyony, 130
Amorites, 30, 38, 52, 64, 182, 219
Annales school, 133. *See also* settlement
   patterns
Aphek, 68, 69
ʿApiru, 73, 74, 131, 171, 174-79, 181
Arad, 24, 29, 30
Aramaeans, 70, 132, 218, 219
Arnon gorge, 24, 29, 30, 32
art, 125, 128
Ashdod, 70

Asherah, 65
Ashkelon, 70, 202
Asiatics, in Delta, 10, 12, 15
assemblage, 101, 102
Azekah, 37

Baʿal, 128
Baʿalat Beer, 27
Baʿal-perazim. *See* Giloh
bamôt ("high places"), 24
bands, 111, 112
Bashan, 24, 32
bedouin, 28, 50-52, 72, 130, 163, 164, 177.
   See also pastoral nomads; Shasu; tribe
Beeroth, 75
Beersheba, 23, 26, 29, 87, 88, 162, 181
Beersheba Valley, 214-16
Benjamin, tribe of, 230
bet-ʾav. See family compound
Bethel, 39, 44, 47, 88
Bethel, in Negev, 27, 28
Beth-horon, 37
Beth-shan, 196, 212
Beth-shemesh, 70, 126
biblical archaeology, 4, 5, 41
bones, animal, 27, 78, 108
"Bull Site," 126-28. *See also* religion

Index of Scripture References